U.S.-
Latin
American
Relations

U.S.- Latin American Relations

THIRD EDITION

Michael J. Kryzanek

PRAEGER

Westport, Connecticut
London

Library of Congress Cataloging-in-Publication Data

Kryzanek, Michael J.
    U.S.–Latin American relations / Michael J. Kryzanek. — 3rd ed.
      p.   cm.
    Includes bibliographical references (p.   ) and index.
    ISBN 0–275–95083–2 (hc : alk. paper). — ISBN 0–275–95084–0 (pb)
    1. Latin America—Foreign relations—United States. 2. United
States—Foreign relations—Latin America. I. Title.
    F1418.K78   1996
    327.7308—dc20   95–31399

British Library Cataloguing in Publication Data is available.

Library of Congress Catalog Card Number: 95–31399
ISBN: 0–275–95083–2
       0–275–95084–0 (pbk.)

First published in 1996

Praeger Publishers, 88 Post Road West, Westport, CT 06881
An imprint of Greenwood Publishing Group, Inc.

Printed in the United States of America

⊗™

The paper used in this book complies with the
Permanent Paper Standard issued by the National
Information Standards Organization (Z39.48–1984).

10 9 8 7 6 5 4 3 2 1

TO MY DAUGHTERS

Laura, Kathryn, and Ann

Contents

Introduction: The Political, Economic, and Social Setting

Latin America, much like the rest of the world in the post–Cold War era, is undergoing immense change. Where once the region was defined in terms of authoritarianism, huge state enterprises, and trade protectionism, the Latin America of the 1990s is democratic, increasingly privatized, and open to foreign investment and the global economy. The changes that have come to Latin America have also had an impact on relations with the United States. Not only have the countries south of the border embraced our governmental framework and become eager participants in the market economy, they have put aside (at least for a time) the animosity and mistrust that marked the ties between them and their enormously rich and powerful neighbor to the north.[1]

In light of this transformation of the Latin American landscape, the United States, both in the public and the private sectors, has reconfigured the hemispheric relationship. Today, U.S. government officials talk about a "mature relationship" with the Latin Americans, and business executives, bankers, and investors are descending on the region in hopes of reaping the benefits from a radically different economic and financial climate. This is clearly a time of cooperation and conciliation in the region as the North Americans and the South Americans enter a period that is filled with promise.[2]

In many respects, it is astonishing how the region and the relationship between the United States and Latin America has changed in a few years. Ten years ago President Ronald Reagan was warning the American people about the communist threat in Nicaragua and revolution in El Salvador. The United States was pumping billions of dollars into Central America to contain or, if possible, destroy the Marxist left. Although the United States did much to champion the electoral process in Latin American countries, governing institutions were weak, support was still unformed, and human rights abuses remained a constant.[3]

Besides the strategic and political concerns of the United States during the mid-1980s, Washington policy makers faced a region on the brink of insolvency as massive indebtedness and inflation made it difficult for many Latin American countries to rebound from what was termed the "lost decade of development."[4] With much of the debt held by U.S. banks and weakened currencies affecting the purchasing power of millions of Latin Americans, the Reagan administration recognized the urgency of resolving these critical financial issues. Through a series of negotiated agreements that restructured the debt and vigorous encouragement of private investment, the United States hoped to forestall Latin America's decline before the "lost decade" expanded its reach into the 1990s.

As both the United States and Latin America head into the last years of the twentieth century concern over communist expansionism, authoritarianism, and state-dominated economies seem quite distant. Marxist guerrillas now run for political office with the blessing of Washington policy makers, U.S. military assistance has been replaced by U.S. corporate investment, and a confident Latin American business sector talks about a hemispheric free trade zone (from Anchorage to Antarctica) to rival that of Europe and the Pacific Rim. The old models and traditional perceptions have given way to a new dynamism in the hemisphere, because not only has Latin America changed but also the way the United States looks and works with Latin America has changed.

This is an exciting time to examine U.S.–Latin American relations, but it is also a period of dramatic adjustment in the relations as the changes brought forth in the 1980s will require that North and South America build on the successes of recent years. President Clinton's Assistant Secretary of Inter-American Affairs Alexander Watson may have placed this new "mature relationship" in its proper context when he said,

No one will ever accuse U.S.–Latin American relations of being boring. Many of the reforms that have taken place are still fragile. But this convergence of values is of historic proportions and offers us the opportunity to forge patterns of behavior and fashion institutional settings that will promote, if not guarantee, peaceful and cooperative resolution of disputes and facilitate common approaches to issues that concern us all.[5]

Declaring that the relationship between neighbors has entered a new, more promising phase will still require extraordinary efforts to solidify the recent gains. Despite the fact that the Latin Americans have been loyal diplomatic allies, eager trading partners, welcome hosts for our tourists, and stalwart defenders of the region, there is an undercurrent of anger and frustration among the Latin American countries. These emotions are the legacy of the neglect and arrogance that have marked the relationship of the more powerful North with the developing South. The United States has often taken Latin America for granted

Latin America

Map sketched by Donna G. Atwood

and turned its attention to the affairs of this region only when our own interests were in danger. The fact that we share a nearly 2,000-mile border with Mexico and that beneath that border live 355 million Latin Americans seems more of an afterthought to most people in the United States. Policy makers in Washington often think of Latin America as "peripheral" to our primary international objectives and the American public remains mired in traditional stereotypes of its neighbors to the south.

It is interesting to note, however, that while the United States has, in the past, paid only scant attention to its neighbors in the hemisphere, the situation is reversed when one examines the view from south of the border. The people of this region, unlike their counterparts in the North, are experts on the effect of sharing the hemisphere with the world's greatest power. Few Latin Americans care to define their relationship with the United States as amicable and based on principles of fairness and equity. There have been too many differences of opinion and out-look, too many conflicts over goals and directions, and too many inequalities of growth and development.

As a result, the United States and Latin America have developed what Venezuelan writer Carlos Rangel calls a "love-hate" relationship.[6] Despite the many areas of common experience and the countless formal arrangements and informal contacts that have fostered an enormous font of goodwill, people in these countries do not hesitate to point to the dangers of living next to what they see as a power-hungry giant bent on domination. The view from the South is thus not only one of renewed interest, conciliation, and maturity but also one of extreme caution and concern over ties with a neighbor often described as the "Colossus of the North." The great Mexican novelist Octavio Paz has perhaps said it best,

[The North Americans] are always among us, even when they ignore us or turn their back on us. Their shadow covers the whole hemisphere. It is the Shadow of a giant. And the idea we have of that giant is the same that can be found in fairy tales and legends; a great fellow of kind disposition, a bit simple, an innocent who ignores his own strength and who we can fool most of the time, but whose wrath can destroy us.[7]

POLITICAL RELATIONS:
INDEPENDENCE AND INTERVENTIONS

Despite their differences and the interpretations of their relationship, the United States and the Latin American states derive surprisingly from a common political heritage. Both the United States and the Latin American nations were born as a result of revolution against a foreign master. The United States fought to break away from English domination, while the Latin Americans were separating from Spanish rule. Furthermore, the principles that formed the basis for these revolutions were quite similar. The founding fathers in the United States and the liberators of Latin America had visions of creating democratic republics that guaranteed popular rights. The revolutions in the New World were fought to secure the great principles of democracy, equality, and liberty and thereby set a new course, free from the monarchy and despotism of European society.[8]

Once the fighting ended and the independence leaders assumed the task of running governments, the similarities between the United States and the Latin American states began to fade. The most obvious difference could be seen almost immediately after Bolívar's final victories in 1823. Instead of being able to establish a unified nation from a number of independent fiefdoms headed by local military leaders or *caudillos*, Bolívar saw his dream of a United States of Latin America vanish.

What was an even more serious setback for the Latin American revolution was that the ideals of democracy, equality, and liberty began to disappear or were compromised. In country after country military strongmen rejected the new rights and formed governments that merely replaced the Spanish crown with a more indigenous form of monarchy. While the United States had by the mid–1990s established an expanding nation with increasing signs of democratic practice, the Latin Americans were slipping into a pattern of instability and authoritarian rule.[9]

The vast gulf between the governing conditions in the United States and in the nations of Latin America would eventually have a crucial influence on how this country viewed its role in the hemisphere. In particular, the unstable leadership situation in Latin America, coupled with the frequent outbursts of violence, weakened the economies of these nations. Without strong and stable governments able to protect themselves, the Latin American nations became, at least from the U.S. perspective, targets of foreign governments anxious to spread their political influence or gain access to vital resources.

But if the United States saw danger in the unstable political conditions in Latin America, it also saw new opportunities. The dismal economic circumstances in these countries spurred both public and private interests in the United States to enter Latin America as a financial backer and corporate developer. Quite simply, there was money to be made despite the instability.

Eventually U.S. presidents found more reasons (or excuses) to involve this country in the affairs of Latin American nations. We did everything for the Latin Americans from collecting taxes to building bridges, from solving border disputes to paying off foreign debts, from running elections to financing railroad and telephone communications.

In some instances we were welcome guests, especially when the host government was desperate for financial or economic assistance, but in general our neighborly concern was viewed as blatant interventionism. No matter how we couched our involvement, the relationship between the United States and the Latin American states had turned from one based on a common revolutionary heritage to one based on inequality of power and frequent intervention to preserve political and economic interests.

Although the United States has been able to maintain its dominant position in the hemisphere, its political relations with the countries of Latin America have undergone some important changes. Where in the past U.S. policy makers looked at Latin America as a series of preindustrial "banana republics" led by "tin horn" dictators who could be easily intimidated, today the political systems in this region cannot be categorized so simplistically. The United States can also no longer operate in this region with the confidence and ease that were once possible. The Latin Americans of today seem more willing to protect their national integrity from U.S. intervention or from unfair trade and investment arrangements. Gone are the days of quiet resignation to U.S. dominance. There is now a new sense of independence in the region and a willingness to take risks without seeking the approval or involvement of the United States.

But even though the internal character of Latin America has changed through the years, the foreign policy objectives of the United States have not undergone any major transformation. This country continues to hold to the belief that its relationship to Latin America must be founded on the principles of political stability, defense against foreign intervention, and cooperative economic ties. What is even more important is that this country continues to hold to the view that the absence of diminution of these three conditions could require some action on the part of the United States to ensure that our preeminence in the region and our economic interests are not jeopardized. Occasionally an administration may loosen the requirements a bit or add new ones, such as President Jimmy Carter's emphasis on human rights, but in the main this country has been the model of consistency on dealing with Latin America. As Latin Americanist Howard Wiarda states:

Since approximately the turn of the century . . . the interests of the United States in Latin America—and especially in the Caribbean Basin—have been almost constant. It has not mattered a great deal, except in terms of emphases and nuance, which Administration was in power. The fact is there has been remarkable consistency in the bedrocks of United States policy toward the area over the past eighty years. These historic continuities of policy are perhaps as strongly present even now as they were nearly a century ago.[10]

Despite new leaders, new economic conditions, new social forces at work, and new ideas, the political ties between the United States and Latin America remain grounded in the belief that because we are neighbors and "superior," this country has the right and the responsibility to influence the development of the nations to its south. It is an awesome and troublesome responsibility that the United States has felt it must bear if it is to remain secure in the hemisphere. On the other hand, it is also a responsibility that the Latin Americans wish the United States would relinquish or at least ignore.

ECONOMIC RELATIONS:
DEPENDENCY AND COMPETITION

Even though U.S. political activities in Latin America have often received the lion's share of public attention, our economic ties form a critical component of inter-American relations. The day-to-day contact between governments and private-sector institutions, whether in the area of trade, economic assistance, debt financing, or investment, have had a greater long-term impact on U.S.–Latin American relations than the periodic political entanglements.

To begin, the economic relationship between the United States and Latin America cannot be understood unless one recognizes that it is a relationship between unequals. The United States is an advanced industrial nation with enormous natural resources and an economy that has provided its people with the highest standard of living in the world. The Latin American nations on the other hand cannot be described through generalizations. Some, like Brazil, Mexico, and Chile, are emerging industrial giants that may soon step forward from the ranks of the developing nations, while others, like Bolivia, Honduras, and Haiti, are so poor that their people consume thirty to fifty times fewer goods in a lifetime than their counterparts in the United States.

Yet despite the vast differences that can be found among the economies of Latin America, the overall picture is one of only limited development. The countries of Latin America are today often defined as having "middle range" economies—not as desperately poor as many of the countries of Asia and Africa, but nowhere near the strength and prosperity found in the industrial nations of Europe and North America. As Table I.1 points out, the United States greatly outdistances its Latin American neighbors in terms of gross national product and per capita gross national product, the two standard indices of national wealth.

One's immediate reaction upon seeing Table I.1 may be to ask why this great disparity in wealth exists. The answer is not an easy one, but an important part of it lies in the level of industrialization found in the United States and Latin America and the impact of that industrialization on overall economic strength. In the United States the industrial revolution arrived in the post–Civil War era, while in Latin America the movement from an agricultural economy to an industrial one did not generally occur until after World War II. Countries like Argentina,

Table I.1
Key Economic and Social Indicators

Country	Population mid–1992 (millions)	GNP per capita Dollars 1992	Average annual growth percent 1980–92	Life expectancy at birth 1992	Adult illiteracy 1990
Argentina	33.1	4,450	–3.7	54	39
Bolivia	7.5	680	–1.5	60	23
Brazil	153.9	2,770	0.4	66	19
Chile	13.6	2,730	3.7	72	7
Colombia	33.4	1,330	1.4	69	13
Ecuador	11.0	1,070	–0.3	67	14
Guyana	0.8	330	–5.6	65	4
Paraguay	4.5	1,380	–0.7	67	10
Peru	22.4	950	–2.8	65	15
Surinam	0.4	4,280	–3.6	69	5
Uruguay	3.1	3,340	–1.0	72	4
Venezuela	20.2	2,910	–0.8	70	8
Canada	27.4	20,710	1.8	78	1
Costa Rica	3.2	1,960	0.8	76	7
Dominican Republic	7.3	1,050	–0.5	68	17
Cuba	10.8	—	—	76	6
El Salvador	5.4	1,170	—	66	27
Guatemala	9.7	980	–1.5	65	45
Haiti	6.7	365	–2.4	55	47
Honduras	5.4	580	–0.3	66	27
Mexico	85.0	3,470	–0.2	70	13
Nicaragua	3.9	340	–5.3	67	—
Panama	2.5	2,420	–1.2	73	12
United States	255.0	23,240	1.7	76	1

Source: World Bank.

Brazil, Chile, and Uruguay have had active industrial sectors since the turn of the century, but even in these nations the impact of the factory on the overall economy was until recently less than that of the farm.

While the United States was becoming the industrial giant of the world, Latin American economies remained based primarily on agriculture or raw resources. Latin American nations developed reputations as agricultural suppliers of coffee (Brazil and Colombia), sugar (Cuba and the Dominican Republic), and bananas (Guatemala and Costa Rica), or as rich centers of natural resources such as tin (Bolivia), copper (Chile), silver (Mexico), alumina (Jamaica), and oil (Venezuela).

As the United States grew in population, industrial production, and wealth, Latin America became the source of the staple goods and natural resources we needed to meet the demands of our consumers and our factories. Once this traditional relationship developed, the Latin

Americans found themselves dependent on economic decisions and trends in demand within the United States. Since most of these countries had but one or two major export items which provided a substantial portion of their national revenue, the U.S. economy played a critical role in determining the prospects for development and financial solvency in much of Latin America.

Over the years this dependent relationship did little to bridge the gap between the wealthy industrial North Americans and the poor agricultural Latin Americans. With world prices for their commodities and resources fluctuating continuously and costs for imported goods increasing, the nations in this region found themselves facing burgeoning trade imbalances, heightened levels of inflation, weakened national currencies, and, most seriously of all, skyrocketing debts. By the late 1980s Latin American debt hovered near $400 billion with countries like Brazil (a debt of $120 billion) and Mexico ($100 billion) mired in a sea of obligations to U.S. and European banks. Table I.2 provides a recent listing of foreign debt obligations by the major Latin American countries.

The solutions to these economic problems have covered the spectrum of public to private initiatives from so-called import substitution policies designed to make Latin American countries less dependent on the external markets and sources of technology to the current panacea, the market economy, with its emphasis on privatization and free trade. In the end, however, the Latin Americans recognize that the solution to their economic woes lies in the creation of a diversified industrial base that can compete effectively with the advanced economies, while being strong enough to provide for the consumer needs of its people.

Beginning with the 1960s the Latin Americans began addressing their industrial deficiencies and lessening their dependency on the United States. As a result, the percentage of the Latin American population working in manufacturing and service capacities began to rise, while the growth in nonagricultural sectors of the economy became substantial. As Table I.3 shows, gross domestic product (GDP) for Latin America, a common index of economic growth, increased dramatically from 1960 to the early 1990s in areas unrelated to agriculture. In particular, the GDP for manufacturing and electricity realized the greatest growth, while areas such as commerce, transportation, and financial services more than tripled their growth. Also, with increased foreign investment in the 1990s, the push for tariff reduction, and the rise in many countries of export processing zones, Latin America has quickly expanded into a number of new areas of economic and financial enterprise from high technology to communication to insurance and public relations.

The desire of the Latin Americans to diversify their economies is now also joined with an eagerness to trade with countries other than the United States. It is not unusual today to find Japanese, West

Table I.2
Selected Latin American Trade Statistics (in billions of dollars)

Country	Trade with	1992			Percentage of total trade[1]		Percentage change 1991–92	
		Exports	Imports	Balance	Exports	Imports	Exports	Imports
Mexico	United States	32.6	40.6	-8.0	76.3	69.4	12.4	21.9
	EEC	3.3	7.3	-4.0	7.7	12.5	—	23.7
	W. Hemisphere[2]	2.0	2.1	-0.1	4.7	3.6	17.6	57.9
	Asia	0.9	2.6	-1.7	1.9	4.4	-11.1	25.0
	World	42.7	58.5	-15.8	na	na	8.9	23.7
Brazil	United States	7.1	5.8	1.3	20.0	25.0	11.0	7.4
	EEC	10.7	5.2	5.5	30.0	22.3	8.9	-0.8
	W. Hemisphere[2]	8.2	4.0	4.2	22.6	17.3	54.7	-7.0
	Asia	3.3	0.7	2.6	9.1	3.0	6.5	10.0
	World	36.2	23.3	12.9	na	na	14.6	—
Venezuela	United States	7.9	5.4	2.5	50.3	43.9	1.3	14.9
	EEC	1.6	2.7	-1.1	10.2	22.0	—	17.4
	W. Hemisphere[2]	4.4	1.5	2.9	28.0	12.2	4.8	7.1
	Asia	0.2	0.8	-0.6	1.3	6.5	-8.2	100.0
	World	15.7	12.3	3.4	na	na	—	23.0

Argentina							
United States	1.2	3.5	-2.3	9.7	22.4	—	36.5
EEC	3.8	3.9	-0.1	30.6	25.0	-4.4	110.2
W. Hemisphere[2]	4.0	4.7	-0.7	32.5	30.4	11.0	83.7
Asia	0.8	1.3	-0.5	6.5	8.3	-4.2	70.5
World	12.4	15.6	-3.2	na	na	3.3	88.0
Chile							
United States	1.6	2.4	-0.8	16.0	20.5	—	50.0
EEC	2.9	2.3	0.6	29.0	19.7	—	64.3
W. Hemisphere[2]	1.7	3.0	-1.3	17.0	25.6	30.8	42.9
Asia	1.0	0.4	14.0	8.5	40.0	66.7	51.9
1.4							
World	10.0	11.7	-1.7	na	na	11.1	
Colombia							
United States	2.8	3.6	-0.8	38.9	43.4	—	50.0
EEC	1.9	1.6	0.3	26.4	19.3	—	60.0
W. Hemisphere[2]	1.7	1.5	0.2	23.6	18.1	—	25.0
Asia	0.1	0.2	-0.1	1.4	2.4	18.4	243.4
World	7.2	8.3	-1.1	na	na	—	66.0

[1]Trade with listed regions/countries as a percentage of total trade.
[2]Minus United States and Canada.

Source: International Monetary Fund, *Directions of Trade Statistical Yearbook 1993*, Washington, D.C.

Table I.3
U.S. Direct Investment Position Abroad at Year End (in billions of dollars)

	All industries		Percent change	Manufacturing		Finance & insurance		Banking		Petroleum	
	1991	1992	1991–92	1991	1992	1991	1992	1991	1992	1991	1992
All Countries	461.0	486.7	5.6	180.5	187.3	32.5	129.5	21.2	23.5	55.9	55.9
Latin America and the Caribbean	76.2	88.9	16.7	25.0	26.7	32.5	40.5	6.3	7.7	4.1	4.6
South America	24.1	27.2	12.9	14.9	15.9	2.9	3.5	1.5	2.0	2.0	2.5
Argentina	2.8	3.4	21.4	1.5	1.6	0.3	0.5	0.4	0.4	0.4	0.5
Brazil	14.9	16.1	8.0	11.6	12.0	1.5	1.8	0.6	1.0	0.6	0.7
Chile	1.9	2.4	26.3	0.1	0.3	1.0	1.0	0.3	0.4	—	—
Colombia	1.6	2.1	31.3	0.7	0.7	—	—	—	—	0.4	0.6
Ecuador	0.3	0.3	—	0.1	0.1	—	—	—	—	0.1	0.2
Peru	0.5	0.5	—	—	—	—	—	—	—	—	—
Venezuela	1.4	1.7	21.4	0.8	1.1	0.1	0.1	—	—	0.2	0.2
Central America	23.3	25.5	9.4	9.2	9.8	9.7	10.9	—	—	1.0	1.0
Mexico	12.3	13.3	8.1	8.8	9.2	0.7	0.8	—	—	—	—
Panama	10.4	11.5	10.6	0.1	0.1	9.0	10.0	—	—	0.7	0.7
Caribbean	28.8	36.2	25.7	1.0	1.0	19.9	26.1	4.8	5.7	1.1	1.0
Bahamas	3.8	4.6	21.0	—	—	1.2	1.3	2.0	2.7	0.4	0.4
Bermuda	23.1	25.8	11.7	—	—	22.2	24.8	—	—	—	—
Netherlands Antilles	−5.7	−1.9	—	—	—	−5.9	−2.1	—	—	—	—
U.K. Islands and the Caribbean	5.1	5.0	−0.2	0.1	—	2.3	2.0	2.6	2.9	0.1	0.1

Source: Unpublished data compiled by the U.S. Department of Commerce.

Germans, Taiwanese, Spaniards, Israelis, and representatives of Latin American countries signing multimillion-dollar trade agreements or financing major infrastructure projects. As can be seen in Table 2, Latin American trade with Europe and the Pacific Rim has increased dramatically in recent years.

Not only has increased competition from Europe and the Pacific Basin changed the economic complexion of Latin America, but the burgeoning foreign debt incurred by these countries has had a serious impact on the level of trade with the United States. Although traditionally the United States controlled a large share of the export-import market of Latin America (40 percent of U.S. exports headed for Latin America, while this country imported 37 percent of Latin American goods in the 1960s), U.S. exports to the region fell by some 40 percent after 1981 as the Latin Americans found it more difficult to purchase U.S. goods and pay their foreign debt at the same time. As documented by Abraham Lowenthal, from 1981 to 1983, U.S. exports to Latin America fell from $39 billion to $22.6 billion, which accounted for about one-half of the worldwide decline in U.S. exports in those years. Lowenthal further estimates that the decline in exports cost the United States perhaps as many as 500,000 jobs and a further widening of the massive trade deficit.[11] Table I.4 provides an overview of the trade ties of the United States with the countries of Latin America.

Despite the increased ties with the countries of Europe and the Pacific Rim, the United States continues to be the primary source of trade and investment in Latin America. In 1992–93, U.S. exports to Latin America were $76 billion, a 3.7 percent increase, while U.S. imports of Latin American goods increased by 10 percent to $74 billion. Spurred on by the new free trade climate and by the signing of the North American Free Trade Agreement by the United States, Canada, and Mexico, which created the world's largest economic entity, the movement of goods between the United States and Latin America is expected to continue the strong growth pattern. Table I.4 shows the U.S. trade relationship for 1992–93 for all of the Latin American countries.

The increased trade ties between Latin America and the United States are matched by the explosion of capital investment from companies eager to benefit from the changing economic and political environment in the region. After years of placing barriers to foreign investment and bashing U.S. multinationals in the name of self-determination, the Latin Americans relaxed laws that made investment unattractive and publicly welcomed foreign investors to bid on newly privatized state enterprises. The results have been nothing short of astonishing. U.S. investment in Latin America at the conclusion of 1992 was $88.9 billion, up from $76.2 billion in 1991, which is a 16.7 percent increase. Some of the biggest increases in U.S. investment have occurred in Colombia, with a 31 percent increase, and Venezuela, with

Table I.4
U.S. Trade Status with Latin America (in millions of dollars)

Country	U.S. Exports		U.S. Imports	
	1993	Percentage change 1992–93	1993	Percentage change 1992–93
Total	76,764.5	3.7	74,475.5	10.0
Mexico	41,635.5	2.6	39,929.7	13.5
Brazil	6,045.4	5.3	7,465.6	−2.0
Venezuela	4,599.1	−15.4	8,140.3	−0.3
Argentina	3,771.7	17.1	1,205.9	−3.9
Colombia	3,229.1	−1.0	3,033.2	6.6
CARICOM*	3,203.8	16.1	3,208.1	38.5
Chile	2,605.3	6.1	1,462.2	7.0
Dominican Republic	2,349.5	12.1	2,671.5	12.6
Costa Rica	1,547.3	14.5	1,541.5	−15.4
Guatemala	1,310.3	8.8	1,194.5	11.1
Panama	1,190.7	8.2	281.0	10.8
Ecuador	1,080.2	8.1	1,399.0	4.2
Peru	1,069.2	6.7	754.0	2.1
Honduras	897.7	11.3	914.5	16.9
El Salvador	868.9	17.3	487.9	27.1
Paraguay	520.9	25.5	49.6	40.9
Uruguay	253.1	9.6	265.8	—
Haiti	221.3	2.1	154.3	44.3
Bolivia	215.9	−2.9	191.0	18.5
Nicaragua	149.6	−20.4	125.9	83.5

*CARICOM: Anguilla, Antigua, Bahamas, Barbados, Barbuda, Belize, Dominica, Grenada, Guyana, Jamaica, Montserrat, St. Kitts and Nevis, St. Lucia, St. Vincent, and Trinidad and Tobago.

Source: Unpublished data compiled by the U.S. Department of Commerce.

a 21 percent increase. Brazil continues to lead the region in total U.S. direct investment with $16.1 billion, and Mexico is second with $13.3 billion.[12]

Mexico, in particular, has become a mecca for U.S. investment. In large part because of former President Carlos Salinas de Gotari's willingness to move away from his country's historical antipathy toward the United States, U.S. investors have jumped into the Mexican economy full force, particularly in the so-called *maquiladora* region, a twelve-mile strip along the border with the United States. The government has created the equivalent of hundreds of industrial parks to attract U.S. businesses with favorable pay scales, low taxes, weak environmental standards, and a positive attitude toward investment. The passage of the North American Free Trade Agreement is expected to continue the movement of capital to Mexico as barriers to trade come down and new business opportunities increase.

The most significant change in the economic relations between Latin America and the United States, however, is not found in export-import ratios or investment figures, but rather in the desire of these nations to be treated fairly as trading partners. For years the United States has held all or most of the economic cards. The Latin Americans now want a better distribution of the cards and therefore are asking for better access to U.S. markets and more stable prices for their export goods. The aggressiveness of the Latin Americans as they push toward development poses a real challenge to the United States, which is not used to competition, demands for equity, and nationalistic fervor from this region. Our response will help define the extent to which we are willing to form a neighborly economic relationship based on fairness and cooperation. It is important to remember that the new-found aggressiveness of the Latin Americans exists within a radically changed perception of the United States and the economic system we champion. As Abraham Lowenthal, a long-time observer of inter-American affairs states,

The broad regional turn toward harmonious relations with the United States has been unmistakable. For years many Latin Americans defined their foreign policies primarily in opposition to Washington. . . . Restrictive policies on foreign investment, reserved markets, high tariff barriers, movements toward regional economic integration and diplomatic concetacíon were all forged in part as responses to U.S. power. . . . All this has changed. Most Latin American governments and many opposition movements in Latin America today want stronger links with the United States.[13]

SOCIOCULTURAL RELATIONS: "COCA-COLA-IZATION" AND IMMIGRATION

In introducing U.S.–Latin American relations, it is important to remember the human element. International relations are often examined in terms of governments and trade percentages, and there is a failure to recognize that people interact more frequently than governments or export companies. The true test, then, of our neighborliness may be in how the peoples of the United States and Latin America relate to each other's cultures.

Commenting on the personal and cultural ties between the United States and Latin America is no easy task. These are, after all, two very different regions with two very different populations. As Lawrence Harrison, a former U.S. Agency for International Development Office, one remarked:

The differences between North America and Latin America are enormous, covering virtually all aspects of human life. The North American and the Latin

American have differing concepts of the individual, society and the relationship between the two; of justice and law; of life and death; of government; of the family; of relations between the sexes; of organization; of time; of enterprise; of religion; of morality. These differences have contributed to the evolution of societies which are more unlike one another than our past policy-makers appear to have appreciated. In fact, it can be argued that there are some Asian societies (Japan is an obvious candidate) which have more in common with the societies of North America than do most of the societies of Latin America.[14]

Despite these vast differences the interaction, whether it be personal, economic, cultural, or diplomatic, continues unabated between the 240 million residents of the United States and the 355 million residents of Latin America. Because the human interaction is such an important part of the relationship, it is helpful now to point out some of the commonly recognized results of the years of contact between North and South America.

From the U.S. perspective, the Latin Americans have been the kind of neighbor that one associates with only out of necessity and often only in order to maintain the appearance of cordial relations. Our contact with the Latin Americans has frequently been marked by arrogance and condescension. Just the fact that we call ourselves "American" suggests that we are the true representatives of Americanism. The Latin Americans, sensing the arrogance of this title, prefer to say "North Americans" as a reminder that the residents of the United States are not the only Americans.

The arrogance that underlies U.S. contacts with Latin America has led to the formation of a number of stereotypes. Too often we hear Latin Americans described as "hot-headed" and "hot-blooded" people who put off work until *mañana* and are forever engaged in some type of revolutionary hostility. We do not seem to be willing to meet the Latin Americans on their own terms and recognize the positive qualities of their society. Instead we have often developed images of our neighbors that foster ill will and perpetuate a negative view.

The most serious result of our contact with the Latin American people can be seen in the manner in which U.S. culture has transformed the unique character of this region. Because of our extensive corporate presence, yearly tourist influx, and the fact that the Latin Americans live next to the most advanced, consumer-oriented society in the world today, they have gradually assimilated many aspects of our culture.

One does not have to travel very far in a Latin American country to see signs of Americanization, or as it is sometimes referred to "Coca-Cola-ization." Latin Americans drink our soda, drive our cars, wear our designer jeans, play baseball, buy our gadgets, watch our television programs, and absorb the images, ideas, trends, and fashion that wind their way across the border. We may not control Latin American nations militarily, but we are present in countless ways because of the cultural grafting of the U.S. way of life.[15]

With the onset of regional trade agreements and a rush to implement market economies, Latin America has become even more Americanized. Pizza Hut is now seeking to achieve a corporate strategy that would develop 500 restaurants in Latin America by the end of the century and introduce a food staple that is now synonymous with our popular culture. The retail giant Wal-Mart has built the largest discount store in the world in Mexico City to accommodate shoppers who cannot get enough goods from the United States. And throughout the region, Latin American's are being introduced to the stock market (or *bolsa* as it is called in many countries) with all its frenzied activity, risk taking, and blatant capitalism. After years of trying desperately to avoid embracing the capitalist ethic and all the cultural characteristics that accompany it, the Latin Americans in the 1990s are seemingly running full speed toward the U.S. system of economics and way of life.

It is important, however, to mention that proximity to the United States also means that Americanization is joined by Latin Americanization. The movement of people from Mexico and the Caribbean into the United States as illegal entrants, day workers, or shoppers has had a profound effect on the states that serve as entry points for the influx from the south. California, Texas, and Florida have become "Hispanicized" as the Latin American cultures brought by the new arrivals change the landscape from food to music to language. Los Angeles, El Paso, and Miami have distinct Hispanic communities where it is difficult for casual visitors to determine whether they are in North America or South America.

For those non-Hispanic Americans who have seen their cities and states become Latin Americanized the adjustment has been difficult and has fostered resentment over the costs related to the new arrivals and the changing domestic ambiance. States, such as California, have become battlegrounds for movements to require English as the official language and to deny educational and social welfare benefits for illegal immigrants. And yet, despite the currents of hostility that have arisen over the new Latin American arrivals and the changing character of life in the United States, the movement northward by people in search of a better life continues and puts to the test some fundamental principles of openness, diversity, and equal opportunity that are at the core of the American ethic.[16]

The pervasive cultural transformation of Latin American society by the United States is criticized in nationalistic intellectual and political circles. These critics of the U.S. cultural invasion argue that the Latin Americans must return to their Spanish, or in some countries to their Indian, heritage. Failure to do so would in the minds of these nationalists deprive the Latin Americans of their identity and increase their dependence on the United States. Already there is some evidence that

Latin Americans are seeking to expand their cultural ties to Spain after centuries of hatred and suspicion. It is the Latin American way of returning to their roots.

Despite the efforts to diminish the influence of the United States on Latin American society, it is nearly impossible to control the effect that one neighbor can have on the other, especially if there is a great disparity of wealth. As one Mexican leader was heard to comment on the impact of the United States, "Mexico, so far from God, yet so close to the United States."

One major consequence of the attraction the United States holds for Latin Americans is the steady stream of immigrants who have come to settle here. In the period from 1880 to 1920, when the bulk of the immigration occurred in this country, the new arrivals came primarily from central and southern Europe. Now in the 1990s a large number of immigrants come from Latin America, and particularly Mexico, the Caribbean, and Central America. As documented by statistics from the U.S. Immigration and Naturalization Service (INS), 2.3 million Mexican and 2 million Caribbean immigrants have gained legal entry into the United States in the last 150 years. The legal immigrants are, however, only part of the story. Estimates of the illegal immigrant population in the United States vary considerably with some sources recording 12 million, while the INS states that the figure is in the neighborhood of 6 million. Table I.5 provides a list of Latin American immigrants living in the United States according to 1990 census figures.

To address what has become a serious social and economic problem in this country, Congress, after years of partisan wrangling and intense lobbying from Hispanic and civil liberties groups, passed in 1986 the Immigration Reform Act, which attempted to control illegal entry into the United States by fining employers who knowingly hire illegals, by beefing up border patrols, and by working more closely with Latin American governments to stem the tide of immigration. The act also sought to quiet the criticism of those who pointed to the contributions to the American economy made by illegal immigrants by granting amnesty to those individuals who arrived in this country before 1982 and could prove continuous residence in the United States.

Despite this landmark legislation, the tide of illegal immigration has not stopped. Immigrants continue to come to the United States without proper documentation. Economic hardship, guerrilla warfare, political repression, and most important, the prospect of participating in the American dream make illegal entry into the United States worth the risk. The INS has toughened its stance against illegal entry, especially by making distinctions between those immigrants who come to the United States for what is viewed as purely economic reasons as opposed to those who seek political asylum.

The continued entry of illegals into the United States poses a fundamental question about our nation and what we value. For a country

Table I.5
Hispanic Population in the United States

States with a higher percentage of Hispanics than the national average

New Mexico	38.2
California	25.8
Texas	25.5
Arizona	18.8
Colorado	12.9
New York	12.3
Florida	12.2
Nevada	10.4
New Jersey	9.6

The ten cities with the largest Hispanic populations

New York	1,784,000
Los Angeles	1,391,000
Chicago	546,000
San Antonio	520,000
Houston	450,000
El Paso	356,000
San Diego	230,000
Miami	224,000
Dallas	210,000
San Jose	208,000

Source: U.S. Census Bureau.

like the United States, which has prided itself on opening its doors to the "tired and homeless," the sight of people crawling under barbed wire in the Arizona desert, jumping over walls in San Diego, and fording the Rio Grande in Texas brings up the question of whether this country is going to continue its tradition of providing access to our way of life. What we do as a nation in response to the Latin American immi-gration problem will reveal our sensitivity to the enormous economic and polit-ical pressures that bring these people to our country.

THE UNITED STATES AND LATIN AMERICA: FROM PATRON-CLIENT TO PARTNERS IN DEVELOPMENT

Trying to put the relationship between the United States and Latin America into understandable terms is no easy task. As can be seen from this brief introductory overview, our ties to the Latin American coun-tries are complex and pervasive. However, by relying on one of the oldest social institutions found in this region it may be possible to view how the relationship developed and how it may be moving to a new level.

Because Latin America has traditionally been largely an agricultural society, the farm became a center of national life. In Latin America the farms, or as they are more properly called, *haciendas*, evolved into huge estates, each owned by one wealthy family and employing hundreds, even thousands, of peasants. The relationship between the *hacienda* owners and peasants became one of domination and inequality. The owner, or *patrón*, ruled over his estate as a kind of benevolent dictator, managing the day-to-day concerns of the *hacienda* but also serving as the local power broker, policeman, problem solver, judge, and social overlord.[17]

The peasants or clients of the *patrón* had little opportunity to challenge the system of authority developed around the *hacienda*. They often had to endure long hours, low pay, the inability to own land, and the prospect of never being able to control their own lives. All they could expect was a tolerable existence with little chance for change, upward mobility, or political influence.

Although the *hacienda* system is no longer as predominant as it was in the past, the relationship between the patron and client remains an appropriate analogy for describing U.S.–Latin American relations. The United States has consistently viewed itself as the principle force in the hemisphere, with the Latin American countries playing a lesser role in the overall scheme of regional security and development. Because the hemisphere was ours to control and lead, the United States, much like the *patrón*, assumed many duties to ensure its continued control of events in this sphere of influence. The Latin American clients for their part could do very little to limit the power of the patron. Instead, they accepted the relationship and reaped what benefits they could, while resigning themselves to the periodic meddling of the "Colossus of the North."

But just as the *hacienda* system gave way to an industrial, urbanized, and more complex social system, the United States today is a neighbor to Latin American countries that are unwilling to remain obedient clients to the power politics of their North American patron. The traditional patron-client relationship has broken down domestically in Latin America in a wave of revolution, land reform, peasant cooperatives, and centralized administration. Similarly, U.S. domination and control in this region is no longer accepted without protest. The Latin America of the 1990s is ripe with nationalism, alternative ideologies, foreign competition, and a more independently minded populace.

U.S.–Latin American relations are now in a period of reevaluation and renewal. As the world has changed so have the Latin Americans and their view of the United States. Today the operative words in Latin America and the United States are "community" and "partnership." In fact, there is a recurring theme among government officials and private-sector investors in the hemisphere that suggests both North America and South America evidence what has been called a "substantive symmetry"—a common agenda of concerns and visions. The components of this symmetry were articulated by Richard Feinberg, President Clinton's Special Assistant for Inter-American Affairs on the National Security Council. In a speech to Latin Americanists in 1994, Feinberg said,

Hemispheric relations are entering a new era in which all countries—north and south—face a similar agenda rooted in their common participation in the one-world economy. This is the era of substantive symmetry. . . . At home, we are rebuilding a sense of community and social inclusion. Many Latin American nations are pursuing political reconciliation and democratic deepening. We are making our economy more competitive and promoting exports. Latin America is inserting itself more and more into the global economy. We are reforming our health, welfare and educational systems. Latin America is turning to its own social agenda.[18]

This new substantive symmetry is a marked departure from the days of the patron-client relationship in which the United States treated the countries of the hemisphere as petulant children who needed to be disciplined or mere pawns in an international chess game. The commonality of interest and emphasis on partnership offers both the United States and Latin America a wealth of opportunities to strengthen their economies and their social systems. But because this is a new relationship and a new world, both the United States and Latin America will have to make adjustments from past practice. From the U.S. perspective, this country wants Latin America to institutionalize democratic governance, open their economies to global competition, and develop public policies that encourage growth and trade. The Latin American people want the United States to accept them as equal partners and permit them to fashion their own social and political solutions without interference. In many respects, these are goals that both the United States and the Latin American nations have wanted for years; only now, in the 1990s, is the climate right for both sides to realize their objectives.

NOTES

1. See John Grimond, "Latin America: Yes We Have No Mananas," *The Economist*, November 13, 1993, in *Annual Editions, Latin America*, 6th ed. (Guilford, Conn.: Dushkin, 1994), pp. 140–47.

2. Abraham Lowenthal, "Changing U.S. Interests in a New World," in *The United States and Latin America in the 1990s*, eds. Jonathan Hartlyn, Lars Schoultz, and Augusto Varas (Chapel Hill: University of North Carolina Press, 1992), pp. 64–85.

3. Margaret Daly Hayes, "Not What I Say but What I Do: Latin American Policy in the Reagan Administration," in *Latin America: A Quarter Century of Crisis and Challenge, 1961–1986*, ed. John Martz (Lincoln: University of Nebraska Press, 1988), pp. 98–131.

4.   See Pedro Pablo Kucynski, *Latin American Debt* (Baltimore, Md.: Johns Hopkins University Press, 1987).

5.   Alexander Watson, Address Before the Institute of the Americas, La Jolla, California, March 2, 1994, in U.S. State Department Dispatch, March 4, 1994, p. 154.

6.   See Carlos Rangel, *The Latin Americans and Their Love-Hate Relationship with the United States* (New York: Harcourt, Brace, Jovanovich, 1977).

7.   Octavio Paz, "El esperio indiscreto," as quoted in Carlos Rangel, "Mexico and Other Dominoes," *Commentary*, June 1981, pp. 27–33.

8.   Howard Wiarda, *In Search of Policy—The United States and Latin America* (Washington, D.C.: American Enterprise Institute for Public Policy Research, 1984), p. 24.

9.   See Caludio Veliz, "Centralism and Nationalism in Latin America," *Foreign Affairs* 46 (October 1968): 68–83.

10.   Wiarda, *In Search of Policy*, p. 24.

11.   Abraham Lowenthal, *Partners in Conflict: U.S.–Latin American Relations* (Baltimore: Johns Hopkins University Press, 1988), pp. 56–59.

12.   Washington Report, The Council of the Americas, Fall 1993, p. 66.

13.   Abraham Lowenthal, "Latin America: Ready for Partnership," *Foreign Policy* 72 (1993):77.

14.   As quoted in Lawrence Harrison, *Underdevelopment Is a State of Mind: The Latin American Case* (Lanham, Md.: Madison Books, 1985), p. xv.

15.   Venezuelan President Rafael Caldera once said, "Our radio stations transmit your music and your outlook on life. Our television is full of an imagery that reflects your mode of thinking." As quoted in Robert D. Bond, "Where Democracy Lives," *The Wilson Quarterly* 7 (Winter 1983): 52.

16.   See Christopher Mitchell, ed., *Western Hemisphere Immigration and U.S. Foreign Policy* (University Park: Pennsylvania State University, 1992).

17.   For a more complete discussion of the patron-client relationship see Barrington Moore, Jr., *Social Origins of Dictatorship and Democracy: Land and Peasant in the Making of the Modern World* (Boston: Beacon Press, 1966), pp. 468–83.

18.   Richard E. Feinberg, "Substantive Symmetry in Hemispheric Relations," Address to the Latin American Studies Association, Atlanta, March 10, 1992, in U.S. Department of State Dispatch, March 14, 1994, p. 158.

Part I

THE EVOLUTION OF U.S.– LATIN AMERICAN RELATIONS

1

The Monroe Doctrine and the Emergence of U.S. Power

To look at the extensive political, economic, and social ties that currently bind the United States and Latin America, one might be surprised to find that this close relationship did not always exist. If we examine the earliest days of the U.S. republic, the record will show that despite our proximity to Latin America, the leaders of the new United States of America were not terribly interested in affairs to their south and instead defined this country's foreign policy objectives in terms of circumstances and conditions in Europe.

In many respects this concern with Europe rather than Latin America was a prudent position for the United States to follow. After all, this country was still viewed as a renegade that dared to challenge the power and authority of the British Empire. From the U.S. perspective it was quite possible that the Revolutionary War would enter a new stage, with Britain trying again to regain its colonial possession. The United States thus felt a need to turn its diplomatic attention to Europe as a means of building support for the democratic experiment and to offset any moves by the British to weaken this country's standing in the international community.

The foreign policy priority given to Europe over Latin America was also based on a perception that close ties with our neighbors to the south were not of primary importance to the future development of the United States. The Latin American colonies were, at least until 1810, securely under Spanish rule, and therefore relations would have to be handled in Madrid. Furthermore, the early leaders of this country had yet to achieve a firm bond with Latin America. Speaking a different language and practicing a different religion, the Latin Americans were often seen as a people with colonial experience far removed from that of the United States.

NO TRANSFER RESOLUTION

The United States' reluctance to formulate an active Latin American foreign policy ended once this country sensed the danger to its security from Spanish landholdings along its southern border, especially in Florida. As early as 1810 Americans in West Florida (now southern Alabama and the panhandle of Florida) staged a revolt, replaced the Spanish authority, and asked for annexation to the United States. Although President Madison supported the take over of West Florida, he feared repercussions from the Spanish and from the British, who recognized the Spanish claims. Madison especially feared that the Spanish, seeing their position disintegrating in Florida, would appeal to the British for assistance in protecting their interests.

The United States acted quickly to offset Spanish and British action in West Florida. President Madison, on January 3, 1811, delivered a message to Congress asking permission to "take temporary possession of Spanish territories to deter any foreign nation from transferring their land holdings to another nation." Congress supported Madison's request and passed a resolution that has come to be called the "No Transfer Resolution," recognized as the first major policy statement of the United States toward Latin America. The resolution as passed on January 15, 1811, states:

Resolved by Senate and House of Representatives of the United States of America, in Congress assembled, That the United States under the peculiar circumstances of the existing crisis, cannot without serious inquietude, see any part of the said territory pass into the hands of any foreign Power; and that a due regard to their safety compels them to provide, under certain contingencies, for the temporary occupation of the said territory; they at the same time, declare the said territory shall, in their hands remain subject to a future negotiation.[1]

Although the No Transfer Resolution clearly established a claim on Spanish-held West Florida and sent a signal to the British that we would not tolerate attempts to threaten our southern flank, the question of who owned Florida was not easily solved. In April 1813, the United States formally annexed West Florida, but it was unable to gain a clear title to the remainder of Florida until the signing of the Adams–de Onis Treaty in 1819. During those intervening years the United States was stymied in its efforts to gain control of the remainder of Florida primarily because the British continued their support of the Spanish.

But once relations between the United States and Britain were normalized after the War of 1812, and, more important, as the Spanish lost their grip of their possessions in the hemisphere, the alliance between England and Spain that formed over the Florida issue began to weaken. When the Spaniards could no longer count on British support, the stage was set for negotiations with the Madrid government and for eventual U.S. control over all of Florida.

The Adams–de Onis Treaty is often thought of as the document that gave Florida to the United States, but it also deprived Spain of any claims on what would eventually become Oregon. In return, the United States agreed not to make any claim on Spanish control of Texas. The treaty, besides being a first formal venture into a diplomatic relationship with Latin America, was a victory for the United States. As Lloyd Mecham states, "Thanks particularly to the incomparable diplomatic skills of John Quincy Adams, the United States exploited to the limit the opportunities presented by the Latin American wars of independence to rectify its boundaries and extend its borderlands."[2]

LATIN AMERICAN INDEPENDENCE AND U.S. NEUTRALITY

From 1810 to 1826, when the colonies of Latin America were at war with their Spanish rulers, the United States was faced with the dilemma of how to respond properly to the righting in this region. At first the United States made a few minor gestures of support for the colonial revolutionaries and appointed a handful of representatives to observe the internal situation in countries like Venezuela, Argentina, Chile, and Peru.

Our caution with respect to the wars of Latin American independence stemmed from the fear of antagonizing Spain and ultimately England by openly supporting the rebels. The administrations of Presidents Madison and Monroe followed a position of neutrality toward the fighting in Latin America. But the official neutrality policy did not deter private citizens from trading with the rebels or from helping to finance their cause.

As the Spanish began losing to the rebels in South America more pressure was placed on U.S. presidents to move from neutrality to recognition of the colonial governments. One of the most eloquent and persistent champions of U.S. recognition of the new Latin American states was Henry Clay, who spent nearly ten years advancing this cause in Congress. In one of his greatest speeches, Clay called on his colleagues to support an appropriation of $18,000 to provide salary and expenses for a minister to Buenos Aires. As Clay said:

[The nations of Latin America would be] animated by an American feeling and guided by an American policy. They would obey the laws of the system of the New World, of which they would compose a part in contradistinction to that of Europe. . . . At the present moment the patriots of the south are fighting for liberty and independence—for precisely what we fought for.[3]

Despite his pro–Latin American oratory Clay's bill was defeated, but the desire to have the United States formally support Latin American independence did not diminish. Clay continued to submit legislation designed to achieve recognition, although Congress was reluctant to interfere with what was viewed as presidential prerogatives in the area of foreign policy. Besides congressional reluctance, Clay also faced a formidable foe in Secretary of State John Quincy Adams, who vigorously opposed recognition and stressed the need to remain neutral until it was clear who would win the war. Adams's opposition reveals the ideological and cultural gulf between the United States and Latin America that prevailed in the early days of this relationship. In his memoirs Adams states:

I have not yet seen and do not now see any prospect that they will establish free or liberal institutions of government. . . . They have not the first elements of good or free government. . . . We shall derive no improvement to our own institutions by any communion with theirs. Nor is there any appearance of a disposition in them to take any political lesson from us.[4]

Although Clay was unsuccessful in attaining early U.S. recognition of Latin American independence, the inability of the Spanish to hold onto their colonial possessions gradually swung the Monroe administration away from its policy of neutrality. On May 4, 1822, President Monroe asked Congress for $100,000 to support diplomatic representatives in La Plata (Argentina), Chile, Peru, Great Colombia, and Mexico. With the overwhelming congressional approval for the appropriation, the United States began receiving ministers from the new Latin American states and sending its own representatives southward. Even though the process of moving from neutrality to recognition was a long one and filled with partisan disagreements, the United States became the first country to recognize formally the independent states of Latin America.

THE MONROE DOCTRINE

President Monroe's decision to recognize the newly independent nations of Latin America signaled to the European powers that the United States was now interested in playing a larger role in the affairs of this region. The response from Europe, however, showed little respect for our policy and even less for the independence movements of Latin America. The European monarchies reacted to the new-found independence of the Latin American colonies by organizing alliances that threatened to reestablish their hold in the hemisphere. In particular, Russia, Austria, Prussia, and France (and for a time England) formed what came to be called the Holy Alliance, which proposed to crush the newly established Latin American states. From Europe, rumors spread that a combined French and Spanish fleet would soon sail to the

Americas to regain the continent and return the revolutionary governments to the hands of the monarchs.

The United States, although not directly threatened by the Holy Alliance, took an active role in defending the hemisphere when Czar Alexander I of Russia issued a decree (*ukase*) in which he warned foreign vessels not to come within 100 miles of the coast of Alaska (Russian America). During the early years of the Republic, the northwest was still unchartered territory and Alexander's decree was not perceived as requiring vigorous diplomatic response. Yet the Monroe administration feared that this *ukase* was but a first step in a concerted effort by the Holy Alliance to intimidate the independent democracies of the New World.

The U.S. response to the threats of the Holy Alliance is contained in what is now viewed as the basic statement of Inter-American relations: the Monroe Doctrine. On December 2, 1823, President Monroe, speaking in his annual address to Congress, enunciated his now-famous statement setting apart the New World from the old, warning against any new colonial incursions, and serving notice that any threat to these new republics would be viewed as a threat to the United States. The important sections of the Monroe Doctrine are provided below.

In the wars of the European powers in matters relating to themselves we have never taken any part, nor does it comport with our policy so to do. It is only when our rights are invaded or seriously menaced that we resent injuries or make preparations for our defense. With the movements in this hemisphere we are, of necessity, more immediately connected, and by causes which must be obvious to all enlightened and impartial observers. The political system of the allied powers is essentially different in this respect from that of America. This difference proceeds from that which exists in their respective governments. And to the defense of our own, which has been achieved by the loss of so much blood and treasure, and matured by the wisdom of these most enlightened citizens, and under which we have enjoyed unexampled felicity, this whole nation is devoted. We owe it, therefore, to candor, and to the amicable relations existing between the United States and those powers, to declare that we should consider any attempt on their part to extend their system to any portion of this hemisphere is dangerous to our peace and safety. With the existing colonies or dependencies of any European power we have not interfered and shall not interfere. But with the governments who have declared their independence and maintain it, and whose independence we have, on great consideration and on just principles, acknowledged, we could not view any interposition for the purpose of oppressing them, or controlling in any other manner their destiny, by any European power, in any other light than as the manifestation of an unfriendly disposition toward the United States. In the war between these new governments and Spain we declared our neutrality at the time of their recognition, and to this we have adhered and shall continue to adhere, provided no change shall occur which, in the judgment of the competent authorities of this Government, shall make a corresponding change on the part of the United States indispensable to their security.[5]

With the presentation of this policy of hemispheric sovereignty the United States officially declared itself the protector of the Western Hemisphere and the principal power to be dealt with in this region. In retrospect this was a bold move on the part of the United States, because its defense of Latin America could not be enforced with any degree of certainty. The United States was in no position in 1823 to back up its threats to the Holy Alliance with a credible naval or military show of force or, for that matter, to assume the task of protecting each Latin American country from recolonization efforts or other forms of intervention. Actually, the British were the bona fide master of Latin American sovereignty and had interests in this region that overshadowed those of the United States.

Despite the limitations of U.S. power in 1823, the Monroe Doctrine was promulgated at a time when this country was beginning to experience feelings of nationalism and had visions of playing a larger role in international affairs. President Monroe's speech was well received; Congress lent its support and newspapers trumpeted the new-found evidence of U.S. power that the doctrine represented. Although the doctrine may have been unenforceable, it served to rally the nation behind President Monroe and the principle of hemispheric independence.

Needless to say, the Monroe Doctrine was not received favorably in the capitals of continental Europe. The monarchies of Europe were not used to being issued directives by an "upstart" nation, much less being ordered to refrain from further colonial interventions in the Western Hemisphere. Dexter Perkins, an expert on the Monroe Doctrine, quotes the French foreign minister, who summed up the European reaction to President Monroe's speech:

Mr. Monroe, who is not a sovereign, has assumed in his message the tone of a powerful monarch, whose armies and fleets are ready to march at the first signal. . . . Mr. Monroe is the temporary president of a Republic situated on the east coast of North America. This republic is bounded on the south by possessions of the King of Spain and on the north by those of the King of England. Its independence was only recognized forty years ago, by what right then would the two Americas today be under its immediate sway from Hudson's Bay to Cape Horn.[6]

The condescending statement of the French foreign minister underestimated the impact of the Monroe Doctrine and its potential as a means of protecting the sovereignty of the Latin American republics. As diplomatic historian Thomas Bailey states: "It is possible—though by no means probable—that there would be somewhat more European territory in the Americas today if the Monroe Doctrine, or some similar doctrine, had not been proclaimed. It became an increasingly potent stick behind the door."[7]

Two final words about the Monroe Doctrine. The assurances of the U.S. president did not engender great enthusiasm in Latin American capitals. Latin American leaders were already wary of U.S. motives and were cognizant of the fact that they could easily become pawns in a contest for regional domination. A few countries immediately sought military and economic alliances with the United States, but these requests were turned down. The United States seemed more interested in words of cooperation than in naval flotillas to protect the hemisphere. After all the furor surrounding the doctrine died down, the Latin Americans still faced the threat of foreign intervention, only now they could expect such intervention might trigger some sort of response from the United States. The only problem was that the actual character of the response remained unclear.

The president's speech did not become known as the Monroe Doctrine until the 1850s. In fact, within weeks of its delivery the Monroe Doctrine faded from the headlines and did not become an integral part of our Latin American foreign policy until the United States was recognized as a more respected and feared participant in world affairs. Yet it is difficult to ignore the importance of this policy statement. The Monroe Doctrine in effect brought the United States into the mainstream of international power politics. By publicly declaring its intention to protect the hemisphere, the United States went on record as saying that it wanted to be recognized as an emerging world power. The fact that the United States was unable to enforce its claims effectively is less important than that we were taking the first step toward enhancing our position among the major European powers. From this point onward, the United States sought to control events by declaring itself the dominant force in the hemisphere, rather than merely reacting to events in Europe.

TEXAS AND THE WAR WITH MEXICO

With the Monroe Doctrine in place, it now remained to be seen whether the United States was willing to live up to its promise of protecting the hemisphere from foreign intervention. But in the years following 1823 the United States showed that it was not so much interested in protecting Latin America as in spreading its influence and control over the region.

The first hint of U.S. designs on Latin America came with the move to annex Texas. Thanks to an earlier agreement with the Spanish government, the United States gained the rights to settlement in what was to become Mexican territory. These Texans, as they came to be called, were a hardy and independent group of settlers who eventually refused to be bound by the dictates of the Mexican government, headed by General Antonio Lopez de Santa Anna. The Mexican government was adamant in its insistence on holding onto Texas and refusing to be intimidated by the settlers or by the frequent attempts of the Jackson administration to purchase the territory.

By 1835 the two sides were in a warring spirit and the Mexicans' attempt to establish their authority set off a series of battles that have now become part of U.S. history and legend. At first Santa Anna, using overwhelming force, defeated the Texans at the Alamo. Jim Bowie, Davy Crockett, and 200 other Texans fought to the last man. Despite the tragic defeat, General Sam Houston rallied his men and struck back at Santa Anna near the town of San Jacinto. The cries of Houston's men to "Remember the Alamo" have become part of U.S. mythology.

The victory at San Jacinto and the capture of Santa Anna brought quick results. On May 14, 1836, the Mexican dictator agreed to leave Texas territory and cease all hostility. In 1837, Texas was recognized by the U.S. government as an independent nation and remained independent for nearly a decade.

While Texas maneuvered for annexation to the United States, President James Polk's administration set its sights on an even bigger prize: California. President Polk has often been associated with the era of Manifest Destiny, during which the United States began to expand its border westward. The Polk administration's action in the 1840s showed how far this country would go in order to increase its territory.

The determination of the new state of Texas to expand to the Rio Grande into what was Mexican territory started another round of conflict. This time, however, the emissaries of President Polk sought not only to claim the new enlarged Texas but also to purchase New Mexico ($5 million) and California ($25 million). Having lost Texas, the Mexican government was not receptive to the offer, even though the nation was near bankruptcy. The mission of President Polk's representative, John Slidell, was, as expected, a failure and the Mexicans, anxious to reassert their dominance in the area, prepared for war. On January 13, 1846, President Polk ordered General Zachary Taylor to take his troops into disputed Texas territory. This action, designed to take the initiative in the dispute, revealed the Polk administration's determination to acquire the remainder of Texas, New Mexico, and California by whatever means.

The Taylor expedition spurred the Mexicans into military action against the U.S. troops. On May 11, 1846, President Polk submitted a declaration of war to Congress which said in part:

The cup of forbearance had been exhausted. . . . But now, after reiterated menaces, Mexico has passed the boundary of the United States, has invaded our territory and shed American blood upon American soil. She has proclaimed that hostilities have commenced and that the two nations are now at war.[8]

President Polk got the support he needed from Congress to engage in war and $10 million to pay for it, but the circumstances surrounding our claim to this territory provoked criticism of the administration and its efforts to extend our borders at all costs. Because of the domestic pressure, President Polk hoped to avoid a long and bloody war and felt he had an ally in General Santa Anna, who was living in exile in Cuba. Hoping that Santa Anna could be convinced to sell the disputed territory, Polk permitted him to enter Mexico. However, instead of setting up negotiations, Santa Anna began war preparations and forced the United States to seek a military solution.

President Polk acted quickly to achieve his objectives. Armed columns were sent to control the disputed Mexican territory. General Kearney moved westward from Missouri to claim Texas, New Mexico, and California; Captain John Fremont sailed up the Pacific coast to secure California and to meet up with Kearney. The real fighting, though, was in Mexico where the armies of Generals Taylor and Winfield Scott captured Buena Vista in the north and the capital, Mexico City, in the central part of the country. In a matter of ten months the fighting was over, as the better organized and trained U.S. troops defeated the Mexicans.

The U.S. invasion of Mexico was in the view of some analysts unnecessary, because Kearney and Fremont had already gained control of Texas, New Mexico, and California. For the Polk administration, however, it was essential to inflict a military defeat upon the Mexicans and thereby limit their ability to engage in further incursions into the newly acquired U.S. territory. The fall of Vera Cruz and eventually of Mexico City created enormous hostility toward the United States among Mexicans, feelings that are still called forth today by nationalistic extremists. Nevertheless, the Mexicans were soundly defeated and the United States had its territory and scores of war heroes, from future president Zachary Taylor to a young officer named Robert E. Lee.

The Mexican defeat was formalized in the Treaty of Guadalupe Hidalgo. Under the terms of the treaty, signed on February 2, 1848, Mexico lost approximately one-third of its territory. In return the United States agreed to pay Mexico $15 million and to assume payment of the claims of its own citizens against the Mexican government, a sum of about $3.2 million. The fact that the Polk administration agreed to pay Mexico $15 million even though it had lost the war was interpreted as a face-saving gesture to soothe the Mexicans, who had suffered a humiliating defeat and whose cooperation would most likely be needed in the future.

That need for cooperation became apparent very soon, as the United States sought Mexican land to build an east-west railroad to California, where gold had been found in 1848. On December 30, 1853, President Pierce's representative to Mexico, James Gadsden, purchased for $10 million a slice of land through what is now Arizona and New Mexico for the railway right-of-way. Luckily for the United States, the Mexican government was again led by the corrupt General Santa Anna and badly in need of money. The deal caused hardly a ripple of negative public opinion in either the United States or Mexico.

The Gadsden Purchase ended for the moment the U.S. drive to acquire new land. Thanks to the aggressiveness of President Polk, the United States was now a two-ocean nation and had increased its territorial holdings (with the inclusion also of Oregon) by two-thirds. It is important, though, to remember that the United States was able to achieve these results only through use of raw military power and a reluctance to compromise with a neighboring nation state. The U.S. actions during the Texas episodes and the war with Mexico revealed to the Latin Americans that the threat to the hemisphere and their national integrity might come not from Europe, but from their northern neighbor.

THE UNITED STATES BEGINS TO LOOK FOR A CANAL

Although the Panama Canal was not completed until 1914, the international maneuvering to gain control of the isthmus began during the Polk administration. The early efforts of the United States to establish a claim to the isthmus tell much about both the application of the Monroe Doctrine in Latin America and the influence of Great Britain in hemispheric affairs.

The struggle for the canal began when Great Britain developed a colony in Central America. By controlling what is today the eastern coast of Honduras, Nicaragua, and Costa Rica, the British posed a threat to the Monroe Doctrine. Moreover, their colony placed the British in an excellent position to control the isthmus and the trade that could potentially pass through this narrow slice of land.

The United States, in concert with the government of New Granada (today known as Colombia), worked quickly to outmaneuver the British in this area. In 1848, the U.S. Senate ratified the Bidlack Treaty, which granted this country the right of transit across the Isthmus of Panama for lawful commerce. In return, the government of New Granada (which controlled modern-day Panama) received assurances that the "United States would guarantee the rights of sovereignty and of property which New Granada has and possesses over the said territory."

The signing of the Bidlack Treaty with New Granada showed our intention to compete with the British for the right to gain sole access to the isthmus and the opportunities for future trade that went with that access. In order to attain this goal, the United States found itself reemphasizing President Monroe's determination to protect the hemisphere from foreign intervention. In fact, as historian Samuel Flagg Bemis states, "[the Bidlack Treaty] is the only occasion in the nineteenth century in which the United States accepted the overture of a Latin American state to defend its sovereignty."9

The Bidlack Treaty opened the floodgates of competition for a waterway to link the two oceans. British representatives now turned their attention to a Nicaraguan route in an attempt to counter the U.S. treaty with New Granada. Competition over the isthmus and a future canal led the United States and Great Britain to work out a compromise, resulting in the Clayton-Bulwer Treaty of 1850, which stipulated that any future railway or canal linking the two oceans would be built under the joint control of the United States and Great Britain. The treaty further established that the isthmus would remain neutral, that transit tolls would be equal for both countries, and that neither country would fortify, colonize, or assume any dominion over Central America.

Although seemingly a fair resolution of the competition for the isthmus, the Clayton-Bulwer Treaty was viewed as a concession by the United States because it accepted joint control of a future canal and failed to force the British out of the region. With war fever increasing in England, historians agree that the administration of President Zachary Taylor was reluctant to challenge the British presence in Central America. In the process of reaching a diplomatic settlement with its major competition in the hemisphere, the United States compromised the clear intent of the Monroe Doctrine.

LATIN AMERICAN POLICY DURING THE CIVIL WAR

The onset of the Civil War in the United States created a foreign policy vacuum that European powers sought to exploit. While the Lincoln administration was preoccupied with the conduct of the war, Spain and France made efforts to reestablish colonies in the hemisphere.

In 1861, the Spanish government of Queen Isabella II moved to reannex the Dominican Republic, stationing 25,000 troops in the tiny nation that had only gained independence from Spain in 1844. Despite the size of its military presence, the Spanish were unable to maintain control, as local Dominican opposition was strong. The Spanish eventually left the Dominican Republic in 1865.

The Dominican reannexation attempt by Spain bears examination not so much because of what the Lincoln administration did in response to this clear violation of the Monroe Doctrine, but rather because of its inaction. The failure of President Lincoln and Secretary of State William Seward to move beyond a written protest of the Spanish invasion shows this country's unwillingness to challenge a foreign power while in the midst of its own civil war. Although there is some evidence that Secretary Seward suggested involvement in a war against Spain as a means of uniting the North and the South, President Lincoln felt that fully implementing the Monroe Doctrine would be dangerous and could seriously weaken the ability of the armed forces to wage war against the Confederacy. The inability of the Spanish to hold the Dominican Republic removed questions about the viability of the Monroe Doctrine from center stage, but it was becoming increasingly clear that the United States lacked the ability and will to implement its Latin American policy.

The Spanish challenge to Dominican sovereignty and the Monroe Doctrine was minor compared to the French intervention in Mexico in 1861. Encouraged by British and Spanish support, French Emperor Napoleon III sent his army to invade Mexico and placed Austrian Archduke Maximilian on the throne. The new monarchy was quickly recognized by the great European powers, who still harbored visions of creating European-controlled colonies in the New World. The Lincoln administration, for its part, saw the French invasion of Mexico as a serious threat to its national security.

At first the monarchy of Maximilian was secure in its new home, even prompting plans for enlarging the empire to include all of Central America and eventually much of mainland South America. But as the Civil War in the United States moved to a close and the words of Secretary Seward grew more harsh, the new French empire began to weaken. In April 1864, a unanimous resolution of Congress demanded enforcement of the Monroe Doctrine. Later General Sheridan of the Union army was sent with 25,000 men to the Mexican border. By 1867, in the face of heightened pressure from the United States and a well-organized internal opposition, the French left Mexico and gave up their dream of a New World empire.

The French withdrawal from Mexico was a resounding victory for the effective use of the Monroe Doctrine. Even more important, the doctrine enjoyed its proudest moment during a period when this country's foreign policy capabilities were severely restrained. It can be argued that the Monroe Doctrine was effective because the Spanish and French colonizers were inept and faced strong local opposition, but there is also evidence that the Spanish and French were aware of the doctrine and fearful of possible U.S. action, especially once it was clear that the Civil War was coming to an end.

U.S.–LATIN AMERICAN RELATIONS
IN THE POSTWAR PERIOD

During the post–Civil War era, the United States built upon its new-found confidence in fending off hemispheric trespassers by again casting its eyes on expansion. This time the target was the Caribbean. In 1867 Secretary Seward signed a treaty with the Dutch government to purchase the Virgin Islands for $7.5 million, subject to the approval of the residents on the island. Despite overwhelming approval by the inhabitants, Congress was in no mood to spend the money. Once

President Grant came into office in 1869 the treaty was formally shelved and Seward's dream of spreading the flag to the Caribbean was put off to a later date.

But President Grant was also in the mood to acquire real estate, and in 1869 the Grant administration signed an annexation treaty with the Dominican Republic. Seriously in debt and easily susceptible to foreign speculation, the Dominican Republic was viewed favorably by Grant, his business cronies, and U.S. naval officials who had always coveted the Samaná peninsula of the Dominican Republic as a Caribbean base.

Grant lobbied vigorously in Congress to have the treaty ratified, but he was unable to convince Massachusetts senator Charles Sumner who was chairman of the Senate Foreign Relations Committee. Sumner, sensing questionable economic motives on the part of the Grant administration, spoke out against the treaty and was instrumental in its defeat in June 1870.

In both the Virgin Islands and Dominican Republic treaties, the attempt to expand U.S. influence through annexation faced critical public reaction and staunch congressional opposition. The U.S. mood in this postwar period was one of reluctance to assume an aggressive posture. The accent was on defending the hemisphere, rather than on controlling its destiny.

THE RISK OF INTER-AMERICAN DIPLOMACY

During the years following the Grant administration, the United States experienced enormous industrial and commercial growth. As a result of this internal growth, relations with Latin America were minimal and confined to issues related to the building of the Panama Canal and the formation of closer economic ties. The primary architect of U.S. foreign policy toward Latin America during this era was Secretary of State James Blaine, who, like Henry Clay, had a strong interest in the Latin American nations. Blaine's major contribution to inter-American affairs was his plan to host an international conference that would bring the nations of the hemisphere together to discuss common issues and resolve problems. Blaine first presented his idea for a pan-American conference during the Hayes administration, but intra-party differences placed the meeting in limbo.

Not until the administration of Benjamin Harrison, when Blaine was again named secretary of state, was the conference idea adopted. In October 1889, representatives from seventeen Latin American nations met in Washington. Blaine zealously urged the delegates to think in terms of regional cooperation, particularly on the issues of lowering trade barriers and developing a method for resolving disputes, but was unable to convince them to ignore their national interests and move toward closer hemispheric ties. All that Blaine was able to achieve in this first attempt at inter-American cooperation was the formation of the Pan American Union, an organization that would serve to encourage close relations through exchange of information and increased contacts. Although Blaine failed to achieve his primary objectives, the creation of the Pan American Union was an important step in the formation of an international body that viewed the hemisphere as one and sought to address its problems in a multilateral setting.

THE OLNEY DOCTRINE

The U.S. effort to promote inter-American cooperation and diplomacy as a means of resolving conflict was tested during the second administration of President Grover Cleveland. At issue in 1893 was a boundary dispute between Venezuela and neighboring British-held Guyana. The dispute, which dated back to 1840, involved control of the mouth of the important Orinoco River, Venezuela's major outlet to the sea.

Although the British made a number of attempts to achieve an acceptable settlement, the Venezuelans refused to agree to the British offers and looked instead to the United States for assistance. The Cleveland administration, for its part, was at odds with the British as a result of a previous trade dispute and was not predisposed to accept British claims of goodwill toward the Venezuelans. Also, renewed British activity in Central America increased the pressure on Cleveland to restate the principles of the Monroe Doctrine.

The official response of the Cleveland administration concerning the boundary dispute came from Secretary of State Richard Olney, who was not known for his diplomatic skills. The Olney message to London on July 20, 1895, threatened the British with the Monroe Doctrine and demanded that the British submit to international arbitration to settle the dispute. The importance of the Olney statement lay not only in its content but in its tone. Rather than framing the message in cautious diplomatic language, the secretary of state boasted about U.S. power in the hemisphere and suggested that the British interference in the affairs of Venezuela would be viewed as an unfriendly act. An example of the Olney rhetoric is perhaps the best guide:

Today the United States is practically sovereign on the continent, and its fiat is law upon the subjects to which it confines its interposition. Why? . . . because in addition to all other grounds, its infinite resources combined with its isolated position render it master of the situation and practically invulnerable as against any or all other powers.[10]

The Olney letter set off a series of responses in the United States and of course in England. Lord Salisbury, the British foreign secretary, engaged in "one-upmanship" by declaring that the Monroe Doctrine did not apply to this border dispute and that the United States had no right, either in international law or as a result of common practice in international relations, to impose a solution in a boundary dispute between two sovereign nations. The central position of Lord Salisbury is provided below:

The disputed frontier of Venezuela has nothing to do with any of the questions dealt with by President Monroe. It is not a question of the colonization by a European power of any portion of America. It is not a question of the imposition upon the communities of South America of any system of government devised in Europe. It is simply the determination of the frontier of a British possession which belongs to the Throne of England long before the Republic of Venezuela came into existence.[11]

Historians have commented on the logical and legal strength of the Salisbury response, but President Cleveland and the U.S. public would have none of the British unwillingness to acknowledge the hallowed Monroe Doctrine and the dominance in our hemisphere that the doctrine symbolized. Responding swiftly to the Salisbury note, President Cleveland asked Congress for an appropriation of $100,000 to form a boundary commission. Meanwhile legislators talked of U.S. military intervention, and public opinion, fed by an active press, clamored for a forceful response to the British.

Fortunately cooler heads prevailed on both sides of the Atlantic. The British in particular were unwilling to pursue further confrontation with the United States in South America, especially since they were facing more serious challenges to their vast empire in South Africa and possible threats in Canada. As a result, the British agreed to submit the boundary dispute to arbitration by signing a treaty with Venezuela in February of 1897. The border dispute was not settled until two years later, and ironically enough the British retained most of what they had originally claimed.

The Venezuelan border crisis is a prime example of the growing tendency of the United States to claim the hemisphere as its own and to use the Monroe Doctrine as the legal basis for extending its influence. One begins to see the blustering and bullying that a number of presidential administrations resorted to in an effort to assure the success of our policies. By the turn of the century, the United States was beginning to realize that other countries were impressed with our economic strength and rising prestige in the international community. We began to use our power, but only in that region where we were likely to be successful and only where foreign powers had marginal interests.

THE SPANISH-AMERICAN WAR

A much more important demonstration of this new U.S. power occurred in Cuba. Since the conclusion of the Civil War the United

States had paid increasing attention to the island colony of Spain off the Florida coast. Not only was the United States concerned about the frequent instances of unrest in Cuba, but by the 1880s this country had developed considerable commercial ties ($50 million in investments and $100 million in trade). In particular, the United States saw Cuba as a prime supplier of sugar; during 1894, for example, Cuba produced 1 million tons of sugar with most of that output destined for the United States.

The dual concerns of political stability and continued commercial relations caused the United States to become actively involved in the internal revolution that broke out in 1895. The insurrectionists, who were seeking to rid Cuba of Spanish control, engaged in a vicious campaign of violence and destruction that eventually had a detrimental effect on U.S. economic holdings. The Spanish, intent on maintaining their last stronghold in the Americas, sent the infamous General George Weyler, who instituted a policy of indiscriminate imprisonment of Cubans in large concentration camps as a way of suppressing the revolt. The imprisonment policy did little to control the disturbances, but the harshness of the Spanish actions angered many in the United States.

At first President Cleveland was reluctant to become involved in the struggle, but the Congress, pressured by business interests, passed a resolution recognizing the rebel cause and suggesting that Spain grant full independence to Cuba. Meanwhile the so-called yellow press in the United States drummed up support for Cuban independence by printing exaggerated reports of Spanish cruelty. Even though Spain recalled Weyler and began to moderate its policies toward the rebels, the anti-Spain attitude in the United States was formed and this country was posed for action.

The catalyst for our involvement came on February 15, 1898, when the U.S.S. *Maine*, on a visit to Havana, was blown up with a loss of 260 lives. Although the cause of the explosion was never established, cries of "Remember the *Maine*" were heard throughout the country. President William McKinley, who succeeded Cleveland, was himself reluctant to have the United States become embroiled in the Cuban independence struggle and thus made a serious attempt to achieve a diplomatic solution. McKinley proposed to Spain that it accept an armistice with the insurgents, an arbitration of the dispute, and an end to the concentration camps. In return the United States pledged not to attempt to annex Cuba.

Although the Spanish eventually accepted the terms of the McKinley proposal, the war momentum had already begun. The Cuban insurgents were willing to accept nothing short of complete independence; Congress was in a war mood and the U.S. public was anxious to avenge the *Maine*. On April 11, 1898, President McKinley sent to Congress a resolution that permitted the United States to take military action to end the hostilities, force a withdrawal of Spanish authority, and gain independence for the Cuban people. In the debate that ensued Congress pledged not to annex Cuba, but only to stay on the island for as long as it took the Cubans to win independence. This so-called Teller Amendment satisfied those in Congress who feared a new expansionist posture in the McKinley administration, but as our Cuban policy developed it became clear that the United States would be actively involved with internal Cuban affairs despite legislative assurances.

As to the war itself, superior U.S. military forces overwhelmed the Spanish outposts in Cuba. After three months of sporadic fighting the war was over and Spain sued for peace. By the terms of the Treaty of Paris, on December 10, 1898, the United States forced Spain to make three concessions: (1) to grant Cuban independence, (2) to cede Puerto Rico and the Pacific Island of Guam, (3) to sell the Philippine Islands for $20 million.

AFTERMATH OF WAR: THE PLATT AMENDMENT

Aside from the victory in Cuba and the acquisition of some valuable real estate, the Spanish-American War had a positive impact on U.S. public opinion. The country's mood was one of exhilaration and national pride as victorious soldiers arrived home and new war heroes like Theodore Roosevelt were named. There was indeed much to celebrate. The United States had not only defeated a European power (albeit a weak one) and expelled it from this hemisphere, but it also had become a colonial power itself with caretaker responsibilities that would require an involvement in the internal affairs of its neighbors. The United States has become the unquestioned force in the Western Hemisphere.

The United States quickly assumed its new caretaker role by establishing a military government in Cuba. Under the guidance of General Leonard Wood, the U.S. military contingent on Cuba ensured political stability, improved health conditions, and began the process of leading the Cubans toward constitutional governance.

The highly effective performance of General Wood and his men, however, was counterbalanced by the Cuban resistance to U.S. intervention in their affairs. When in 1900 General Wood ordered elections to be held and the drafting of a new constitution, which was to include provisions for establishing a more permanent U.S. role in Cuba, the Cubans balked and began questioning the real extent of their independence.

Their questions were answered when in March 1901, upon the request of Secretary of War Elihu Root, Congress approved what has come to be called the Platt Amendment. Originally attached to a military appropriations bill and named after that chairman of the Senate Foreign Relations Committee, the Platt Amendment became the first indication of U.S. intentions toward Cuba and of the lengths to which this country was willing to go in order to protect and guide the nations in this hemisphere.

Because the Platt Amendment is an important document in U.S.–Latin American relations, it is appropriate to present the full text of this congressional act. It provides:

I. That the government of Cuba shall never enter into any treaty or other compact with any foreign power or powers which will impair or tend to impair the independence of Cuba, nor in any manner authorize or permit any foreign Power or Powers to obtain by colonization or for military or naval purposes, or otherwise, lodgment in or control over any portion of said Island.

II. That said Government shall not assume or contract any public debt to pay the interest upon which, and to make reasonable sinking-fund provision for discharge of which, the ordinary revenues of the Island, after defraying the current expenses of the Government shall be inadequate.

III. That the Government of Cuba consents that the United States may exercise the right to intervene for the preservation of Cuban independence, the maintenance of a government adequate for the protection of life, property, and individual liberty, and for discharging the obligations with respect to Cuba imposed by the Treaty of Paris on the United States, now to be assumed and undertaken by the Government of Cuba.

IV. That all acts of the United States in Cuba during its military occupation thereof are ratified and validated, and all lawful rights acquired thereunder shall be maintained and protected.

V. That the Government of Cuba will execute, and as far as necessary extend, the plans already devised or other plans to be mutually agreed upon, for the sanitation of the cities of the Island to the end that a recurrence of epidemic and infectious diseases may be prevented, thereby assuring protection to the people and commerce of Cuba, as well as to the commerce of the Southern ports of the United States and the people residing therein.

VI. That the Isle of Pines shall be omitted for the proposed constitutional boundaries of Cuba, the title thereto left to future adjustments by treaty.

VII. That to enable the United States to maintain the independence of Cuba, and to protect the people thereof, as well as for its own defense, the Government of Cuba will sell or lease to the United States lands necessary for coaling or naval stations at certain specified points, to be agreed upon with the President of the United States.

VIII. That by way of further assurance the Government of Cuba will embody the foregoing provisions in a permanent treaty with the United States.

The Platt Amendment formally turned Cuba from an independent nation into a protectorate of the United States. This country obtained the rights to approve treaties, control finances, intervene militarily, lease land, and generally control the destiny of the island-nation. The Cubans were naturally upset with the legislation, but in order to end U.S. military occupation, they reluctantly approved the act and agreed to have its language included as an appendix to their constitution.

In retrospect, the Platt Amendment represents the exertion of raw power and arrogance on the part of the United States. Claiming to champion Cuban independence and democratic development, the United States became a suprasovereign caretaker and, as we shall see, a meddler in Cuban international affairs. But as is the case with most historical analysis, it is important to judge our Cuban policy in terms of the times in which it was formulated. The United States at the turn of the century was on the threshold of world prominence. The European powers, for the most part, had given up active competition with the United States in the Western Hemisphere. Moreover the three vital sectors in the formulation of U.S. foreign policy—the presidency, the Congress, and public opinion—were in general agreement on the need for this country to play a larger role in hemispheric affairs. Add to this the fact that the actions of Latin America, especially in the Caribbean, were in either economic or political disarray, and the motivation for an aggressive U.S. role in this region becomes understandable.

Judged by today's standards the proper U.S. response to problems such as the Venezuelan border dispute or the Cuban independence struggle would be quiet diplomatic consultation and self-determination, but at the turn of the century it was not easy for a country like the United States to forsake an active role in its own region in favor of moderation and self-restraint. The temptation to become a leader in world affairs and to control the future direction of neighboring states was just too great. The United States was on the move on its homefront and was intent on continuing this movement in foreign policy. This was a heady era, and it was only beginning.

NOTES

1. D. Hunter Miller, ed., *Secret Statutes of the United States* (Washington, D.C.: U.S. Government Printing Office, 1918), pp. 5–6.

2. Lloyd Mecham, *A Survey of United States–Latin American Relations* (Boston: Houghton Mifflin, 1965), p. 29.

3. Calvin Colton, ed., *The Works of Henry Clay* (New York: Federal Edition, 1904) 6: 140 (March 24, 1818).

4. Charles Francis Adams, ed., *Memoirs of John Quincy Adams*, 12 vols. (Philadelphia: 1874–77) 4: 28; 5: 176.

5. J. D. Richardson et al., eds., *Messages and Papers of the Presidents* (Washington, D.C.: 1896) 2: 209 (December 2, 1823).

6. *L'Etoile*, January 4, 1824, quoted in Dexter Perkins, *Monroe Doctrine, 1823–1826* (Cambridge, Mass.: 1927), p. 30.

7. Thomas Bailey, *A Diplomatic History of the American People* (New York: Appleton-Century-Crofts, 1964), p. 190.

8. J. D. Richardson et al., *Messages and Papers*, 4: 442.

9. Samuel Flagg Bemis, *The Latin American Policy of the United States* (New York: Harcourt, Brace and World, 1943), p. 105.

10. *Foreign Relations* (1895) 1: 558 (Olney to Bayard, July 20, 1895).

11. *Foreign Relations* (1895) 1: 564–65 (Salisbury to Pauncefote, November 24, 1895).

2

Interventionism, Cooperation, and Revolution

Twentieth-century hemispheric relations begin with the United States further expanding its power base in the region and even more anxious to direct the internal political and economic development of neighboring nation-states. The continuation of the expansionist and interventionist policies so reluctantly implemented by President McKinley found a ready advocate in his successor, Theodore Roosevelt. Fresh from his exploits with the Rough Riders in the Spanish-American War, Roosevelt catapulted from the vice-presidency to national leadership in 1901 upon the assassination of McKinley.

There is perhaps no president in this century who created so much controversy in his dealing with Latin America as Theodore Roosevelt. Roosevelt became the embodiment of the new-found confidence and aggressive spirit that characterized the United States at the turn of the century. His tough talk, impatience with detail, and willingness to use military force in order to accomplish foreign policy objectives became the characteristic traits of his administration.

Under Roosevelt the United States began to view the Caribbean and Central America as an area that this country has an absolute right to control, whether through financial management, business investment, governmental reorganization, or outright military presence. There was little room for hand-wringing debates about our proper role in this region. President Roosevelt was determined to move the United States into its rightful place among the world powers and quite prepared to follow almost any course to achieve that goal.[1] Theodore Roosevelt is in large part responsible for guiding the United States into a position of world prominence; unfortunately, Latin America became the means through which this goal was achieved.

THE FINAL PUSH FOR THE CANAL

By the Roosevelt presidency, trade opportunities, engineering capabilities, and political pressures had combined to make the building of the Panama Canal a real possibility. But before work on the canal that would link the Pacific with the Caribbean could begin, the United States had to take a series of steps designed to remove both British and Colombian claims to the isthmus.

British claims were contained in the Clayton-Bulwer Treaty of 1850, in which the United States and England agreed to joint construction and maintenance of a future canal. In 1901, however, the British were no longer interested in competing with the United States for the right to build and operate an inter-oceanic canal. As a result the first Hay-Paunceforte Treaty was negotiated between Secretary of State John Hay and Lord Paunceforte, the British ambassador to the United States. In the treaty the British granted the United States sole right to construct the canal, but not to construct fortifications.

Although many in Washington felt the British position was a fair one, there was much opposition to the treaty from Democrats anxious to show themselves even more aggressive on this issue than the Republicans and from a jingoistic press that was becoming increasingly vocal about the canal. The protests forced a renegotiation of the treaty. In November 1901 a second Hay-Paunceforte Treaty was concluded in which the Clayton-Bulwer agreement was replaced with an understanding that the United States would have the right to build, control, and fortify a future Panama canal. The willingness of the British to negotiate a second treaty seems to have been the result of foreign policy concerns elsewhere and a desire to maintain cordial relations with the United States.

Now that the British were out of the canal picture the United States could turn its attention to negotiating with the two countries that were in the running for the canal: Colombia and Nicaragua. Even though the inter-ocean canal had consistently been discussed in terms of Panama, a route through Nicaragua was actually viewed by experts as more feasible and cheaper. It was in this competition between the Panamanian route and the Nicaraguan route that the "push for the canal" became frought with politics, money, arrogance, and dishonesty.

The principal characters in the canal saga were Theodore Roosevelt; the French representative of the canal company, Phillipe Bunau-Varilla; Secretary of State John Hay; and the Colombian chargé d'affaires in Washington, Tomás Herrán. At first the Nicaraguan route received official government support and appeared to have the inside track. The Walker Commission, appointed by President McKinley, reported in favor of the Nicaraguan canal. To bolster the Nicaraguan route, the House of Representatives voted by a sizable margin to accept the findings of the Walker Commission.

At this point, pressure politics replaced reasoned investigation in the determination of the canal route. Phillipe Bunau-Varilla was able to convince President Roosevelt that the Panamanian route was far superior. But it was not Bunau-Varilla's charm alone that shifted opinion. Financial backers of Bunau-Varilla in the Republican party increased their contribution to the party's campaign chest while simultaneously advising the president of their desire to have the canal built in Panama. The combination of aggressive public relations and financial contributions was successful. Not only did Roosevelt become an ardent supporter of the Panama route, but the U.S. Senate, in June of 1902, authorized the president to negotiate with the Colombian government for a right-of-way to build a canal in its Panamanian province.

Up to this point the acquisition of the right-of-way for the Panama Canal had been relatively smooth and conflict free. The next step, separating Panama from Colombian control, would pose a more difficult test and would provide the Latin Americans with their first glimpse of Theodore Roosevelt's temperament. First the Roosevelt administration sought to entice the Colombians with a financial offer for the Panamanian territory. Secretary of State John Hay successfully completed a treaty with the Colombian representative, Tomás Herrán. The Hay-Herrán Treaty ceded a canal zone six miles wide on either side of the canal in return for $10 million and an annual payment of $250,000 beginning in ten years. The lease was renewable and could be extended in perpetuity.

This treaty, which was so favorable to the United States, was resoundingly rejected by Colombia. The Colombians not only saw the treaty as a blatant effort to take away their territory but also felt that the price agreed to by Herrán was far too small, especially in light of the vast commercial potential of the canal. The refusal of the Colombians to accept the terms of the Hay-Herrán Treaty and their willingness to wait for a better offer aroused the ire of President Roosevelt, who, unable to suppress his displeasure with the Colombian "jack-rabbits," prepared to take matters into his own hands.

With the Colombians stalling for more money, the Roosevelt administration looked to their friend Phillipe Bunau-Varilla to help speed up the negotiations for the canal. Bunau-Varilla's approach was not diplomatic. From New York he organized a ragtag Panamanian liberation army that with U.S. support would stage a revolution, declare its independence from Colombia, and sign a treaty with the United States to achieve what negotiations could not. Although there is no clear evidence of collusion between Roosevelt and Bunau-Varilla concerning the Panamanian liberation army, the two met on a number of occasions and Roosevelt let it be known that he was in favor of Panamanian insurrection. Bunau-Varilla, being an astute entrepreneur, interpreted Roosevelt's attitude as a clear sign of administration consent. He thus initiated the Panamanian revolution.

On November 2, 1903, the U.S.S. *Nashville* docked in Colón, Panama—and one day later the Panamanian rebels revolted against Colombian rule. Intimidated by the presence of the U.S. navy, the Colombians chose not to suppress the uprising. On November 4, 1903, Panama declared its independence, and on November 6, President Roosevelt recognized the new nation of Panama. Only one more step was needed to complete the taking of Panama and that occurred on November 18, 1903, when Phillipe Bunau-Varilla, a French citizen, represented the Panamanian nation and signed the Hay–Bunau-Varilla Treaty by the terms of which the United States paid the new government $10 million and $250,000 a year for a zone that had been widened from six to ten miles.[2] Most important, the treaty granted the United States sovereign rights in the canal "in perpetuity." After some bitter debate, the Senate approved the treaty 66 to 14. The United States had finally gained this valuable piece of commercial and strategic real estate, although the manner in which it was acquired left many saddened over the blatant use of our power.

Looking back over the Panama Canal episode, historians have speculated about the possible motivation behind Roosevelt's actions. Some are baffled by his refusal to accept the Walker Commission recommendation to build the canal in Nicaragua, where there was no need to sponsor a revolution. Others wondered why Roosevelt could not have waited one more year, when the Colombians would have been in a position to gain an additional $40 million from the sale of the French canal holdings to the United States, again without recourse to revolution. The answer to these questions is perhaps contained in a 1911 address of Theodore Roosevelt who said:

I am interested in the Panama Canal because I started it. If I had followed traditional conservative methods I would have submitted a dignified State paper of probably 200 pages to Congress and the debates on it would have been going on yet, but I took the Canal Zone and let Congress debate: and while the debate goes on the Canal does also.[3]

And so Theodore Roosevelt "took" the canal and in the process showed the people of the United States and the Latin Americans how he intended to handle trouble spots that limited our ability to expand further in this region. The Panama Canal episode, though, was but the prelude to a host of other actions by President Roosevelt as he sought to advance our interests.

THE BIG STICK IN THE CARIBBEAN

Theodore Roosevelt continued his Latin American "offensive" when in a message to Congress on December 6, 1904, he enunciated his own version of the Monroe Doctrine. This speech has appropriately come to

be called the Roosevelt Corollary, and it represents the strongest statement to date of U.S. intentions in Latin America. The corollary speech
is pure Roosevelt: arrogant, caustic, and filled with supreme confidence
in our right to control the destiny of the Latin American nations. The
key portion of the speech is offered below:

Chronic wrongdoing, or an impotence which results in a general loosening of
the ties of civilized society, may in America, as elsewhere, ultimately require
intervention by some civilized nation, and in the Western Hemisphere the
adherence of the United States, however reluctantly . . . to the exercise of an
international police power.[4]

With the Roosevelt Corollary the United States went beyond the
Monroe Doctrine, which was largely defensive in nature, and began
to assume the responsibility of bringing political and financial order
to the hemisphere. Wherever there was "chronic wrongdoing" or the
example of a "general loosening of the ties of civilized society," President
Roosevelt pledged the United States to intervene or, as he termed it,
exercise our "international police power." The Roosevelt Corollary
ushered in the period often described as the Big Stick era, during which
the Roosevelt administration employed its new-found role of hemispheric policeman by intervening in Caribbean nations whose financial
and political affairs were in disarray.

The first instance of this new doctrine at work occurred in the
Dominican Republic, which by 1904 had amassed a national debt of $32
million. In early 1905 the United States pressured the Dominican
government to "invite" the United States to administer the collection of
revenues from its customhouses and to oversee the payment of the
country's creditors. In the agreement the Dominican government
accepted a U.S. administrator as the receiver of its custom duties. The
task of the receiver was to ensure the financial solvency of the Dominican Republic by controlling its primary source of revenue. The formula
agreed to by the Dominicans was that 45 percent of the revenue was to
revert directly to the government, while the remaining 55 percent was
to be deposited in U.S. banks to be used for payment of outstanding
foreign debts. In effect the United States became the official customs
collector and national banker of the Dominican Republic.

After a few years the receivership program did bring a semblance of
order to Dominican finances, but internal instability in the country
caused the United States to seek an even larger role in its financial
affairs. On a number of occasions the United States refused to provide
the Dominican government with additional funds for fear of increasing
the national debt. These refusals led to internal upheavals since governments could not make good on political promises to initiate new
programs. The United States had entangled itself sufficiently in the

Dominican financial picture that it was also influencing the course of national politics.[5]

While the United States was collecting customs revenues in the Dominican Republic, the Roosevelt administration carried its Big Stick to Cuba. In 1905 the government of Tomás Estrada Palma was engaged in a violent partisan revolt. The Cuban leader, fearing for his new government, appealed to the United States for assistance. After Secretary of War William Howard Taft surveyed the situation and declared it to be chaotic (Estrada Palma had resigned the presidency without naming a replacement), President Roosevelt sent in over 7,000 marines to occupy and govern the nation. The United States stayed in Cuba until 1909. During its occupation, the military government of Governor Charles Magoon created much resentment among the Cubans, who charged the marines with harsh treatment of civilians and encouraging official corruption.[6]

The Big Stick intervention in the Dominican Republic and Cuba served to establish the Roosevelt Corollary firmly as U.S. policy and even to legitimize intervention as an appropriate method of solving internal problems in the hemisphere. By the end of Roosevelt's term in office, the United States had a string of protectorates in the Caribbean and Central America and was increasingly viewed in Latin America as a country that would not hesitate to meddle in the affairs of another nation in order to protect its interests. More important, the United States was beginning to emphasize maintaining stability in the region. Although Roosevelt complained about "chronic wrongdoing" and "impotence," his main concern was the loss of stable political and economic relations that resulted from these conditions. This accent on stability indicated that the United States now considered dangers from social, economic, or political disruption to be more important than any concern for recognizing the right of these nations to develop in their own manner and without outside intervention.

TAFT AND DOLLAR DIPLOMACY

President William Howard Taft entered the White House in 1908 and carried forward the interventionist policies of his predecessor. There was, however, one major difference between Roosevelt and Taft. While Roosevelt's interventions were carried out to alleviate "chronic wrongdoing," Taft sought, as Federico Gil states, "the promotion and expansion of the hold of United States financial and banking interests."[7] U.S. concern with monetary interests in Latin America became known as Dollar Diplomacy.

The practice of Dollar Diplomacy can best be examined in our dealings with Haiti and Nicaragua. Haiti, much like the Dominican Republic, was, in the period from 1910 to 1920, experiencing severe economic problems. Moreover, the near bankruptcy of Haiti coincided with domestic political upheaval. During this unstable period, the National City Bank of New York acquired an interest in the Banque Nationale, the official treasurer for the Haitian nation.

Encouraged by the Taft administration, the U.S. bank expanded its involvement in the Banque Nationale and also joined with other interests to finance a railroad in Haiti. But the increased U.S. participation in Haitian financial affairs was not enough to forestall European creditors who were demanding payment of their loans. Eventually the United States became increasingly concerned about the possible intervention of the French and the Germans, who had considerable interests in Haiti. Rather than become militarily involved at this stage in the crisis, President Taft and his secretary of state, Philander Knox, chose to let U.S. banking and commercial representatives in Haiti try to fend off the Europeans.[8] But as we shall see this reluctance to use force would be only temporary.

The U.S. involvement in Haitian economic affairs coincided with a more traditional form of internal meddling in Nicaragua. The government of Nicaraguan dictator José Santos Zelaya refused to grant the United States rights to lease and build a naval base in the Gulf of Fonseca on the Pacific Ocean side of Nicaragua. Zelaya also encouraged the harassment of U.S. businessmen, who were quite active in the country. These actions of Zelaya spurred U.S. business interests in Nicaragua to support an overthrow attempt. There is also evidence that shows that the U.S. embassy had prior knowledge of the anti-Zelaya revolt. In the ensuing uprising, the United States broke relations with the Zelaya government and sided with the rebels.

With U.S. financial and diplomatic support, Zelaya was overthrown and the United States was able to negotiate an agreement with the new leadership group. The resulting agreement was called the Knox-Castrillo Convention and it provided for a $15 million loan to the Nicaraguans in return for the right to control the country's customs. The U.S. Senate refused to ratify the convention, fearing undue influence from the banking community, but this did not deter the Taft administration from seeking a financial foothold in Nicaragua. The banks privately negotiated the loan agreement and had the new government of Adolfo Díaz create a position of customs collector that would be under the direct control of the U.S. secretary of state.

The financial intervention of the United States in Nicaragua did not, however, ensure either economic or political stability. President Díaz soon faced armed revolt and requested military assistance from the United States. President Taft responded by sending eight warships and some 2,000 marines. With the presence of U.S. military personnel, the uprising against Díaz was repressed, ensuring that pro-American and pro-banking interests would remain in power in Nicaragua.[9]

Although the Taft administration sought to spread our influence in the Caribbean and Central America through these less conspicuous financial arrangements, U.S. foreign policy had not really changed that much. Rather, Dollar Diplomacy served as a kind of midpoint in what has come to be called the "era of intervention." Placed between Roosevelt's Big Stick and Wilson's extensive involvement in Latin American affairs, the actions of the Taft administration in Haiti and Nicaragua are merely variations on a common theme. The goals of economic penetration and maintenance of political stability were still the same; the means, however, now became a little more diverse as businessmen joined militia commanders and civilian administrators in solidifying our hold in the hemisphere.

WILSON'S "CIVILIZING" INTERVENTIONS

The Democrats under the idealistic leadership of Woodrow Wilson regained the presidency in 1912 after sixteen years of Republican dominance. But despite the lofty and humanitarian views of the new president, Latin America experienced what can only be termed an "epidemic" of U.S. economic and military intervention. During his administration Wilson sent troops to control unstable situations in Haiti, the Dominican Republic, Nicaragua, and Cuba; he sought to influence the course of the Mexican Revolution and ordered General Pershing to invade the country. Finally, he forced a treaty on the Nicaraguans and in the process alienated the countries of Central America.

All this intervention on the part of President Wilson stemmed from his firm belief that the United States must take the initiative to ensure that constitutional democracies be established and protected in Latin America. This commitment to democracy led Wilson to propose that the United States follow a new policy of nonrecognition of revolutionary governments. As Wilson put it, in order "to teach the South Americans to elect good men . . . no Latin American government should be recognized that had not been formed along constitutional lines."[10]

With his belief in civilizing people through democracy and refusing to reward revolutionary governments with diplomatic recognition, President Wilson became a grave disappointment to the Latin Americans. Although initially impressed with his public commitment to republican government, they came to realize that his commitment would be a smokescreen for continued U.S. efforts to expand our markets and enhance our security.

Because the interventions of President Wilson are important not only as a chronicle of U.S. policy toward Latin America but as actions that have had profound effects on our contemporary relations with these countries, let us review the instances of U.S. involvement during this period.

Haiti

The Taft administration's involvement in the credit problems and railroad development of Haiti brought the U.S. military on the scene. Military intervention was triggered by the collapse of the government of President Vilbrun Gillaume Sam in January 1915. When President Sam was dragged out of his hiding place in the French legation and beaten to death by an angry mob, the country lapsed into a period of internal chaos. President Wilson wasted no time in ordering U.S. troops to establish calm and to offset any possible attempts by the French, British, or Germans to land their troops.

While the U.S. forces occupied Haiti, the Wilson administration sought a new president who would accept the U.S. plan to solve the country's financial problems. The search ended when Philippe Sudre Dartiguenave was elected by the Haitian congress in August of 1915. The United States immediately submitted a draft treaty to Dartiguenave that secured our presence in the country. The U.S. representative in Haiti boldly informed the new president that he would have to accept the treaty without change.

The U.S.–Haitian Treaty of 1915 authorized President Wilson to name a customs receiver, prohibited the increase of the public debt without the approval of the president of the United States, created a constabulary force led by a U.S. officer, prohibited the sale or lease of any Haitian territory, and permitted the United States to take action to maintain "a government adequate for the protection of life, property and individual liberty." The treaty with Haiti was extended for twenty years in 1917 and amended in 1918 to allow U.S. approval of all proposed legislation. With this treaty the United States had gained another protectorate.[11]

During its occupation of Haiti, the United States did attempt to develop the semblance of constitutional government and made numerous improvements in the areas of health, public works, and bureaucratic administration. But these efforts did little to satisfy the Haitians, who grew increasingly rebellious and contemptuous of the U.S. presence in their country. Contrary to Wilson's ideals, the Haitians did not see the United States as providing them with an opportunity to develop democracy, but rather as a powerful neighbor instituting a new form of colonialism.

The Dominican Republic

President Wilson found to is dismay that Roosevelt's customs receivership in the Dominican Republic did not ensure political stability. In 1911 a period of political calm was shattered with the assassination of popular President Ramón Cáceres. A new period of unrest began as various political factions fought. When an anti-American faction took power, President Wilson sent in troops.

At first the U.S. presence was limited and designed to maintain order, but when the Dominicans refused to accept new terms for our control of customs revenues and the formation of a national police force under our direction, President Wilson ordered a complete occupation with the U.S. military commander assuming day-to-day legislative and executive functions.

The United States remained in the Dominican Republic for eight years and, as in Haiti, was responsible for a number of structural improvements. The United States modernized Dominican society in the areas of health, sanitation, roads, education, and financial management. The U.S. forces also formed and trained a new police force that was intended to replace the marines as keepers of internal order.[12]

Despite some well-intentioned reforms, the United States was not a welcome occupation force. The Dominicans voiced considerable opposition and staged small but effective guerrilla attacks on marine encampments. By the end of Wilson's term in office in 1920, the United States was reevaluating its role in the Dominican Republic and seeking ways to leave the country without losing its control of fiscal affairs. The United States left the Dominican Republic in 1924 but continued to influence the country's internal development. Moreover, the constabulary formed by the United States would in a few short years be headed by a young lieutenant named Rafael Trujillo, who was destined to become "dictator for life" and a constant friend of the United States.

Cuba

By the Wilson administration, intervention in Cuba had become commonplace. Using the Platt Amendment as a basis for action, the United States periodically involved itself in Cuban affairs. The situation during the Wilson administration was no different. In 1917, when the Liberal party in Cuba disputed the election of a Conservative candidate, a revolt erupted and the United States, under Wilson's direction, sent in 2,600 marines to maintain order and to ensure that the Conservative candidate (who was also pro–United States) would remain in power.

At the close of the Wilson administration General Enoch Crowder was sent to Cuba to supervise election reforms and to revise the electoral code. When Crowder left the country in 1923, he had expanded his role from one of institutionalizing democratic government to one of managing the Cuban national finances.[13] As was the case in other countries, constitutional reform was often the pretext used by the United States to inject itself into other sectors of the country, in particular the financial sector.

Nicaragua

U.S. relations with Nicaragua during the Wilson years centered not on military intervention, although a small contingent of troops remained from the Taft occupation, but rather on acquiring territorial rights. In 1914 President Wilson's secretary of state, William Jennings Bryan, concluded a treaty with the Nicaraguan government in which the United States paid the Nicaraguans $3 million in exchange for: (1) exclusive rights in perpetuity to construct an inter-oceanic canal through the country; (2) a ninety-nine–year lease on the Great and Little Corn Islands in the Caribbean and on the long-sought naval base sight on the Gulf of Fonseca; and (3) the option to renew both leases for another ninety-nine years.

The signing of the Bryan-Chamorro Treaty and its ratification in 1916 aroused a storm of protest in Central America. Countries like El Salvador and Honduras viewed the acquisition of the leases as a direct threat to their sovereignty, because both claimed the Gulf of Fonseca as their own territory. These two countries along with Costa Rica, which had claims connected with the building of a proposed canal, took their issue to the Central American Court of Justice and received a favorable judgment.

The United States refused to recognize the court decision, an action that intensified Latin American protest because this country was instrumental in forming the court in 1907 and had pledged publicly on a number of occasions to abide by the principle of judicial settlement of disputes. President Wilson, however, was adamant in his desire to establish a permanent foothold in Nicaragua as a means of securing peace in that country and offsetting any possible European intervention.

The Bryan-Chamorro Treaty unfortunately did not bring political stability to Nicaragua. The United States played a dominant role in both the 1916 and 1920 election periods as a supporter of unpopular and minority regimes in order to maintain the peace. As for the marines, they remained in Nicaragua until 1933, except for one short period in 1925. Although Wilson merely continued the military occupation of Nicaragua during his term in office, his efforts to acquire Nicaraguan territory remained a sore spot in our relations with Nicaragua and indeed with all of Central America.

Mexico

The Mexican Revolution in 1910 caused great concern in the United States. Not only did Mexico share a border with the United States, but we have considerable oil, mining, and utility interests in that country. Since the regime of the Mexican dictator Porfirio Díaz (1876–1910), U.S. investment was estimated at $1 billion. The collapse of the Díaz regime and the restoration of democracy under Francisco Madero in 1910 prompted the Taft administration and its ambassador in Mexico, Henry Lane Wilson, to support an overthrow of the Madero government so as to ensure the safety of our business interests. In 1913 Victoriano Huerta, with U.S. support, staged a coup against the Madero government.

When Woodrow Wilson entered the White House, policy shifted from cooperation with Huerta to antagonism. Mexico became the primary testing ground of Wilson's nonrecognition policy. Wilson was heard to state with reference to the Huerta regime, "We have no sympathy with those who seek to seize the power of government to advance their own personal interests or ambitions."

President Wilson's posturing about democracy and recognition did not seem to influence Huerta, who refused to be removed from power by the United States. President Wilson, however, would not be stymied. In November 1913 Wilson demanded that Huerta resign, and when this failed he permitted the sale of arms to Huerta's major opponent, Venustiano Carranza. Wilson became further embroiled in the Mexican Revolution when in April 1914 he ordered the bombing of the port city of Vera Cruz when the Huerta government refused to apologize for arresting some U.S. naval officials. Eventually Huerta fell from power in mid–1914, but his departure did not extricate the United States from the Mexican Revolution; in fact it brought this country further into the fighting.

The direct cause of our further involvement in the Mexican Revolution was the action of the outlaw rebel Pancho Villa, who in 1916 crossed the border and entered Columbus, New Mexico, where he killed seventeen U.S. citizens. The attack by Pancho Villa raised an enormous public outcry in the United States, and forced President Wilson to send General John Pershing and 10,000 troops into Mexico to hunt down the rebel leader. After over a year of fruitless pursuit, the troops were recalled.[14]

The conclusion of the bloodiest phase of the revolution in 1917 removed the need for active U.S. military intervention, but it began a new phase of hostility over the proper role of U.S. business interests in Mexico. At the center of the controversy was Article 27 of the 1917 constitution, which stated that the government of Mexico controls the subsoil rights to precious minerals and resources and that these rights are not transferable to foreign governments or corporations. Although during the remaining years of Wilson's administration the issue of subsoil rights did not seriously hamper U.S.–Mexican relations, the Republican presidents of the 1920s would be forced to deal with nationalistic leaders intent on protecting their country's natural resources from foreign control. Eventually the Harding administration in 1923 was able to negotiate the Bucareli Agreement in which Mexico stated that it would not apply Article 27 retroactively to U.S. oil and mineral properties in its country.

The Wilson Legacy in Latin America

Much has been written about the inner conflict of President Wilson's approach to Latin America. In the name of democracy and civilization, Wilson intervened in the internal affairs of sovereign nations and in many cases did more to solidify dictatorial regimes than to encourage the practice of constitutional governance. The rhetoric of teaching the Latin American republics "to elect good men" never really was put into practice, because the United States continued to support leaders on the basis of expediency and not democratic principles. In the final analysis, Wilson may have differed from Taft in that he paid less attention to commercial expansion and from Roosevelt in that he claimed to be acting in the interest of higher values rather than raw power. But in the implementation of policy we find that President Wilson was above all else a staunch proponent of intervention as the most effective tool of U.S. foreign policy.

One major consequence of the Wilson interventions was that the nations of the Caribbean and Central America became politically dependent on the United States and in many cases actually sought out our counsel or invited our involvement. As Dana Munro, the foremost historian of this period, said, "local leaders got into the habit of looking to Washington for the settlement of political problems. A belief that the faction favored by the United States would usually come out on top . . . gave an excessive importance to every indication or fancied indication of the attitude of American officials."[15] By the conclusion of the Wilson administration this heightened political dependence placed the United States at the center of the power structure in many Central American and Caribbean sectors. A conservative aristocracy supported by a U.S.–trained repressive military held power and worked closely with the United States to maintain stability and enhance our commercial and financial interests. Although the formula suited our objectives at the time, this triumvirate would cause the United States enormous difficulty in future years.

LATIN AMERICAN POLICY IN THE POST-INTERVENTIONIST PERIOD

The Republican administrations of Harding, Coolidge, and Hoover have often been seen as concerned primarily with domestic economic issues, but in terms of inter-American affairs these three presidents were responsible for moving this country away from a policy of active intervention. One must be careful not to heap false praise on these presidents, for the United States was still guided by the same philosophy as under the "great interventionists." The Republican presidents, however, were more conscious of the price that was being paid in hostility to the United States among the Latin American community of nations and more particularly in those countries that had experienced interventions. It simply became prudent policy for the United States to loosen its grip on these protectorates and return home. Furthermore, the United States had successfully trained local constabularies who would maintain order and position people favorable to the United States in national leadership offices. Leaving would thus not pose a great risk to our national security or our economic interests.

As a result the United States gradually and cautiously began to dismantle its hold on the Caribbean and Central American protectorates. The first country to regain its sovereignty was the Dominican Republic in 1924, although as with Haiti, removal of the military was not linked with a lessening of our control of Dominican fiscal affairs. Negotiations for the ending of our military presence with neighboring Haiti were vigorously supported by President Herbert Hoover. The United States completed a treaty with Haiti that granted the country partial sovereignty during the waning days of the Hoover administration. However, the treaty was rejected by the Haitian congress because of continued U.S. involvement in the country's fiscal affairs. The failure to achieve an agreement kept U.S. troops in Haiti until 1934 when a new agreement that lessened fiscal control was included in the terms of departure. The final lifting of fiscal controls did not come until about 1940.

Finally, Nicaragua, which had had almost continuous U.S. military presence since 1912, conducted elections under the supervision of the Hoover administration and as a result saw the marines depart in early 1933. Nicaragua, like the Dominican Republic, was one of those countries in which the United States organized and trained a local constabulary that maintained order and responded positively to U.S. initiatives. Also, like the Dominican Republic, the Nicaraguan National Guard (as it came to be called) was headed by a ruthless despot named Anastasio Somoza who conspired to assassinate his populist adversary, Augusto Sandino, and created a family dynasty that controlled the country until 1979.[16]

The Republican presidents' desire to reverse the interventionist policies of the past was reflected in what has come to be called the Clark Memorandum. Written in 1928 by Undersecretary of State J. Reuben Clark, the document repudiated the Roosevelt Corollary as a justification for military intervention (although it did not repudiate intervention per se). The memorandum received little public attention at the time, but over the years historians have pointed to its condemnation of the corollary as one indication that our policy was evolving from a position of aggressive involvement in the hemisphere to one of restraint.

It is also important to point out that the Republican presidents did not concern themselves only with removing U.S. military units from the Caribbean and Central America. The period from 1920 to 1932 was also marked by extensive contacts with Latin American nations over matters of trade and debt refinancing. Issues in the area of our commercial ties with Latin America were the protective tariffs put into place after World War I and the huge debts that the Latin Americans now owed U.S. rather than European banks.

The attention to trade and debt problems was necessitated by the changes wrought in the world economy after World War I and the dominant economic position that the United States had assumed in the hemisphere. As Irwin Gellman observes:

Without much planning the United States assumed the largest share of the market (in Latin America), filling the void created by European nations. . . . By 1929 United States exports to Latin America were a third of the United States total, and Latin American exports to the United States grew to 20% of their total. Investments showed an even sharper rise. By 1929 they reached $5,430,000,000, representing a third of all United States foreign investments.[17]

But with the Latin Americans increasingly dependent on U.S. trade, the large tariffs coupled with their highly speculative bond purchases prior to the Depression made it nearly impossible for the Latin Americans to settle their debt problems. Faced with these difficulties, the Latin Americans resorted to international forums to plead their case and to denounce U.S. protectionism. As a result the regular pan-American conferences in the late 1920s became settings for extensive criticism of our trade policies and our refusal to address the debt problems of the Latin American nations.

In this Republican era, President Herbert Hoover deserves the greatest attention and a considerable amount of credit for placing U.S.–Latin American relations on a new course. Besides rejecting the Wilsonian interventionist stance and moving forward with the dismantling of our protectorates, Hoover became actively involved in settling border disputes between Peru and Colombia, and Bolivia and Paraguay. Furthermore he was one of the few presidents up to that date to tour Latin America and take an interest in its concerns. As Edwin Lieuwen comments, Hoover, "brought a new attitude toward Latin America's problems and demands . . . and he seemed to appreciate the possible future significance of Latin America to the security of the United States."[18]

Despite these contributions, Hoover became associated with placing obstacles in the way of Latin American trade and development. As the president who signed the Hawley-Smoot Tariff Act of 1930 and the equally protectionist Revenue Act of 1932, Hoover was seen in Latin

America as responsible for limiting the ability of these countries to cope more effectively with the worldwide depression. Hoover left office in 1932 not only as the "father of the Depression" but also as someone who had turned his back on the economic needs of his neighbors.

ROOSEVELT AND THE GOOD NEIGHBOR POLICY

The assumption to the presidency of Franklin Delano Roosevelt in 1933 brought significant changes to our Latin American policy. That a new spirit of cooperation rather than intimidation was beginning in hemispheric relations became evident in Roosevelt's inaugural address of March 4, 1933. In that address the president outlined his vision of our relationship to other countries in the world:

In the field of world policy, I would dedicate this nation to the policy of the good neighbor—the neighbor who resolutely respects himself and, because he does so, respects the rights of others—the neighbor who respects his obligations and respects the sanctity of his agreements in and with a world of neighbors.[19]

This new spirit was shown to be more than mere political rhetoric when Secretary of State Cordell Hull at the Seventh Pan American Conference in 1933 surprised the Latin American delegates by supporting a proposal that placed the United States on record as opposed to intervention in the internal affairs of another nation. Further, the United States agreed that the territory of hemispheric nations could not be the object of military occupation. The combination of support for nonintervention and opposition to military occupation signaled to Latin Americans that the United States indeed had embraced a new policy toward the hemisphere.

The first tangible sign of this change came in 1934 when the Platt Amendment was abrogated and Cuba for the first time since 1901 was able to exercise its sovereign rights as a nation-state. It is important, however, to point out that the United States still retained significant economic control over Cuba in terms of loan agreements, sugar import quotas, land holdings, and extensive commercial investments.

The Roosevelt administration did not stop with Cuba. In 1936 Secretary Hull negotiated a treaty with Panama in which the United States withdrew its right to intervene in Panamanian internal affairs and in effect gave the country its independence. We, of course, still maintained the Canal Zone, but this treaty laid the groundwork for a greater degree of cooperation and ensured greater political stability.

The major test of our new noninterventionist stance came in 1938 when the Mexican government of President Lázaro Cárdenas, using Article 27 of the constitution, expropriated U.S. oil properties in a dispute over labor conditions. The U.S. companies, which had earlier refused to abide by Mexican court decisions upholding the rights of workers, now appealed the expropriation decision to President Roosevelt and asked for U.S. intervention. President Roosevelt held firm on his nonintervention policy and rejected the oil companies' request. The expropriation issue was eventually settled at the World Court when the Mexican government agreed to pay the companies for the expropriated properties.

The positive image created by the Roosevelt administration with its noninterventionist policy was further enhanced by its efforts to break down trade barriers. The key legislation that achieved this objective was the Reciprocal Trade Agreement Act of 1934, which gave the president the power to lower tariffs with individual countries by as much as 50 percent. The goal of this legislation was to reduce tariffs on our part so as to foster a similar reduction on the part of other trading partners. In effect the law sought to achieve an atmosphere of mutually agreed upon reductions that might revive hemispheric trade and help stimulate the depressed economies both in this country and in Latin America. As a result of the act, the United States signed a series of bilateral trade agreements with Latin American countries that included these tariff reductions.

The Roosevelt administration expanded its economic revival plan for Latin America by creating the Export-Import Bank in 1934. The bank lent money to Latin American countries with the stipulation that the funds be used to purchase imports from the United States or from U.S. businesses in Latin America. Although the objective of the bank was basically to help the U.S. economy, the transfer of millions of dollars to Latin America provided the necessary capital for a number of modernization projects that would not have been started without this new lending institution.

The renewed spirit of cooperation initiated by the Roosevelt administration became more important as war threatened the hemisphere. The Latin Americans, at first, were reluctant to become entangled in a potential European war and were suspicious of U.S. attempts to have them commit their governments to anti-Axis policies. At the Eighth Pan American Conference in 1938, Secretary Hull tried to convince his fellow ministers that the Axis powers posed a threat to the region and that unified action was necessary to bolster hemispheric defenses. The efforts of the secretary of state did not produce the desired results, especially among the so-called ABC countries—Argentina, Brazil, and Chile—which have strong commercial and military ties to Germany and Italy.

As World War II broke, and with the invasion of Poland and fall of France and the Netherlands, the Latin Americans became more concerned about the possible spread of the war to this hemisphere. In Panama in 1939 they agreed to a 300-mile-wide neutrality zone that was intended to be free of "hostile acts by warring nations." In 1940 the Latin American foreign ministers adopted the Act of Havana, which stated that any territorial possession belonging to a non-American state (that is, France, Netherlands, and Great Britain) that was forcefully taken over by another non-American state (that is, the Axis powers) would be protected and administered by American states.

Although the Latin Americans initially showed great reluctance to shed their neutral position, they gradually developed closer military and economic ties to the United States. The United States sent scores of military and naval advisors to Latin America as a means of lessening the influence of Axis military representatives who for years had served as the primary source of instruction for many of these countries. The Latin Americans also purchased weapons from the United States in greater volume than in the past and agreed to lease military bases for naval and air transport purposes. Finally, the United States stepped up its purchases of Latin American strategic materials such as rubber, tin, and tungsten, which greatly aided the balance of payments situation in these countries.[20]

The Latin Americans stepped beyond the bounds of neutrality after the Japanese attack on Pearl Harbor. By early 1942 most of the Latin American nations had either declared war on the Axis powers or had severed diplomatic relations. Only Chile and Argentina, with their close ties to the Axis powers and influential fascist groups within their military, did not declare war on Germany and Italy until 1945, when it was clear that the Allies would be victorious.

The cooperation of the United States and Latin American states in conducting the war was established at the Rio Conference in 1942, when the foreign ministers agreed to break all commercial ties with the Axis powers and gear their economies for a war effort. The Rio Conference also established the Inter-American Defense Board, which sought to create a multilateral approach to hemispheric defense. As a result of the support that the United States received at the Rio Conference a number of bilateral defense agreements, most notably with Brazil and Mexico, were signed. The agreements provided military equipment in exchange for various defense commitments. As a result, over $260 million in equipment found its way into Latin American hands.[21]

As far as actual involvement of the Latin Americans in the fighting, their contribution was minimal. The Brazilians, who were the most committed, sent an infantry division to Italy, while the Mexicans sent an air squadron to the Philippines. In the main, the Latin Americans concerned themselves with assisting the United States by providing military bases (in Brazil, Panama, Cuba, and Ecuador) and by selling their resources to the Allies.

The wartime cooperation between the United States and Latin America covered the wounds that had been made during the "era of intervention." By the end of the war the United States was working closely with the Latin Americans in the defense of the hemisphere, in expanding trade opportunities, and in providing funding for modernization projects such as the Pan American Highway. Much of this cooperative spirit was the work of President Roosevelt and Secretary Hull, who viewed U.S.–Latin American relations differently from past administrations. Granted that some of this cooperation was a result of World War II and the mutually felt threat from Germany, but nevertheless there is sufficient evidence to show that Roosevelt meant what he said about being a good neighbor. His death in 1945 and the rise of communism would shift policy once more and find the United States defending the hemisphere against a leftist revolution.

POSTWAR COMMUNIST CONTAINMENT

U.S.–Latin American relations in the postwar era were based on issues quite different from those of past periods. Latin America in the late 1940s and 1950s was a region in the throes of social, economic, and political transition. Sectors of society that had previously remained passive and politically unorganized began to exert pressure on governments for fundamental change. In particular land reform, income redistribution, labor rights, and guaranteed freedoms became important concerns in many Latin American nations.

At the same time that these pressures for reform were being expressed, Soviet communism was flexing its muscle in Europe and threatening to spread its influence to less developed nations in Asia, Africa, and Latin America. The possibility of a communist threat to Latin America became a primary concern to Washington policy makers. Both Presidents Truman and Eisenhower began to define this country's chief responsibility in Latin America as one of protection against communist encroachment and support for governments who were seeking to quell revolutionary movements deemed to be communist inspired. There was little sympathy at this date for the view that revolution resulted from generations of inequality and injustice. The position taken by U.S. leaders during this era was that communism must be stopped and that we must support anti-communist governments.

In order to achieve these goals the United States and the Latin American nations signed a series of agreements. In 1947 in Rio de Janeiro the nations of the hemisphere signed the Inter-American Treaty of Reciprocal Assistance, often known as the Rio Treaty. This agreement, which was an offshoot of an earlier pact signed in Mexico City (the Chapultapec Agreement), created a permanent military alliance among the nations of the hemisphere. The important aspect of the Rio Treaty was its accent on collective security. The signatories pledged that an attack on any member state would be viewed as an attack on all and that collective measures would be taken to protect the hemisphere.

The Rio Treaty served as a model for other mutual defense pacts like the North Atlantic Treaty Organization. Although the Latin Americans did not yet see the Rio Treaty solely as a deterrent against Soviet-initiated expansionism, the United States envisioned the agreement as part of a larger strategy to prevent the Soviet Union or its agents from spreading their influence to the hemisphere.

The United States continued to emphasize collective action when it lent its support to the founding of the Organization of American States (OAS). Formed in 1948 in Bogotá, Colombia, as a successor to the Pan American Union, the OAS was designed to cement further hemispheric solidarity during the growing cold war period while also fostering democratic governance and economic cooperation through closer ties with Latin America.

The establishment of the OAS followed closely on the heels of the founding of the United Nations and provided a regional body to complement the work of the worldwide unit. Moreover, the OAS gave a greater voice to smaller states than did the United Nations and did not permit veto powers to hamper its ability to respond to hemispheric problems. Most important, the OAS gave the Latin Americans a new and more prestigious forum to air their grievances and settle disputes. The OAS would be used extensively in the coming years to challenge U.S. policy.

A side note to the Bogotá conference was the failure of the Latin Americans to get a commitment from the United States to offer them something akin to the European Marshall Plan for economic reconstruction. Latin American leaders were becoming more and more concerned over the impact of poverty and lack of modernization in their countries and wanted the United States to rescue them as we had the Europeans. The United States turned a deaf ear to these requests. The Latin Americans thus settled for the formation of the diplomatic forum with its opportunities for greater contacts with the United States and for more organized pressure to emphasize key issues of economic development.

The trade and aid complaints of the Latin Americans did not sway the United States from its main concern: the communist threat. In 1951 the United States sought Latin American involvement in the Korean conflict. The Truman administration was anxious for the Latin Americans to participate actively in this "police action." The Latin Americans were not interested and did not see the danger to them of communist aggression thousands of miles away. The United States was able to convince the Colombians to send a token fighting unit to Korea, but the remainder of the countries agreed only to bolster their defenses against a possible communist threat.

In 1954 the United States got a sampling of what can happen when social and economic problems are left untouched. After a left-wing revolution in Guatemala in 1944 the government began to institute a number of fundamental reforms. In 1951 Jacobo Arbenz succeeded the architect of the revolution, Juan José Arévalo, and pushed the nation further along the path of change. Arbenz supported a vigorous program of land redistribution, expansion of labor rights, and nationalization of foreign-owned properties.[22]

In 1952 Arbenz took the bold step of nationalizing the United Fruit Company, which had considerable banana holdings in Guatemala. President Eisenhower's secretary of state, John Foster Dulles, viewed the actions of Arbenz as a sign of growing communist involvement in the hemisphere and a direct threat to our national security.

At first the Eisenhower administration sought to pressure the Arbenz government publicly to return the United Fruit properties and to lessen its ties to known Guatemalan communists. When this failed to move the Arbenz government, Secretary Dulles asked for Latin American cooperation in putting an end to the leftist regime. The Latin Americans, who for years had been fighting to keep the United States out of their internal affairs, would have none of this talk of intervention.

With these approaches unsuccessful, the Eisenhower administration relied upon its military ties to Guatemala's neighbors, Honduras and Nicaragua, as a means of putting an end to Arbenz. Employing funds from a series of military aid agreements called Mutual Defense Assistance Pacts, the United States used Honduras and Nicaragua as staging areas for a covert attack sponsored by the U.S Central Intelligence Agency to bring the Arbenz government down. The U.S.–sponsored invasion was led by a deposed Guatemalan military leader named Carlos Castillo Armas. With 1,000 men and U.S. weapons, the Armas forces successfully overthrew the Arbenz government and returned the country to its prerevolutionary state.[23]

The invasion was by some standards a success, but the crushing of the Guatemalan revolution did not quiet the social and economic pressures that were building in Latin America. The United States continued to take a narrow view of revolutionary change, choosing to blame only communist influence for triggering the unrest. The frequent complaints by the Latin Americans that the United States must address the root causes of unrest went unheeded.

The Eisenhower administration got some sense of the antagonism that was building in Latin America when Vice President Richard Nixon was attacked and nearly injured by an angry student demonstration in Caracas, Venezuela. This incident caused the president to send his brother Milton Eisenhower on a fact-finding tour of Latin America. His report sparked a total review of existing U.S. economic policy toward Latin America.[24]

One of the results of this review was the formation of the Inter-American Development Bank (IDB), which would act as a lending institution providing low-interest loans for modernization projects in Latin America. The bank began operation in 1959 with $1 billion, of which 55 percent came from Latin American nations and the remainder from the United States. The bank immediately became an important addition to regional economic development efforts and today is a mainstay of multilateral assistance programs for Latin America.

The establishment of the IDB, although praised by the Latin Americans and long overdue, was not the cure-all for the economic ills of the region. The loans distributed by the IDB would merely scratch the surface of Latin American development needs and do little to correct the flaring inequalities and injustices that were causing heightened tensions and numerous signs of revolutionary activity.

As the decade of the 1960s approached, the United States would face heightened revolutionary activity and more pressure from Latin Americans to address the social and economic sources of the unrest. But government leaders remained wary of the communist threat posed by leftist guerrillas and continued to view violent disruptions in terms of communist expansion. U.S. foreign policy thus took on a more complex character with concern for development issues now beginning to compete with containment as the official response to revolutionary change in Latin America. This fundamental dichotomy in our relationship with Latin America would serve as the background for this country's greatest test in the hemisphere: the Cuban revolution of Fidel Castro.

NOTES

1.   For the most complete picture of this era see Dana G. Munro, *Intervention and Dollar Diplomacy in the Caribbean 1900–21* (Princeton, N.J.: Princeton University Press, 1964).

2.   See Philippe Bunau-Varilla, *The Creation, Destruction and Resurrection* (New York: 1914).

3.   *New York Times*, March 25, 1911.

4.   *Congressional Record*, 58th Cong., 3rd sess., p. 19.

5.   See Sumner Welles, *Naboth's Vineyard: The Dominican Republic, 1844–1924* (New York: Payson and Clark Ltd., 1928), for a complete discussion of this intervention.

6.   David F. Healy, *The United States in Cuba 1898–1902* (Madison: University of Wisconsin Press, 1963), provides the best discussion of the U.S. occupation.

7.   Federico G. Gil, *Latin American–United States Relations* (New York: Harcourt Brace Jovanovich, 1971), p. 71.

8.   Hans Schmidt, in his book, *The United States Occupation of Haiti 1915–1934* (New Brunswick, N.J.: Rutgers University Press, 1971), offers the most detailed study of U.S. policy in Haiti.

9.   Neill McCauley, *The Sansino Affairs* (Chicago: Quadrangle, 1967), pp. 226–65.

10.   R. S. Baker, *Woodrow Wilson: Life and Letters* (Garden City, N.Y.: Doubleday, 1931) 4:289 (Wilson to Sir William Tyrrell, November 13, 1913).

11.   See David F. Healy, *Gunboat Diplomacy in the Wilson Era: The U.S. Navy in Haiti, 1915–1934* (Madison: University of Wisconsin Press, 1976).

12.   See Bruce J. Calder, *The Impact of Intervention: The Dominican Republic During the U.S. Occupation of 1916–1924* (Austin: University of Texas Press, 1984).

13.   This period is documented in Louis Perez, *Intervention, Revolution and Politics in Cuba 1913–1921* (Pittsburgh, Pa.: University of Pittsburgh Press, 1978).

14.   Robert Freeman Smith's *The United States and Revolutionary Nationalism in Mexico, 1916–1932* (Chicago: University of Chicago Press, 1972) is the most complete discussion of the U.S. role in the Mexican Revolution.

15.   Munro, *Dollar Diplomacy*, p. 542.

16.   Richard Millet, *Guardians of the Dynasty: A History of the U.S. Created Guardia Nacional de Nicaragua and the Somoza Family* (Maryknoll, N.Y.: Orbis, 1977), is considered the authoritative source on the rise of the Somoza dynasty.

17.   Irwin F. Gellman, *Good Neighbor Diplomacy* (Baltimore, Md.: Johns Hopkins University Press, 1979), p. 7.

18.   Edwin Lieuwen, *U.S. Policy in Latin America* (New York: Praeger, 1965), p. 59.

19.   Franklin D. Roosevelt, Inaugural Address, Washington, D.C., March 4, 1933.

20.   See Gellman, *Good Neighbor Diplomacy*, pp. 93–169, for an expanded discussion of this military agreement.

21.   See Gil, *Relations*, pp. 168–84.

22.   See Juan José Arévalo, *The Shark and the Sardines*, translated by June Cobb and Raul Osegueda (New York: Lyle Stuart, 1961), for a more complete discussion of the nationalist reforms in Guatemala.

23.   See Stephen Schlesinger and Stephen Kinzer, *Bitter Fight—The Untold Story of the American Coup in Guatemala* (New York: Doubleday, 1982), pp. 191–226.

24.   Milton Eisenhower, *The Wine is Bitter: The United States and Latin America* (Garden City, N.Y.: Doubleday, 1963).

3

Castroism and the Challenge to U.S. Power

On January 1, 1959, the guerrilla forces of Fidel Castro entered Havana and proclaimed a new Cuban revolution. After years of hardship and struggle in the Sierra Mestra Mountains of eastern Cuba, Castro, the lawyer turned revolutionary, defeated the U.S.–trained troops of President Fulgencio Batista. The Castro victory electrified Latin America and provided inspiration to other leftists in the region who saw revolution as the only means of bringing about economic change and social justice.[1]

Fidel Castro's revolution caused much apprehension in the United States, not only in official circles but also in the business community, which had invested heavily in the island's sugar and tourist industries. Over the years the United States had developed a good working relationship with the Batista government and counted on his firm grip of national politics to ensure our continued influence in Cuba. Batista's reputation for harsh rule and corrupt administration was largely overlooked by the United States, which valued the stability and the friendly investment climate of his regime.

During the first year of the revolution, relations between the United States and Cuba were cautious but cordial. Castro, on a number of occasions, assured the United States that he was not a communist and would not steer Cuba into the communist orbit. These assurances became less believable as Castro gradually developed closer ties to the Soviet Union and other Eastern bloc countries.[2]

Castro's embrace of communism became a hotly debated issue in U.S. governmental and academic circles. Some analysts believe Castro was forced into developing ties with the Soviet Union because the United States refused to accept his brand of nationalism. Others claim that Castro always harbored Marxist views and was intent on moving Cuba toward communism no matter how the relationship with the United States turned out. This debate became less significant when Castro took decisive steps to redistribute private land holdings, expropriate U.S.–owned businesses, and implement policies designed to redress peasant and working-class grievances. Within one year of the revolution, Castro had taken Cuba down the road toward socialism.

By mid–1960 U.S. relations with Cuba were becoming hostile. Castro's open questioning of our right to control the Guantánamo naval base on the island and his sugar-for-oil agreement with the Soviets prompted the Eisenhower administration to stop the importation of Cuban sugar. Eventually the United States cut off all imports from Cuba as Castro increasingly looked to the Soviets and the Chinese for trade. The final break in formal ties to Cuba came in the waning days of Eisenhower's presidency, when we ended diplomatic relations with the Castro government and took our embassy personnel out of Havana.[3]

As John F. Kennedy entered the White House in January 1961, he faced a Cuban nation that was clearly anti-American and moving closer to the Soviet sphere of influence. An even more serious consequence of Castro's revolution was that it provided Latin America with a viable alternative to our democratic-capitalist development model. With Cuba moving closer to the Soviet Union and gaining popularity in the hemisphere, there was great pressure on the new president to counteract this new Marxist state off our coast.

THE BAY OF PIGS INVASION

Early in his administration President Kennedy was informed of plans made by the Central Intelligence Agency (CIA) and approved by President Eisenhower to stage an invasion of Cuba using anti-Castro rebels. The rebels would be trained in clandestine camps in Guatemala and Nicaragua and would invade Cuba from the south at a place called the Bay of Pigs. CIA analysis of the Castro regime showed that the Cuban leader was vulnerable to such a surprise attack, and that once the rebels landed, they would line up with other "freedom fighters" to quickly put an end to the revolution.

Although Kennedy had reservations about U.S. involvement in this invasion, he gave the go-ahead for the plan. On April 19, 1961, some 1,500 rebels landed from a makeshift armada off the Cuban coast. Almost immediately the invasion proved to be ill advised and poorly planned. The rebel forces faced intense resistance from the local militia; no popular support for the invaders materialized and the promised air cover from U.S. planes was insufficient. Within hours the invasion was over and 1,200 of the rebels were captured.[4]

The result of the Bay of Pigs invasion was exactly opposite to what the United States had intended. The Castro government became even more entrenched, with the whole nation now united in defense of its homeland. The Latin Americans were outraged at this new example of U.S. intervention and more supportive of the Castro regime, despite its commitment to socialism. Finally, the Kennedy administration was disgraced; its failure to effectively analyze Castro's strength and direct the invasion raised questions about the new president's ability to manage foreign affairs.

THE ALLIANCE FOR PROGRESS

While the Kennedy administration was making preparations for the Bay of Pigs invasion, it was also developing plans to unveil a massive assistance program that would combine U.S. foreign aid with support for democratic reform. President Kennedy was convinced that it was time to address Latin America's long-standing economic and social ills with deeds rather than study commissions. More important, the Kennedy administration realized that this country could no longer ignore the relationship between revolution and poverty in Latin America. If future Cubas were to be avoided, the United States would have to use its economic power and democratic principles to challenge communism.

On March 13, 1961, one month before the Bay of Pigs, President Kennedy, speaking to a gathering of Latin American diplomats and members of Congress, introduced his new program for Latin America, which he called the Alliance for Progress. The Alliance for Progress was an ambitious effort to create a joint working relationship with the Latin Americans to meet their development problems and bring badly needed change to their societies. As President Kennedy said on that day, "Unless necessary social reforms, including land and tax reforms, are freely made—unless we broaden the opportunity of all our people—unless the great mass of Americans share in increasing prosperity—then our alliance, our revolution and our dream will have failed."[5]

In his address, President Kennedy presented a ten-point program that revealed the broad scope of the Alliance for Progress:

1. A decade of "maximum effort."
2. A meeting of the Inter-American Economic and Social Council to "begin the massive planning effort which will be the head of the Alliance for Progress."
3. An initial U.S. contribution of $500 million for the Social Progress Fund, formed by Eisenhower in 1960 for social investment in Latin America.
4. Support for Latin American economic integration through a Latin American free-trade area and the Central American Common Market.
5. U.S. cooperation in "serious, case-by-case examinations of commodity market problems" to stabilize prices in the Latin American countries.
6. Expansion of the Food for Peace emergency program to supply U.S. surplus food to Latin America for school lunches and hunger areas.
7. Sharing of advances in science and research through cooperation among universities and research institutions, and inclusion of Latin American

instructors in U.S. science teacher-training programs.

8. Expanded technical training programs and assistance to Latin American universities to supply the trained personnel "needed to man the economies of rapidly developing countries."

9. A renewal of the U.S. pledge to defend all American nations "whose independence is endangered" through the collective security system of the OAS [Organization of American States], enabling these nations "to devote to constructive use a major share of those resources now spent on instruments of war."

10. An educational and cultural exchange program to increase appreciation in the United States of Latin American accomplishments in thought and the creative arts.

President Kennedy's speech announcing the Alliance for Progress combined with his later request for $500 million to fund the Social Progress Trust Fund aroused great interest in Latin America. It also set the stage for an OAS-sponsored Inter-American Economic and Social Council meeting in Punta del Este, Uruguay, in August 1961, where delegates awaited more specific commitments from the United States within the new Alliance for Progress. The U.S. representative to the conference, Secretary of the Treasury C. Douglas Dillon, showed the seriousness of the Kennedy administration's resolve to assist Latin American development when he announced that the United States would allocate $1 billion in aid to the region in the first year of the program. Furthermore, Dillon stated that Latin America could expect to receive $20 billion in external aid over the next ten years, most of which would come from the United States.

Although the proposed financial commitment of the United States to Latin America was substantial, Dillon's message to the delegates emphasized cooperation in attaining development goals. The United States was prepared to assist the Latin Americans, but Dillon made it clear that Latin American nations must "formulate the plans, mobilize the internal resources, make difficult and necessary social reforms and accept the sacrifices if their national energy is to be fully directed to economic development."[6]

With this commitment from the United States, the delegates went to work to draft a charter that laid the foundation for a permanent and on-going alliance for Progress. The charter of the alliance for Progress contained two sections. The first, a "Declaration of the Peoples of America," presented the goal of the member nations under the alliance and reflected the delegates' concern with social and political reform. The major goals as set by the delegates were as follows:

1. The improvement and strengthening of democratic institutions.

2. The acceleration of economic and social development.

3. The implementation of urban and rural housing programs.

4. The attainment of comprehensive land reform.
5. The abolition of illiteracy.
6. The promotion of health and sanitation programs.
7. The stimulation of private enterprise.
8. The reform of tax laws.
9. The development of fair wage legislation and the guarantee of satisfactory working conditions.
10. The control of the inflationary spiral.

The second part of the document was the official charter, which set specific development "targets" in the areas of economic growth (2.5 percent per capita per year), illiteracy (elimination by the year 1970), and infant mortality (50 percent reduction over ten years). The charter also emphasized the importance of intensifying efforts to diversify Latin American economies through rapid industrialization while also increasing agricultural production, achieving economic integration among the member nations, and forming agreements to bring some stability to commodity pricing arrangements.

The Punta del Este conference was a major success for the United States and helped this country regain the confidence of the Latin American leaders. Despite some caustic exchanges between Secretary Dillon and the Cuban delegate, Ernesto "Che" Guevara, in which the United States was accused of using the alliance as a new form of "economic imperialism," the delegates left the conference with the view that the United States was committed to a comprehensive programmatic assault on the social and economic ills of this region.

THE CUBAN MISSILE CRISIS

The Alliance for Progress, with its huge aid package and pledges of democratic reform, did not intimidate Fidel Castro or lessen his revolutionary fervor. In fact, by 1962 the Cuban leader was bringing his revolution into close alignment with the objectives of the Soviet Union. Besides extensive trade and assistance ties with the USSR, Cuba also began accepting military and technical personnel along with new and sophisticated weapons. Cuba quickly became the second most powerful military force in the hemisphere, and a Soviet military outpost 100 miles from the United States.

The Soviet arms buildup in Cuba soon led to one of the most dangerous instances of confrontation between the United States and the Soviet Union since the conclusion of World War II. In October 1962, U.S. reconnaissance flights over Cuba took pictures of newly constructed missile emplacements that Pentagon analysts were convinced could be used to launch an attack against this country.

After seeing the aerial photos, President Kennedy brought together a team of his most trusted advisors to develop a strategy of response. The members of this team argued over possible options, including conducting a so-called nuclear surgical strike on Havana. Eventually President Kennedy's brother Robert prevailed in his view that a naval blockade of Cuba would be the most effective and least threatening method of challenging the Soviets.

As a result, President Kennedy placed the U.S. military on alert and sent navy ships to establish a quarantine of Cuba so that no additional weapons would reach the Castro regime. At the same time Kennedy called for an urgent meeting of the OAS and requested that collective action be taken to rid the hemisphere of the Soviet nuclear presence. The OAS responded with a call for dismantling and withdrawal of all missiles and urged its member nations to support the U.S. blockade.

The tough stance taken by the Kennedy administration placed the hemisphere and indeed the world on the brink of nuclear war. The Soviets fortunately were not willing to challenge the U.S. show of force and agreed to discontinue work on the missile sites and dismantle those missiles already in place. Soviet premier Nikita Khrushchev, however, demanded that the United States cease its naval blockade and pledge not to invade Cuba. The sight of Soviet cargo ships leaving Cuba with the missiles ended this highly charged period in U.S.–Soviet relations.[7]

The missiles were gone, but Fidel Castro remained in power and continued to be the beneficiary of Soviet advice, assistance, and trade. Castro came out of the missile crisis a little apprehensive about having his country the site of an East-West nuclear confrontation, but he remained firmly committed to his revolutionary principles. What public relations victory the Kennedy administration may have achieved by standing up to the Soviets was diminished somewhat by the fact that this country still faced a shrewd communist leader dedicated to spreading Marxism throughout the hemisphere.

UNITED STATES RESPONSE TO CUBAN-INSPIRED REVOLUTION

In the years immediately following the missile crisis, Castro ventured forth and lent support to revolutionary movements in other Latin American countries. Venezuela with its newly founded democracy was the first target. In the period between 1963 and the presidential elections of 1964, Castro supplied arms to left-wing guerrillas who were intent on disrupting and even canceling the elections. When Venezuelan authorities found a huge cache of Cuban arms, the government asked for an OAS investigation. Upon OAS verification that the arms were from Cuba, the United States seized the opportunity to seek new sanctions against Castro. (Cuba had already been banished from participating in the OAS as a result of a 1962 vote of the membership.)

At a 1964 meeting of Latin American foreign ministers, Cuba was officially condemned for its activity in support of Venezuelan leftists, and by a vote of 15 to 4 the ministers agreed to break diplomatic relations and cease commercial trade with Cuba. Only trade for humanitarian reasons was permitted. Despite four negative votes (Bolivia, Chile, Mexico, and Uruguay) and an Argentine abstention, the two-thirds rule for taking such action was met and the vote became official OAS policy. Cuba thus stood virtually alone in the hemisphere. Only Mexico maintained diplomatic relations with Cuba in violation of OAS policy.

But even though the economic and diplomatic boycott of Cuba severely damaged its standing in the hemisphere, the Castro regime was able to survive. Besides the Soviet "connection," Castro continued to maintain economic relations with many European states along with Japan and Canada. As for his revolutionary fervor, Castro eventually turned his attention inward toward economic development objectives. There were still the calls for revolution, the training facilities for communist revolutionaries, and isolated instances of active support for guerrilla warfare, such as Che Guevara's unsuccessful foray into Bolivia, but by the time President Kennedy was assassinated the Cuban "menace" had become more a code word for Castro's ability to irritate the world's most powerful nation than a realistic appraisal of his power to spread revolution successfully.

The containment of Cuban communism was also the result of U.S. efforts to better prepare governments in this region in counterinsurgency. During this period the United States began providing assistance and training to countries threatened by revolution. The objective of these programs was not only to prepare Latin American military units to fight guerrilla-style wars but to impress upon them the importance of combining counterinsurgency with what the Kennedy administration termed "civic action." As was the case with our widening presence in Vietnam, the Kennedy administration felt that communist revolution can best be stopped by using the military as a means of pacifying the countryside. Latin American militaries were thus encouraged to foster development projects as a means of winning the hearts and minds of the rural peasants.[8]

THE DOMINICAN INTERVENTION

The assassination of President Kennedy in November 1963 brought his vice-president, Lyndon Johnson, into office. The president's death cast a pall over Latin America, because many reform leaders felt that the momentum for change initiated by John Kennedy would now begin to weaken. Once the new Johnson administration established itself in office, the fears of the Latin Americans seemed to be justified. President Johnson turned his attention inward toward domestic issues, and when he ventured into hemispheric affairs it was not so much to further the Alliance for Progress goals as to respond aggressively to the threat of communist revolution. The Johnson administration became known for its willingness to use the U.S. military as a kind of international police force to combat communism or stabilize situations that could lead to a communist takeover.

In Latin America, and particularly the Caribbean, President Johnson was firm in his belief that the United States must prevent a "second Cuba" from occurring. If the United States could not topple the Castro regime, it could at least ensure that his influence would not spread any further. It is within this frame of reference that the events of the spring and summer of 1965 in the Dominican Republic can be understood.

The Dominican Republic, which shares the Caribbean island of Hispaniola with Haiti, was deeply divided in 1965 between those who wanted a return to civilian democracy and those who feared the consequences of a liberal regime. During the Kennedy years, Juan Bosch, a liberal democrat, held office for nine months, but was removed from the presidency by a military coup. Although Bosch left for exile in Puerto Rico, his loyal supporters in the Party of the Dominican Revolution yearned for the day when he would return and reestablish his presidency.

The opportunity came in April 1965, when the government of a civilian puppet president named Donald Reid Cabral collapsed amid mounting opposition. In the power vacuum that resulted, the Party of the Dominican Revolution, with support from students, urban laborers, progressive military officers, and some elements of the professional middle class, led an uprising that sought to restore Bosch and constitutional government. On April 24, 1965, fighting erupted in the capital city of Santo Domingo as the so-called constitutionalists took over the National Palace and proclaimed themselves the new Dominican government.

The revolt of the "constitutionalists" did not go unanswered. Conservative military officers responded by bombing the National Palace and sending tanks into the city to end the uprising. The counterattack inflicted heavy loss of life on the rebels and turned Santo Domingo into an urban battleground. When the revolution began on April 24, the Johnson administration took a "wait and see" posture, secure in the fact that U.S.–trained and equipped Dominican military would be able to defeat the rebels. But as the fighting continued, the "constutionalists" proved to be a far better organized and determined fighting force than the United States had anticipated. In a decisive battle on April 28, the rebels drove the military out of Santo Domingo and seemed on the verge of victory.[9]

At this point the U.S. embassy began sending urgent messages to Washington describing the "constitutionalists" as heavily infiltrated by communists. Although there were some communist sympathizers among the rebels, the vast majority were strongly democratic and in many cases were pro-American. The U.S. embassy and the Johnson administration, however, were not inclined to make distinctions between left-wing reform democrats and left-wing communist sympathizers. The major concern of Washington was that a civil war in a Caribbean nation was creating instability at a time when the United States still feared the prospect of a "second Cuba." On April 26 President Johnson ordered U.S. military personnel into Santo Domingo, ostensibly to protect U.S. citizens but in reality to help the military regain the offensive against the "constitutionalists."

Within days U.S. forces in the Dominican Republic had risen to 23,000 men. U.S. troops immediately sought to neutralize the rebels by containing them within the old sections of Santo Domingo. The presence of the U.S. forces changed the character of the fighting: pitched battles gave way to a kind of tense stalemate among the rebels, the Dominican military, and the U.S. peace keepers.

As expected, U.S. intervention raised widespread opposition in Latin America. In an attempt to deflect the criticism, the Johnson administration formed the Inter-American Peace Force. Using the auspices of the OAS (under extreme pressure), the United States was able to convince a number of Latin American countries, all right-wing dictatorships except for Costa Rica, to send peace-keeping contingents to the Dominican Republic to join up with our forces. The Inter-American Peace Force did little to assuage Latin American critics, who saw the peace-keeping units as merely aiding the United States in crushing a popular revolution.

The stalemate between the "constitutionalists" and the coalition of peace keepers lasted throughout the summer. Fighting took the form of periodic sniper attacks and localized firefights. After months of negotiations between the rebels and the U.S. representative Ellsworth Bunker, an agreement, which called for an interim president and new elections to be held in June 1966, was reached on August 31. The "constitutionalists" publicly decried the settlement but signed the Act of Reconciliation primarily because they had no choice—they were surrounded in a small section of the city and saw little chance of defeating the forces arrayed against them. With the signing of the agreement, most of the U.S. forces soon left the Dominican Republic.[10]

The election of June 1, 1966, brought Joaquín Balaguer into the Dominican presidency. Balaguer, a friend of the United States, won an easy victory in large part because his opponent, Juan Bosch, feared for his life and therefore did little campaigning. It was clear that Balaguer was the choice of the Johnson administration, because the United States bestowed millions of dollars in aid on the new government and did little to criticize the harsh tactics that were used against opposition groups.

The Dominican intervention was, from the Johnson administration's viewpoint, a "success." The United States got in and out of the country in a relatively short period of time and achieved its main objective of stopping what it felt was a potential "second Cuba." Unfortunately "success" is a matter of perspective. The Dominicans suffered greatly in the war, not only in loss of life and property but in dashed hopes about the possibility of attaining liberal democratic government on their own terms.

THE END OF THE ALLIANCE FOR PROGRESS

By the time Lyndon Johnson left office in January 1969 it was clear that the impact of the Alliance for Progress on Latin American development had fallen short of expectations. Many saw the goals set in early 1961 by the Kennedy administration as unrealistic. In the areas of per capita growth, income distribution, agricultural productivity, literacy, and housing construction, Latin America experienced little if any improvement.

This is not to say that the influx of U.S. dollars ($10.2 billion from 1961 to 1969) and expertise did not have impact, but rather it reflects the difficulties of attaining any real growth in a region with yearly population increases of 3 percent. The United States found that despite economic growth the rising population made it very difficult to achieve significant development. Also, the architects of the alliance realized that calling upon Latin Americans to cooperate in bringing about economic and social reforms does not always ensure compliance. U.S. officials encountered great reluctance on the part of governing and economic elites to move forward in the areas of land reform, tax equalization, and the formation of social welfare programs. Finally, there was an underlying mistrust among Latin Americans toward this new grand scheme of the United States. Latin Americans had heard these promises before and were not overly anxious to get on the alliance for Progress bandwagon.

Despite the demographic problems and the resistance to change, it would be unfair not to point out the accomplishments of the alliance. Significant progress was made in the areas of public health, tax collection, and sanitation in many Latin American countries. Although illiteracy remained high, school-age enrollment increased dramatically during the alliance years. Land reform finally received recognition as a policy issue that needed immediate attention and in some countries initial steps were taken to redistribute property. Most important, though, the Alliance for Progress impressed upon Latin America a new spirit of development and sense of urgency that would be essential if these countries were to meet the challenges of modernization. As Jerome Levinson and Juan de Onis, two authors highly critical of the alliance, state:

Without the Alliance the Latin American experience in the 1960's might have been even more turbulent. . . . It was a dramatic and noble crusade, deriving from excessive idealism and over optimism, a momentum that was slowly but indisputably dissipated in encounter with harsh realities—economic, political and social.[11]

Although in many respects the Alliance for Progress brought on its own demise, the Johnson administration did little to carry forward the sense of mission that characterized U.S. relations with Latin America during the Kennedy administration. By 1967 Congress, with quiet approval of the White House, began making cuts in aid appropriations to Latin America. In 1969 aid to Latin America reached a low of $336.5 million, a significant departure from the glowing promises of Secretary Dillon at Punta del Este.

The decline in aid for Latin America during the Johnson presidency also reflected changing priorities in our foreign policy. The Vietnam conflict was now at center stage and demanding the president's full attention and also a large proportion of our budgetary resources. Latin America was again placed on the back burner of U.S. foreign policy concerns as our national leaders chose to fight communist revolution in Southeast Asia rather than devote foreign aid to the staggering and perhaps unsolvable development problems of our neighbors.

But perhaps the most serious change ushered in by the Johnson administration was its decision to downplay the support for democratic governance and accent the need for combating the spread of Marxist revolution. In 1966 Thomas Mann, President Johnson's Assistant Secretary of State for Latin American Affairs, articulated a new policy position for the United States (often called the Mann Doctrine) which suggested that military or rightist regimes would be tolerated, especially if they followed a strongly anti-communist line. This position of tacitly accepting authoritarianism as essential in the fight against communism would remain in place for the next ten years and serve as one of the key foundations of harsh military rule.[12]

NIXON AND THE "SPECIAL RELATIONSHIP"

The Nixon presidency brought new and quite different challenges to U.S.–Latin American relations. The sweeping aid programs developed under the Alliance for Progress had come to an end and the emphasis now was on replacing public grants with increased private investment and multilateral lending. In the area of trade, the dependent ties that had developed during the 1930s were changing as European and Japanese business interests sought to make inroads in the hemisphere. Finally, the Latin Americans were anxious to express their independence of the United States and were no longer reluctant to show their hostility or fearful of following a course of action that ran contrary to U.S. interests. Our hold in the hemisphere was gradually loosening.

The beginning of a new decade also saw the United States involved in a number of problem areas that heretofore had not been given a great deal of attention. In particular, the illegal migration of Latin Americans into the United States; the smuggling of huge quantities of marijuana and cocaine from countries such as Mexico and Colombia; concerns over the possible misuse of nuclear technology by Argentina and Brazil; and bothersome fishing disputes between West Coast fishermen and Peru, Ecuador, and Mexico created periods of tension and controversy. This expansion of the inter-American agenda to include new issues unfortunately came at a time when there seemed to be less willingness on the part of Latin America to cooperate with this country in resolving these problems. In many cases the Latin American countries either dragged their feet in negotiations with the United States or took defiant stands to prove their independence.[13]

President Nixon got an early taste of the new Latin American mood when he asked former New York governor Nelson Rockefeller to head a study commission to report on ways to improve our relations in the hemisphere. In his travels to Latin America Rockefeller encountered repeated protests and demonstrations in many of the countries on his tour. In some instances his visit had to be cancelled for fear of serious disruptions.

Upon his return to the United States, Rockefeller presented his report on the "Quality of Life in the Americas" to President Nixon. The report discussed many of the economic issues that were causing strained relations between the United States and Latin America including debt rescheduling, commodity agreements, trade opportunities, and of course the request for more aid assistance. In the area of government and politics the report reinforced the position taken by the Johnson administration that military governments may be appropriate stabilizers in countries where economic recession and social polarization has created conflict and stalemate. Among its eighty-three recommendations, the Rockefeller Commission called for a doubling of trade with Latin America by 1976 and the dismantling of many of the trade barriers that had been set up to deny access to Latin American agricultural and finished products. The report also picked up on the theme that our failure to recognize the severe economic conditions experienced in Latin America would eventually lead to instability and revolution.[14]

President Nixon gave only cautious approval of the report, and instead pledged a new era of cooperation with heavy reliance on multilateral assistance, private enterprise, and greater efforts to break down trade barriers. The focus of the Nixon position was that the United States could not try to promise more than it could deliver and that we would look to Latin America for consultation on the proper course of action. This was the essence of what was termed our "special relationship" with Latin America. While some have called the Nixon position on Latin America "benign neglect," the Republican approach to development in the Third World sought to reduce direct government involvement in dealing with these difficult economic issues and to rely on the corporate sector as the "engine of change."

Although the United States under President Nixon turned away from the Alliance for Progress approach to Latin American development, the administration did not reject our traditional concern about the spread of communism in the hemisphere. At issue was the 1970 election of Salvador Allende as president of Chile. After two unsuccessful bids for the presidency, Allende, a socialist, won a slim plurality of the votes over two more moderate candidates. Allende's rise to the Chilean presidency signaled danger to U.S. business interests like the Anaconda and Kennecott copper companies, International Telephone and Telegraph, Ford, General Motors, and others. Allende's campaign platform stated his intention to nationalize property held by foreigners and begin redirecting the economy toward socialism.

The Nixon administration was also concerned about Allende because of his commitment to Marxist principles, which made it likely that he would develop closer ties with Cuba and the Soviet Union. A Marxist government in Chile could, in the view of the administration, serve as a base for spreading left-wing revolution to surrounding states like Bolivia and Peru. Because communism had not succeeded in establishing a foothold in South America, President Nixon was determined to take appropriate measures to weaken the Allende regime and limit its ability to evolve into a socialist state.

Our involvement in Chile during the Allende years has been described as "destabilizing." The Nixon administration utilized an extensive array of economic, financial, and covert tactics in its campaign to cause unrest in Chile and promote uncertainty within the Allende regime. In response to Allende's nationalization of U.S. copper holdings and his refusal to pay just compensation, the Nixon administration decreased foreign assistance to Chile and used its veto power in multilateral lending agencies to deny key loans to the government. The Nixon administration also made it difficult for Chile to obtain vital spare parts to maintain its factories and transportation systems. Furthermore, in the three years while Allende was in power the United States spent some $7 million to support opposition newspapers and organizations. Finally, recent investigations of the Nixon presidency reveal that White House officials initiated a full range of covert operations including support for assassination plots against Chilean leaders, bribery of opposition politicians, and active encouragement of conspiracies to bring the government down.[15]

In September 1973, with the Chilean economy in shambles and the military fearful of a further extension of socialism, the Allende government was brought down in a violent coup in which the president and his personal guards fought to the death. A new military junta headed by General Augusto Pinochet quickly established order and ushered in a period of stern authoritarian rule unusual in Chilean history. Left-wing associates of Allende were rounded up, many were imprisoned, some disappeared, Eventually relations between Chile and the Nixon administration returned to normal: economic loans were restored, trade was renewed and compensation issues relating to our holdings were resolved with little difficulty.

Much has been written about the reasons for Allende's downfall. Some observers feel that the United States was directly responsible for Allende's overthrow. They argue that our economic, financial, and trade restrictions created enormous dislocations in Chilean society and that our covert support of the opposition strengthened its resolve to bring down Allende.[16]

Others feel that Allende brought about his own downfall by mismanaging his revolution and being a captive to ideology. If Allende, so this version goes, had worked with U.S. business interests to come to an equitable agreement on the copper holdings and had not alienated the Chilean middle class with his socialist program, he could have avoided the ultimate showdown with the military.[17]

Although the fall of Salvador Allende along with his experiment in "democratic Marxism" captured the interest of many, both in Latin America and the United States, the important lesson from this failed Chilean revolution is the Nixon administration's choice of destabilization as a strategy for protecting our business interests and containing communist expansion. Because the communist threat was thousands of miles away and not in our Caribbean–Central American sphere of influence, the United States chose not to employ military force, but rather to pursue a course of action that limited Allende's ability to govern. By weakening the economy, seeking out and encouraging right-wing conspirators, influencing domestic opinion, and drumming up international opposition to Chile, the United States helped create an internal political climate where overthrow became inevitable. Allende found that he faced two enemies: the conservative elites and the Nixon administration.

The storm of protest that followed the military overthrow of Allende and the investigative reporting of our role in that overthrow by the press and other sources further hampered relations with Latin America and gave liberal critics of the Nixon administration even more ammunition with which to criticize the president. By the fall of 1973 President Nixon himself was facing an ouster movement over the cover-up employed in the Watergate break-in. U.S. policy toward Latin America became a minor concern in light of the domestic furor that engulfed the Nixon White House, but the value system and ethical standards that helped to foster the Watergate crisis can be directly connected to our involvement in Allende's Chile. As Seymour Hersh, in his study of the Nixon White House, states:

With Chile as with Watergate, cover-up payments were sought for CIA contacts and associates who were caught in the acts of crime. With Chile as with Watergate, records were destroyed and documents distorted. With Chile as with Watergate, much of the official testimony provided to congressional investigating committees was perjury. With Chile as with Watergate, the White House was in league with unscrupulous and violent men.[18]

THE FORD INTERLUDE

The resignation of Richard Nixon in August 1974 may have resolved the Watergate crisis, but it did little to brighten relations between the United States and Latin America. In fact Nixon's successor, Gerald Ford, occupied the presidency at a time when the Latin Americans heightened their criticism of the United States trade policies and broke with this country's longstanding isolation of Cuba.

The major source of conflict with Latin America during the brief tenure of Gerald Ford was the passage of the Trade Reform Act of 1974. Although President Ford disliked the protectionist nature of the legislation, he was unable to stop passage. The Latin Americans in particular took issue with the section of the bill that curtailed so-called preferential or most-favored-nation trade status to members of the Organization of Petroleum Exporting Countries (OPEC). Because Venezuela and Ecuador were charter members of OPEC, the legislation singled out two trading partners of the United States and denied them traditional advantages extended to other Latin American nations.

This OPEC restriction along with other protectionist barriers against consumer and manufactured goods outraged the Latin Americans and prompted them to form their own hemispheric trade alliance: the Latin American Economic System (SELA). The United States was not included in the twenty-four nation system (Cuba was invited to join), but to date SELA has not had a marked impact on restructuring trade patterns in Latin America. Rather, SELA revealed the extent of Latin American displeasure with our failure to recognize their need for greater access to U.S. markets.

While the Trade Reform Act angered Latin American nations, President Ford's efforts to normalize relations with Cuba were well received. As a result of quiet diplomatic discussions the Ford administration appeared ready to lift its opposition to OAS sanctions against the Castro regime. After a failed effort by OAS foreign ministers in Quito, Ecuador, a resolution was passed in San José, Costa Rica, in July 1975. By a vote of 15 to 3 (with the United States voting with the majority) the sanctions were removed and member nations were advised that they could resume relations in the manner they thought appropriate.

The effort to resume normal relations that led the United States to support the removal of sanctions against Cuba continued, as the Ford administration pressed for more diplomatic talks, permitted foreign-based subsidiaries of U.S. corporations to sell their products to Cuba, and agreed not to impose penalties on nations that traded with Cuba. Unfortunately the positive climate of U.S.–Cuban relations collapsed when the Castro government decided to send combat troops to Angola and to increase their presence in nine other African countries. With Castro unwavering in his desire to assist other revolutionary regimes, the Ford administration backed away from any further conciliatory gestures.[19]

In the November 1976 election Gerald Ford lost a close contest to former Georgia governor, Jimmy Carter. During the campaign, Carter pledged to pay closer attention to the numerous economic concerns of the Latin Americans while also criticizing the Nixon-Ford policy of supporting authoritarian regimes and ignoring human rights violators. As a Democratic president entered the White House for the first time in eight years, there was an air of expectation in Latin America as leaders looked to the new administration to show greater interest in the social and economic problems facing this region.

NEW DIRECTIONS IN THE CARTER ADMINISTRATION

The Latin American policy of President Jimmy Carter is best described as a mix of high principle, human compassion, belief in negotiation, and a reluctance to intervene in leftist revolutions. During his term as president, Jimmy Carter strove to develop a more favorable image of the United States in Latin America.[20] Partly because of his own personal convictions and partly as a reaction to past Republican policies, President Carter was conscious of the fact that the United States had to reestablish its credibility in the hemisphere.

One of the primary means of regaining support in Latin America, especially among the proponents of democratic reform, was the fashioning of a human rights policy by the Carter administration. The president, along with Secretary of State Cyrus Vance and United Nations Representative Andrew Young, stressed on numerous occasions that the United States was firmly behind those governments that protected individual freedom and opposed to those regimes that engaged in harsh, repressive practices in order to limit dissent.

The Carter human rights policy was not mere political speech making. Using the 1976 Foreign Military Assistance Act as a basis for action, the United States began to link credits for military sales to the respect for human rights. As a result, the administration cut back or completely eliminated military assistance to authoritarian regimes in Argentina, Brazil, Chile, Guatemala, Paraguay, and Uruguay. President Carter also sought Senate ratification of the 1969 American

Convention on Human Rights and cooperated extensively with the OAS Inter-American Human Rights Commission, which reported on human rights abuses. The internal foreign policy structure in the United States was also affected by the push for human rights, as the president named a new assistant secretary of state for human rights and supported the publication of a yearly human rights report that described the status of each country in the world with respect to protection of human rights.[21]

Although the accent on human rights is not new to U.S. foreign policy, its vigorous pursuit by the Carter administration caused extensive criticism from conservatives in Congress, who felt that this country would lose support of some of Latin America's most influential governments. The criticism of the Carter policy spread to Latin America, where the military governments affected by the arms restrictions lashed out at what they viewed as a new form of U.S. intervention in their internal affairs. Brazil even went so far as to cancel its military aid treaty with the United States.

While the general fumed, the democratic politicians in Latin America were quite pleased with the Carter emphasis on human rights. Venezuelan president Carlos Andres Perez called the policy the "best message the President of the United States could give Latin America." Many human rights advocates credited the president with helping to revive democratic governance in Latin America and with decreasing repres-sion in the military-run countries. Such claims are hard to substantiate, but there is no doubt that the United States bolstered the spirits of democratic leaders, opposition party activists, and government dissenters in Latin America and caused military officials to reevaluate the wisdom of following a course of action that placed them in opposition to the president of the United States.

The Carter administration continued to rebuild its image in Latin America by finalizing an agreement with Panama over the Canal Zone. After years of negotiations with the Panamanians, President Carter was determined to achieve success. In many respects the opposition to a new treaty came not from the Panamanians but from various interests in the United States. Both right-wing conservatives, who felt a treaty would show weakness and lessen our ability to control this strategic waterway, and the thousands of U.S. employees in the zone who feared for their jobs viewed the prospect of a treaty with great suspicion.

Despite the opposition and the political risks involved, President Carter prevailed. On September 7, 1977, at OAS headquarters in Washington, President Carter and Panamanian leader General Omar Torrijos signed a new Canal Zone treaty. The treaty itself was actually two documents. The first, titled the Panama Canal Treaty, addressed the issue of transfer of control and future responsibility for the operation of the canal. A key section of this document permits the United States to manage and defend the canal until the year 1999, even though

Panama retains jurisdiction over the Canal Zone. There is also provision in this part of the treaty for employee guarantees, rights of passage for ships, and a schedule of payments to Panama. The second treaty, or Neutrality Treaty, addressed the question of transit through and defense of the zone after 1999. In this part of the document Panama pledged to assure perpetual neutrality for the canal and to permit the United States to defend the canal in case of a threat to its neutrality.

Despite the fanfare over the signing of the Panama Canal Treaty in Washington, there were other hurdles that would have to be crossed before implementation. General Torrijos went back to Panama and sought a popular referendum to support the treaty. After a month of internal debate, 66 percent of the Panamanian people gave their consent, a figure much lower than Torrijos had expected. President Carter, as with other treaties, sought senate approval. Again conservative groups fought the ratification. An intense lobbying and public-opinion campaign was waged to stop the treaty. Only after additional changes were made to the treaty, granting the United States rights beyond the year 1999, did the Senate narrowly ratify the agreement.

The Panama Canal Treaty was without question a major foreign policy achievement for the Carter administration. Even though the conservatives bemoaned "giving back what was ours," Carter showed the Latin Americans that it is possible to negotiate with the United States over longstanding disputes. For all the furor that surrounded the Panama Canal Treaty and the conservative prognostications of doom, the agreement received widespread support in both the United States and Panama and is being implemented with little difficulty.[22]

The belief in the power of diplomacy to settle disputes carried over into Cuban-American relations. President Carter, like Gerald Ford, sent out diplomatic "feelers" to the Castro government, hoping to encourage the Cuban leader to refrain from revolutionary activity and establish normal ties with the United States. Even Castro seemed anxious to resume economic ties with the United States because the Cuban economy had stagnated and needed huge infusions of trade and capital investment.

Although there were still deep divisions between the two countries concerning Cuban troops in Angola, the United States naval base on Guantánamo, and of course the trade embargo, the diplomatic contacts did lead to the establishment of "interest-section" offices in Havana and Washington. These interest-section offices were not given embassy status and did not signal the resumption of diplomatic relations, but the fact that these two enemies were beginning to break down barriers was seen as encouraging by many supporters of normalization.

The interest-section agreement was all the normalcy that would be achieved between Cuba and the United States. In 1979 the Carter administration charged that the Soviet Union had assembled a combat unit of some 2,000 to 3,000 soldiers in Cuba. The unit had been in the country for some years, but the Carter administration chose to make an issue of Soviet presence in the hemisphere, and thereby placed a chill on any further diplomatic progress.

Relations between the United States and Cuba during the Carter administration took a strange turn when Fidel Castro permitted thousands of his countrymen to leave the island. Initiated when some 10,000 Cubans stormed the Peruvian embassy seeking asylum, the incident eventually involved the departure of over 120,000 Cubans from that port city of Mariel. President Carter, seeing the propaganda value of the mass exodus, welcomed the Mariel boat people. But while the stream of refugees reflected the troubled times that had come to Castro's revolution, the Cuban leader shrewdly used the migration to clean out his jail and mental institutions. As the refugees landed in the United States, immigration officials were unable to handle the rush of new arrivals and were forced to set up makeshift camps. Although many Cubans entered the mainstream of U.S. society, the Cuban criminal element caused considerable problems for police, especially in Florida where many of the refugees took up residence.

As President Carter headed into the final two years of his administration, this country began to become embroiled in the revolutions erupting in Central America. Long a bastion of conservative pro-American regimes, Central America in the late 1970s was beset by leftist revolution. In particular, the government of Nicaraguan dictator Anastasio Somoza was challenged by a dedicated band of revolutionaries called the Sandinistas.

As fighting raged in his country, President Somoza appealed to the Carter administration for assistance against the rebels. President Carter, however, was reluctant to provide Somoza with aid or public support because the Nicaraguan leader had a record as one of Latin America's most repressive and corrupt dictators. Instead the United States urged Somoza to institute social and political reforms as a means of curtailing rebel activity. Somoza made some cosmetic changes, but continued to rely on his National Guard to achieve a military solution. But when popular opposition journalist Pedro Chamorro was assassinated, what little support Somoza had in the country disappeared.

The erosion of Somoza's power posed a dilemma for the United States. On the one hand the Carter administration wanted to remain true to its human rights policy and not appear to be propping up a dictator, but on the other hand the Sandinista forces were leftists who would certainly take Nicaragua down a path toward Marxism. Faced with two equally difficult alternatives, the Carter administration seemed unsure of the proper course to follow and on occasion showed support for both sides. At one point the administration sought OAS participation in sending a peace-keeping force to Nicaragua and setting up a democratic government that would rest in between Somoza and the Sandinistas. The OAS, remembering its embarrassing participation in the Dominican peace-keeping episode, flatly rejected the U.S. initiative.[23]

The Carter administration's efforts to find the middle course between Somoza and the Sandinistas became unnecessary when the rebels forced the Nicaraguan dictator to leave the country in July of 1979. Once in power the Sandinistas lived up to their revolutionary slogans and began to implement policies that were reminiscent of Cuba in the 1960s. Literacy drives and health-care programs, along with Cuban technicians and anti-American speeches became common in Nicaragua. But despite the swing to the left, the Carter administration hoped that the Sandinistas would moderate their policies and that the United States could still have influence in Nicaragua.

Many of the early debates about U.S.–Nicaragua relations centered on the Carter administration's desire to provide the Sandinistas with $75 million in emergency aid. The aid question divided Congress as conservatives questioned the wisdom of supporting a Marxist regime, while liberals felt that the aid would give the United States a degree of access to the new leadership group and moderate their behavior. The aid package did eventually pass through Congress, but only about $60 million reached Nicaragua as both the Carter administration and Congress began to doubt the propriety of assisting the Sandinistas. With Cuban and Soviet advisors arriving at regular intervals and signs that the new government was fostering revolution in nearby El Salvador, the Carter administration moved further away from its conciliatory approach and began to contemplate a military containment policy.

Nicaragua may have moved in the direction of a Marxist state, but the Carter administration felt that the same fate need not occur in neighboring El Salvador. The view in Washington was that with extensive economic and military assistance the government could turn back the Salvadoran rebel movement. As in Nicaragua, President Carter was torn between unwillingness to support a repressive, anti-reform government and the need to have in place a government that took a strong anti-communist stance.

The Carter administration justified its increased aid and public support of the Salvadoran government by pledging to work with the country's leaders to achieve greater democratization and faster distribution of land to the peasants. The president was convinced that given time and sufficient assistance El Salvador could neutralize the rebels and serve as a counterforce to neighboring Nicaragua. To show his resolve with respect to controlling the revolution, President Carter, in one of his last acts as president, agreed to send fifty advisors to train the Salvadoran military.

As Jimmy Carter left the presidency, his Latin American policy received praise from those who were impressed with the emphasis on human rights and democratic principles and criticism for its failure to recognize the expanding communist threat in the hemisphere. But to many citizens President Carter was perceived as responsible for a general decline in U.S. prestige and influence throughout the world. The fact that Carter strengthened ties with Latin America and gained the respect of those seeking an end to military repression did not help to stem the conservative tide in this country. Increasingly Americans saw revolution spreading in our "backyard," the Soviets gaining new allies, and Latin American leaders harshly condemning this country for everything from trade imbalances to immigration quotas. Despite his accomplishments, President Carter became a target for those like Ronald Reagan, who told the American people that it was time to respond forcefully to the communist threat in the hemisphere and take aggressive steps to protect our national security as he had done so many times before (Table 3.1).[24]

Table 3.1
Instances of Use of U.S. Armed Forces in
Central America and the Caribbean, 1901–1994

1901	Columbia (State of Panama) — November 20–December 4 To protect U.S. property on the Isthmus and to keep transit lines open during serious revolutionary disturbances.
1902	Columbia (State of Panama) — September 17–November 18 To place armed guards on all trains crossing the Isthmus and to keep the railroad line open.
1903	Honduras — March 23–30 or 31 To protect the U.S. consulate and the steamship wharf at Puerto Cortez during a period of revolutionary activity.
1903–14	Panama To protect U.S. interests and lives during and following the revolution for independence from Columbia over construction of the Isthmian Canal. With brief intermissions, U.S. marines were stationed on the Isthmus from November 4, 1903–January 21, 1914, to guard U.S. interests.
1904	Dominican Republic — January 2–February 11 To protect U.S. interests in Puerto Plata and Sosua and Santo Domingo City during revolutionary fighting.
1904	Panama — November 17–24 To protect U.S. lives and property at Aneon at the time of a threatened insurrection.
1906–8	Cuba — September 1906–January 1909 Intervention to restore order, protect foreigners, and establish a stable government after serious revolutionary activity.
1907	Honduras — March 18–June 8 To protect U.S. interests during a war between Honduras and Nicaragua, troops were stationed for a few days or weeks in Trujillo, Celba, Puerto Cortez, San Pedro, Laguna, and Choloma.
1910	Nicaragua — February 22 During a civil war, to get information of conditions at Corinto; May 19–September 4, to protect U.S. interests at Bluefields.

1911	Honduras — January 26 and some weeks thereafter
	To protect U.S. lives and interests during a civil war in Honduras.
1912	Panama
	Troops on request to both political parties, supervised elections outside the Canal Zone.
1912–25	Nicaragua — August–November 1912
	To protect U.S. interests during an attempted revolution. A small force serving as a legation guard and as a promoter of peace and governmental stability remained until August 5, 1925.
1913	Mexico — September 5–7
	A few marines landed at Claris Estero to aid in evacuating U.S. citizens and others from the Yaqui Valley, made dangerous for foreigners by civil strife.
1914	Haiti — January 29–February 9, February 20–21, October 19
	To protect U.S. nationals in a time of dangerous unrest.
1914	Dominican Republic — June and July
	During a revolutionary movement, U.S. naval forces by gunfire stopped the bombardment of Puerto Plata, and by threat of force maintained Santo Domingo City as a neutral zone.
1914–17	Mexico
	The undeclared Mexican-American hostilities following the Dolphin affair and Villa's raids included capture of Vera Cruz and later Pershing's expedition into northern Mexico.
1915–34	Haiti — July 28, 1915–August 15, 1934
	To maintain order during a period of chronic and threatened insurrection.
1916–24	Dominican Republic — May 1916–September 1924
	To maintain order during a period of chronic threatened insurrection.
1917–22	Cuba
	To protect U.S. interests during an insurrection and subsequent unsettled conditions. Most of the U.S. armed forces left Cuba by August 1919, but two companies remained at Camaguey until February 1922.
1918–19	Mexico
	After withdrawal of the Pershing expedition, our troops entered Mexico in pursuit of bandits at least three times in 1918 and six in 1919. In August 1918 U.S. and Mexican troops fought at Nogales.
1918–20	Panama
	For police duty according to treaty stipulations, at Chirique, during election disturbances and subsequent unrest.
1919	Honduras — September 8–12
	A landing force was sent ashore to maintain order in a neutral zone during an attempted revolution.
1920	Guatemala — April 9–27
	To protect the U.S. legation and other U.S. interests, such as the cable station, during a period of fighting between Unionists and the Government of Guatemala.
1921	Panama
	U.S. naval squadrons demonstrated in April on both sides of the Isthmus to prevent war between the two countries over a boundary dispute.
1924	Costa Rica — February 28–March 31, September 10–15
	To protect U.S. lives and interests during election hostilities.
1925	Honduras — April 19–21
	To protect foreigners at La Celba during a political upheaval.

1925   Panama — October 12–23
          Strikes and rent riots led to the landing of about 600 U.S. troops to keep
          order and protect U.S. interests.
1926–33   Nicaragua — May 7–June 5, 1926, August 27, 1926–January 3, 1933
          The *coup d'état* of General Chamorro aroused revolutionary activities
          leading to the landing of U.S. marines to protect the interests of the
          United States. U.S. forces came and went, but seem not to have left the
          country entirely until January 3, 1933. Their work included activity
          against the outlaw leader Sandino in 1928.
1933   Cuba
          During a revolution against President Gerardo Machado naval forces
          demonstrated but no landing was made.
1956–60   The Caribbean
          2nd Marine Ground Task Force was deployed to protect U.S. nationals
          during the Cuban crisis.
1962   Cuba
          President Kennedy instituted a "quarantine" on the shipment of offensive
          missiles to Cuba from the Soviet Union. He also warned the Soviet Union
          that the launching of any missile from Cuba against any nation in the
          Western Hemisphere would bring about U.S. nuclear retaliation on the
          Soviet Union. A negotiated settlement was achieved in a few days.
1965   Dominican Republic
          Intervention to protect lives and property during a Dominican revolt.
          More troops were sent as the United States feared the revolutionary forces
          were coming increasingly under communist control.
1980   El Salvador
          U.S. military advisors sent to instruct government troops in anti-guerrilla
          tactics.
1982   Honduras
          U.S. military advisors sent to train government troops.
1983   Grenada
          U.S. military forces invade Grenada.
1990   Panama
          U.S. troops invade to remove General Manuel Noriega.
1994   Haiti.
          U.S. troops lead peace-keeping mission.

Source: Adapted from U.S. Library of Congress Foreign Affairs Division Committee
Print, 94th Cong., 1st sess. (Washington, D.C.: U.S. Government Printing Office,
1975), pp. 58–66.

NOTES

1. Herbert Matthew's study, *Fidel Castro* (New York: Simon & Schuster, 1969),
remains the most authoritative account of Castro and the days of the revolution.
2. Andres Suarez, *Castroism and Communism 1954–66* (Cambridge, Mass.:
MIT Press, 1967), is the authoritative source of this period of the Cuban revolution.
3. Philip W. Bonsal, *Cuba, Castro and the United States* (Pittsburgh: University
of Pittsburgh Press, 1971).
4. Tad Szulc and Karl E. Meyer, *The Cuban Invasion: The Chronicle of Disaster*
(New York: Ballantine Books, 1962), detail this failed effort to bring the Castro regime
down.

5.   As quoted in Jerome Levinson and Juan de Onix, *The Alliance That Lost Its Way* (Chicago: Quadrangle, 1972), p. 34.

6.   *Reunion extraordinaria del Consejo Interamericana Economico y Social al Nivel Ministerial* (Washington, D.C.: Pan American Union, 1961), OEA/SerH/4:1.

7.   The best account of the Cuban Missile Crisis can be found in Graham T. Allison, *Essence of Decision: Explaining the Cuban Missile Crisis* (Boston: Little, Brown, 1971).

8.   Edwin Lieuwen, *U.S. Policy in Latin America* (New York: Praeger, 1965), pp. 101–4.

9.   The most complete account of the civil war in Santo Domingo is Piero Gleijeses, *The Dominican Crisis: The 1965 Constitutional Revolt and American Intervention* (Baltimore, Md.: Johns Hopkins University Press, 1978).

10.   The negotiation stage of the revolution is documented in Jerome Slater's *Intervention and Negotiation: The United States and the Dominican Revolution* (New York: Harper & Row, 1970), pp. 71–135.

11.   Levinson and de Onis, *The Alliance*, p. 307.

12.   See Edwin Lieuwen, *Generals vs. Presidents: Neo-Militarism in Latin America* (New York: Praeger, 1964), pp. 142–44.

13.   A good overview of the Nixon administration's Latin American policy can be found in Karl Schmitt's "The United States and Latin America," in Robert C. Gray and Stanley J. Michalak, Jr., eds., *American Foreign Policy Since Detente* (New York: Harper & Row, 1984), pp. 114–47.

14.   *The Official Report of a United States Presidential Mission for the Western Hemisphere* (Chicago: Quadrangle, 1969). A critique of the Rockefeller Report can be found in James D. Cockroft, *Neighbors in Turmoil: Latin America* (New York: Harper & Row, 1989), pp. 37–38.

15.   See Seymour Hersh, "The Price of Power: Kissinger, Nixon and Chile," *The Atlantic*, December 1982, pp. 31–58.

16.   The most critical account of U.S. policy in Chile can be found in James Petras and Morris Morley, *The United States and Chile: Imperialism and the Overthrow of the Allende Government* (New York: Monthly Review Press, 1975).

17.   For a more balanced approach see Paul Sigmund, "The 'Invisible Blockade' and the Overthrow of Allende," *Foreign Affairs* 52 (January 1974): 322–48.

18.   Seymour Hersh, *The Price of Power: Kissinger in the Nixon White House* (New York: Summit Books, 1983), p. 638.

19.   Schmitt, "United States and Latin America," pp. 124–26.

20.   A good overview of President Carter's Latin American policy is provided by Abraham Lowenthal's "Jimmy Carter and Latin America: A New Era or Small Change," in Kenneth Oye, Donald Rothchild, and Robert Leiker, eds., *Eagle Entangled: U.S. Foreign Policy in a Complex World* (New York: Longman, 1979), pp. 290–303.

21.   See Howard Wiarda, "Democracy and Human Rights in Latin America: Toward a New Conceptualization," *Orbis*, Spring 1978, pp. 137–60.

22.   See John P. Augelli, "The Implementation of the Panama Canal Treaties," in Jack Hopkins, ed., *Latin America and Caribbean Contemporary Record* (New York: Holmes and Meier, 1982), pp. 162–70.

23.   See William LeoGrande, "The United States and the Nicaraguan Revolution," in Thomas Walker, ed., *Nicaragua in Revolution* (New York: Praeger, 1982), pp. 68–71.

24.   See, for instance, Pedro A. San Juan, "Why We Don't Have a Latin American Policy," *Washington Quarterly* 3 (Autumn 1980): 28–39.

4

Contemporary Relations: Reagan, Bush, and Clinton

Ronald Reagan wasted no time in letting the Latin Americans know that he was going to approach the problems in the region differently from Jimmy Carter. Instead of stressing human rights, Reagan chose to criticize the terrorism of leftist guerrillas; instead of breaking ties with authoritarian regimes, Reagan made new overtures to countries like Brazil, Chile, and Guatemala and offered to restore aid; instead of normalizing relations with Cuba, Reagan lambasted Castro and talked in a manner that suggested a return to the days of confrontation.

One of the first initiatives of the new Reagan administration was to link the revolution in El Salvador to Cuban and Soviet intervention. A State Department report entitled *Communist Interference in El Salvador* sought to portray the revolution in El Salvador as sponsored and supplied by Cuba and the Soviet Union.[1] Using captured documents and aerial reconnaissance photos the report showed that Cuba was using Nicaragua as the main conduit for arms and assistance to the Salvadoran rebels. The report strengthened the administration's view that El Salvador was the next target of the communists in Central America and that the conflict there was not just a struggle for social justice as liberals had claimed.

The Reagan administration continued to press hard on the theme of communist expansion in the hemisphere in a series of verbal assaults against the Castro regime and the Sandinistas. Secretary of State Alexander Haig talked sternly to Cuba about "going to the source" of the revolution in El Salvador, while claiming that the Nicaraguan government was creating a "platform for terror and war in the region." These and many other statements made by the administration cast the revolution in Central America as a contest between competing ideologies, with the United States determined to meet the communist challenge head on.

The extent of our determination to stop the communists from capturing the revolutionary process in Central America was seen in the

Reagan commitment to provide economic and military assistance. From 1981 through 1983 the Reagan administration supplied El Salvador with nearly $700 million in assistance with ever larger percentages of that aid going to military training and weapons purchases. Neighboring countries such as Honduras and Guatemala also benefited from the Reagan fear of communist expansion. Between 1981 and 1983 Honduras received nearly $200 million in assistance, while Guatemala gradually returned to favor with the Reagan administration and saw its share of U.S. aid increase as well.

Although El Salvador occupied much of the president's attention, his administration saw the larger implications of revolution in the hemisphere and responded with both economic and military initiatives. Perhaps the most highly publicized program of foreign assistance since the Alliance for Progress was President Reagan's Caribbean Basin Initiative (CBI) of 1981. Designed as a means of responding to communist-inspired revolution through a comprehensive trade and aid policy, the CBI brought Central America and the Caribbean together as a strategic region (President Reagan called it our "third border") that would benefit from more liberal access to our markets, greater economic assistance, and more incentives for capital investment.

The CBI called for an immediate allocation of $350 million in emergency aid to the region, a twelve-year period of free trade with the United States, and tax benefits to U.S. firms that invested in this region. The emergency aid passed through Congress with little opposition, but the trade and tax initiatives were compromised as special interests limited entry of certain goods (that is, rum and leather products) and replaced the investment credit with greater tax deductions for conventions held in the Caribbean. But despite the changes, the overall package was well received in the Caribbean Basin and helped stimulate a good deal of interest among U.S. companies, which saw the Reagan administration as supportive of their business expansion in this region.[2]

While the CBI sought to offset communist influence through huge injections of capital and a resurgence in trade, the Reagan administration felt it necessary to move beyond its commitment to El Salvador and expand its containment policy by bolstering the military preparedness of Honduras. Besides providing over $50 million in military assistance to Honduras, the Reagan administration worked closely with the Honduran government in conducting joint military maneuvers. From 1982 to 1985 U.S. military personnel (at some points reaching as many as 4,000 soldiers) participated in exercises called Big Pine I, II, and III. These joint exercises were viewed by the administration, not only as part of an overall effort to modernize and professionalize Central American militaries, but as another signal to the Cubans, and especially to the Nicaraguans, that the United States was serious about stopping the spread of Marxist revolution.

The joint military exercises were not as controversial as the Reagan administration decision to use Honduras as a base for a covert war against neighboring Nicaragua. With over 15,000 anti-Sandinista *contras* supplied and trained by Central Intelligence Agency (CIA) operatives, Honduras became a staging area for a guerrilla-style war against Nicaragua. Although a full-scale invasion never took place, the border between Honduras and Nicaragua became the site of numerous skirmishes.

The attacks against Nicaragua from Honduras evoked a new round of congressional opposition. Liberals felt that the funding of the covert war violated the 1795 Neutrality Act, which forbade the United States to support the invasion of another country. Other critics deplored the use of covert forces made up in part of ex-Somoza officers. As a result, Congress debated the funding for the war throughout 1983 and succeeded in limiting the appropriation to $24 million, thereby forcing the president to return to Congress and justify further expenditures. These early debates in Congress on the administration's *contra* aid proposals were fierce as liberals warned that a further commitment to the contras would jeopardize the prospects for a negotiated settlement with Nicaragua and link this country with counterrevolutionaries who commanded little support among their own people. Conservatives lashed back at the failure of liberals to support the *contra* "freedom fighters" against a government that was showing signs of increased Marxist influence and closer ties to the communist bloc.

The legislative defeats of compromises on the *contra* aid package were stunning blows to Reagan, who was used to getting his way with Congress. Despite congressional opposition, Reagan pledged not to give up the fight but to return with even larger requests. Meanwhile, the *contras* continued to fight on with support from private sources and with the hope of eventually "liberating" their homeland. Against them, however, was a larger, better-equipped, and more popular fighting force that had so far proved to be a more than adequate defender of the revolution.

The *contra* aid problems of the president, however, did not handcuff the administration or prevent it from meeting its objectives of weakening the Sandinistas and containing communism in the hemisphere. A few days after the *contra* vote President Reagan signed an executive order that broke off all trade with the Nicaraguan government. The order, which prohibited the entry of Nicaraguan commodities such as bananas and coffee, denied landing rights to Nicaraguan airlines, curtailed U.S. shipments of goods to the Sandinistas, and required all U.S. ships to steer clear of Nicaraguan ports, was designed to further weaken the economy of that country and make Congress recognize that the president was not going to allow the legislative branch to dictate this country's foreign policy.

Although the communist threat to the Caribbean Basin preoccupied the Reagan administration, a number of other issues and policy concerns brought the United States into contact with Latin America. One major point of dispute was our support of Great Britain in the Falklands-Malvinas War. In April 1982, Argentine forces invaded the British Falkland Islands, claiming that the Malvinas (as Argentina calls the islands) belonged to them.

Prime Minister Margaret Thatcher of England, wasting little time in responding to the Argentine action, sent an armada to regain the Falklands. Early on in this conflict over age-old claims of sovereignty, President Reagan decided to assist England by providing satellite photos of the island and working closely with the Thatcher government in other intelligence-gathering areas. Most important, the Reagan administration rejected the Argentine and Latin American claims that we must abide by the Rio Treaty and stop British intervention in the hemisphere. The fact that the Reagan administration viewed Argentina as the aggressor and refused to be bound by the Rio Treaty angered the Latin Americans and further damaged this country's credibility in the region. On June 14 the Argentine military surrendered to the superior British forces arrayed against them and were forced to return to Buenos Aires to face hostile public opinion. The Reagan administration for its part accepted the criticism from Latin American leaders but felt confident in its decision to support a traditional ally rather than a hemispheric neighbor who chose to settle a dispute by armed aggression.

The powerful reach of U.S. influence and control also touched the tiny Caribbean island of Grenada. In the fall of 1983 the socialist prime minister of Grenada, Maurice Bishop, was replaced by a more orthodox faction of his party that pledged to develop even closer ties to Cuba and the Soviet Union. Bishop and his followers sought to regain power but were cut down in a bloody confrontation. The murder of Maurice Bishop touched off a period of uncertainty on the island and moved the Reagan administration to action. On October 25, 1983, President Reagan, citing the need to protect U.S. students on the island (there were several hundred attending medical school in the capital city of St. George's) ordered U.S. military units into the country.

The United States was conscious of its past record of unilateral intervention and thus it was pleased when nations making up the Organization of Eastern Caribbean States requested that the Reagan administration use military means to rid the island of communist influence. U.S. military personnel thus joined with contingents from Barbados, St. Lucia, Dominica, and Jamaica in the invasion force. These Caribbean ministates agreed that a leftist government in Grenada, with ever-expanding ties to Cuba, posed a threat to their security. As for the United States, the safety of the medical students was not our only concern. The Bishop government had accepted a Cuban offer to build an airstrip on the island that the Reagan administration felt would be used in the future to land Soviet jets and troop transports. With Cuba already a Soviet satellite state and Nicaragua headed in that direction, the president felt that it was necessary to stop this latest example of communist expansion.

The invading U.S. forces encountered heavy resistance from Grenadian leftists and from Cuban technicians, many of whom were military officers. After a few days of fighting, the U.S. forces secured the island. Nineteen U.S. soldiers were killed and scores were injured. Cuban casualties were twenty-four dead and hundreds wounded or captured. Searches of warehouses by U.S. troops turned up huge caches of arms and documents showing an increased commitment to the Grenadian government from communist nations such as the Soviet Union, North Korea, and of course Cuba.

Unlike the beneficiaries of many of the previous U.S. interventions, the vast majority of the Grenadians welcomed the U.S. troops as liberators and provided the Reagan administration with a huge public relations boost. Some observers questioned the need to save the medical students and the extent of the threat posed by Grenada's ties to communist countries, but the invasion revealed that the Reagan administration was indeed serious about containing communism and would use military force in order to protect its security interests.

But no matter how complex and far-ranging the other issues of the hemisphere became, the Reagan administration was pulled back to the guerrilla war in El Salvador and the Marxist state developing in Nicaragua. As the fighting in El Salvador continued with the rebels achieving some important victories, and the Sandinista government maintaining its defiant adherence to revolutionary principles, President Reagan sought to generate support both in Congress and through U.S. public opinion for what was certain to be a long-term commitment to contain communist insurgency in Central America.

In order to gain this support President Reagan formed a special commission headed by former Secretary of State Henry Kissinger. The Kissinger Commission, made up of prominent citizens of both political persuasions, was ordered to report to the president on its analysis of the Central American crisis and the proper role for the United States. On January 11, 1984, the commission made public its findings. The report warned of increased Cuban and Soviet influence in the region and urged a comprehensive response to the threat of another communist victory in El Salvador. As the report stated:

The worst possible policy for El Salvador is to provide just enough aid to keep the war going, but too little to wage it successfully. . . . The deterioration in Central America has been such that we cannot afford paralysis in defending our national interests. . . . The more we learned the more convinced we became that the crisis there is real and acute; that the United States must act to meet it and act boldly.[3]

With this belief in the importance of Central America to U.S. interests, the commission made the following recommendations:

1. a five-year, $8 billion economic aid program for the region;
2. a "substantial" increase in the present level of military aid to El Salvador,
3. increased aid to Honduras and resumption of aid to Guatemala,
4. the formations of a Central American Development Organization to promote regional development,
5. 10,000 scholarships to train Central American youth,
6. greater emphasis on addressing the housing needs of the region,
7. a new literacy corps to complement the Peace Corps,
8. emergency food aid,
9. further reduction of trade barriers, and
10. provision of emergency credit to the Central American Common Market Fund to finance trade deficits.

The commission's consensus on the necessity of responding to the communist threat in El Salvador was reflected in its view of the dangers posed by the Sandinistas. By characterizing Nicaragua as a "security threat" to the hemisphere and warning that "Nicaragua must be aware that force remains an ultimate recourse" for the United States, the commission gave the president the support he needed to continue the covert war being waged by the *contras*. Only in the area of human rights certification of the government in El Salvador did the president receive a major setback. The commissioners felt that future assistance to the beleaguered country must be contingent on progress in curbing the right-wing "death squads" that had accounted for thousands of political murders over the years.

The Kissinger report ended with some suggestions for solving the crisis in Central America. The Commissioners recommended that further steps be taken to ensure the democratization of El Salvador. The idea of attempting to incorporate the guerrillas and the current governing elites in a broadly based coalition was dismissed as "not a sensible or fair political solution for El Salvador." As for Nicaragua, the report recommended that all avenues of negotiation be pursued in order to achieve a comprehensive regional peace agreement. But while advocating negotiations with the Sandinistas, a majority of the commissioners also expressed support for the covert war of the *contras*, arguing that the insurgents represented "one of the incentives in favor of a negotiated settlement." Finally, the report acknowledged the work of the so-called Contadora group—Colombia, Mexico, Panama, and Venezuela—in the negotiations process, but the commission saw the United States as taking the primary leadership role in reaching a settlement in Central America. As the report states in its concluding section:

Our task now, as a nation is to transform the crisis into an opportunity: to seize the impetus it provides and to use this to help our neighbors not only to secure their freedom from aggression and violence but also to set in place the policies, processes and institutions that will make them both prosperous and free.[4]

The Kissinger Commission report was another in a long series of studies that have told presidents, Congress, and the U.S. populace about the way this country should conduct its relations with Latin America. Although the report broke some new ground by suggesting greater emphasis on social reform and human rights protection, the major recommendations continued the traditional reliance on aid and arms as the major tools to counteract revolution. The commission recommendations served as a basis for debate within Congress over the proper means of responding to the revolution in Central America. Not surprisingly, liberals saw in the report a justification for their claims that economic aid and human rights were the keys to a solution, while conservatives accented the commission's warnings about the communist threat and the prospect of revolutions erupting elsewhere in the hemisphere if the United States failed to stop the leftists. But although the Kissinger Commission report seemed to contain something for everyone, it was, above all, an attempt to alert Congress and the U.S. populace that Central America had now become a critical region in terms of U.S. foreign policy priorities. What is more, the report stated the obvious: instability, revolution, and communist subversion in Central America were occurring in our sphere of influence and posed a potential threat to our national security.

The Kissinger Commission's prediction that Central America would continue to be a region of great importance to the United States seemed to be borne out throughout 1984 and 1985. Events in both El Salvador and Nicaragua caused concern within the Reagan administration as it sought to contain leftist revolution. In El Salvador the presidential elections posed a major challenge to the administration's plan to defuse the revolution by building democratic institutions. For a country with little practice in Western-style democracy, the election of a president was a monumental undertaking. The situation was complicated by the fact that one of the candidates was Roberto D'Aubuisson, a cashiered military officer who was linked to the squads that had been responsible for an estimated 40,000 political deaths in El Salvador. The election in late March proved inconclusive, because no candidate received a clear majority, and a runoff had to be scheduled. The top two vote-getters in the March election were the reformist Christian Democrat, Jose Napoleon Duarte and D'Aubuisson. The runoff election in May became a contest between the U.S.–sponsored Duarte (who allegedly received CIA campaign funds) and D'Aubuisson, who Washington feared would usher in a reactionary regime committed to conservative interests and was supportive of right-wing terror. Despite numerous election foul-ups, vote-counting delays, and allegations of voter fraud, the Salvadoran people chose Duarte as their president by a slim margin. From the U.S. perspective, Duarte's election proved that democratic reform could work even in a revolutionary environment. But although the victorious Duarte presented the image of a moderate who would bring change to El Salvador, Washington feared that he might not be able to establish firm control of the government and would in effect be a prisoner of the power elite and military interests.

While El Salvador was struggling to develop its democracy, Nicaragua became the scene of expanded U.S. effort to destabilize the Sandinista government. In April 1984 the Reagan administration admitted to a covert CIA operation to mine the Pacific Coast harbors of Nicaragua. Using a CIA mother ship in international waters, the *contra* rebels succeeded in blowing up an oil storage area and damaging a number of foreign ships. The news of this CIA operation caused a major protest in Congress, as both Republicans and Democrats castigated the administration for what they felt was an act of war against a sovereign nation. Nicaragua sought to marshal international opinion against the United States by taking its case to the World Court of Justice in the Hague, where it received a favorable judgment. But by the time the court rendered its decision, the Reagan administration had agreed to stop the mining. Although the mining of Nicaraguan harbors was curtailed, President Reagan's continued support of the *contra* rebels showed that his administration was determined to press forward with its destabilization program. In fact the president stated that his primary objective in Nicaragua was to replace the Sandinista government and rid Central America of communist influence, or as he once said in private, "we want them [the Sandinistas] to say 'uncle.'"

By 1984 the Reagan administration was firmly committed to supporting the *contra* rebels (now called "freedom fighters") as the primary means of bringing the Sandinista regime down. But because of limitations imposed by the Boland Agreement (which forbade this country from engaging in covert activity for the purpose of overthrowing the Nicaraguans), the administration directed its attention toward Congress and a series of appropriations battles over military assistance to the *contras*.

In the fiscal year 1984 appropriations cycle, the administration was successful in gaining $24 million in military aid for the *contras* despite opposition from the Democratic-controlled House of Representatives. Despite this victory, President Reagan pressed forward with an additional request of $21 million in supplemental military assistance. This time, however, liberals, fearful of creating an endless pipeline of aid to the rebels, turned back the request.

The setback in the supplemental assistance package did not deter President Reagan or his supporters. In 1985, with Congress still in an anti-*contra* aid mood, the administration, and in particular National Security advisor Lt. Col. Oliver North, began expanding the network of private support for the *contras*. Relying upon the contributions of conservative benefactors such as Joseph Coors of the Coors Brewery family, the *contras* were able to hold together a fighting force and continue their hit-and-run raids inside Nicaragua. Unfortunately for the administration, the success they achieved with conservatives around the country was not matched in Congress or among the American people. Fear of another Vietnam, negative press reports concerning *contra* atrocities, and a widely held view in government and academic circles that the Sandinistas posed no real threat to the region or U.S. interests limited President Reagan's ability to increase military assistance to the rebels.

By 1986 the mood in Congress shifted on the *contra* aid issue. Sandinistas' leader Daniel Ortega's strident Marxist rhetoric and heightened reliance on the Soviets, plus President Reagan's tireless lobbying efforts in Congress, helped to win the first major victory for *contra* aid. In June 1986 the House of Representatives, in a historic vote, agreed to fund $100 million in aid to the *contras*. The key element in the appropriation was $70 million earmarked for lethal assistance to the rebels. Moreover the vote lifted the restriction on U.S. support to the *contras* by permitting the CIA to once again manage the aid program.

But just as the White House was savoring its victory over *contra* aid, the Iran-*contra* scandal broke. As reported in the press and later in public hearings in Congress, it was revealed that Reagan administration officials, including National Security Advisor Robert MacFarlane, his successor Admiral John Poindexter, and Lt. Col. Oliver North, had engaged in an alleged scheme to divert profits from the sale of weapons to Iran (designed to speed the release of U.S. hostages in Lebanon) to the *contra* rebels. The scandal engulfed Washington and the Reagan administration and weakened its efforts to keep the aid pipeline open. Furthermore, the scandal weakened the image of President Reagan, who nevertheless vigorously denied knowledge of the scheme.

While the Reagan administration turned its attention toward the domestic furor over the Iran-*contra* scandal and Congress again shifted back to a position against providing lethal aid to the *contras*, leaders in the Central American republics were seeking ways to take the initiative and propose a nonmilitary solution to the fighting. In a historic agreement signed in Guatemala City on August 7, 1987, the five nations of Central America (including Nicaragua) signed a regional peace plan. The agreement, painstakingly put together by the determined leadership of Costa Rican president Oscar Arias, called for an internal dialogue with "unarmed internal political opposition groups," guarantees of democratization within all of the countries, a request that each Central American nation and those outside the region end all military support of guerrillas, and creation of an Internal Verification and Follow-up

Commission to ensure compliance with the agreement. The essential elements of the Arias Peace Plan are listed below.

Key Points of the Arias Peace Plan for Central America

1. A movement to achieve national reconciliation which includes:
    a. A dialogue with opposition groups
    b. Amnesty for irregular forces—i.e., the *contras*
    c. A national reconciliation commission to verify the carrying out of the process of reconciliation
2. A cessation of hostilities and the signing of a cease-fire agreement between the combatants.
3. A commitment to begin the process of democratization based on the following:
    a. Complete freedom of the press and electronic media
    b. Complete pluralism
    c. The termination of any state of siege and reestablishment of constitutional guarantees
4. The establishment of a framework leading to free and open elections throughout Central America.
5. A cessation of assistance to irregular forces or insurrectional movements except assistance that provides for repatriation or relocation.
6. The establishment of the principle of the non-use of territory to attack or destabilize other states.
7. The development of an agreement to negotiate matters relating to security, verification, and control and limitation of armaments.
8. Adoption of agreements permitting the development of more egalitarian and poverty-free societies.
9. Urgent attention to the flow of refugees and displaced persons brought about by the crisis.
10. Establishment of a framework for the international verification of the agreement.
11. Creation of a calendar for implementing the agreement.

The Arias Peace Plan was greeted with great joy in Central America and astonishment in Washington, because two days before the signing of the agreement House Speaker Jim Wright, with the approval of President Reagan, presented his own peace plan. The Wright-Reagan proposal was more specific than the Arias plan, especially on the issue of the Sandinista commitment to bring about democratic government. But the Wright-Reagan plan was quickly pushed off center stage as the world marveled at the ability of the Central Americans to put together their own peace proposal in the face of U.S. intransigence. The Arias Peace Plan was significant not only in terms of establishing the framework for peace in the region but for showing the new-found independence and confidence of the Central American leaders.

The Arias plan immediately set in motion a number of political forces. Liberals in Congress began pressing for humanitarian aid to help the *contra* war "wind down." In the fall of 1987 over $6 million in nonlethal aid was provided to the *contras* as Congress sent President Reagan a message that the issue of military assistance was dead. Reagan and Assistant Secretary of State for Inter-American Affairs, Elliott Abrams, continued to warn of Nicaragua's military threat and expansionist designs, but these warnings fell on deaf ears.

The Central American peace agreement and the changed mood in Washington also affected the *contra* leadership, which began to show signs of internal discord and greater willingness to engage in peace talks. Also in the fall of 1987 the top leadership of the *contra* movement and representatives of the Sandinista government met in the tiny Nicaraguan town of Sapoa and ironed out a cease-fire agreement. Those familiar with the *contras* and the *contra* war were not surprised at the agreement, because rebel leaders had come to recognize that Washington was no longer willing to fund the war, while the Sandinistas were running a war-torn country that hungered for peace and even a faint sign of prosperity.

The cease-fire agreement took the *contra* war off the headlines in the United States. President Reagan made some half-hearted attempts to revive military aid to the rebels, but had to settle for humanitarian assistance designed to feed and clothe the fighters while both sides negotiated a permanent peace. Even the 1988 presidential election campaign between George Bush and Michael Dukakis did little to place the conflict back in the forefront of U.S. consciousness. There were some attempts by the media to link Bush to the Iran-*contra* scandal, but substantive discussions concerning revolution in Central America or the strategic implications of a Marxist government in the region were ignored by both candidates.

Although the *contra* war occupied center stage of U.S.–Latin American relations from 1984 to 1987, the Reagan administration was also faced with other challenges. Perhaps the most serious was the controversy involving attempts by the United States to remove Panama's strongman General Manuel Noriega from office. Long suspected as a key link in the shipment of drugs from South America, the United States in 1988 indicted Noriega on a number of criminal charges.

With Noriega safely entrenched in Panama as chief of the National Guard, U.S. officials were aware that convicting the general would be nearly impossible. But advisors to President Reagan in the White House and in the State Department believed that economic and diplomatic pressure from the United States could force Noriega from power and usher in a new, more honest and democratic leadership for Panama.

The U.S. strategy appeared to be working when the constitutional president, Eric Delvalle tried to oust Noriega and lead a popular revolt against the real power in the country. The hopes for a quick turnaround in Panama were shattered when Noriega received strong support from the military and only lukewarm opposition from the people. A gradually escalating policy of economic and financial sanctions against Panama failed to dislodge Noriega and even helped him garner public support. The United States became the nation that was trying to bankrupt Panama, while Noriega became the tough patriot standing up to Washington.[5]

The Noriega affairs became more complex and controversial when Senator John Kerry of Massachusetts released information that showed Noriega as receiving substantial payments from the CIA in return for his support of the *contras* and intelligence information pertaining to the Sandinista government. The Noriega-CIA link called into question the Reagan administration's war on drugs and its willingness to pressure dictators into accepting democratic government. While the *contra* war hardly entered the issue conflicts of the 1988 campaign, the Noriega affair was grabbed by Governor Dukakis as he hit at the administration's commitment to stop drugs from entering the United States and Vice President George Bush's management of drug interdiction from Latin America.

The failed efforts to remove Manuel Noriega from office and replace him with moderate civilian politicians were part of a larger policy position by the Reagan administration in the area of democratization. Often dubbed the Reagan Doctrine, the administration sought to convince military dictators to accept the transition to democracy and permit civilian-led governments to regain national power. One country where the administration worked diligently to achieve this transition was Haiti. The departure of Haitian dictator Jean Claude ("Baby Doc") Duvalier in 1987 opened up the possibility of redemocratization in that poor Caribbean nation. But after months of careful preparation for national elections the process of returning the country to popularly elected rule fell apart as conservative military leaders and remnants of Duvalier's secret police killed scores of Haitians as they waited to vote. The killings forced the closing of the polls and the electoral process. The Reagan administration protested the violence and cut aid to the military government, but it was unable to dislodge the leaders or convince them that open democracy was the proper form of governance.

As Ronald Reagan left office in January 1989 there were many who attempted to put U.S.–Latin American policy in perspective. Surprisingly, most observers came to a similar conclusion: that the Reagan administration made a bold attempt to control events in the hemisphere, but in the end came to realize the Latin Americans were not easily intimidated by the power of the United States and were unwilling to have Washington dictate the solutions to their problems.

The failure of the Reagan administration to bring down the Sandinista government, to deal with a known drug kingpin in Panama, or to effect the process of democratization in a place like Haiti pointed up the limitations of this country's power in the hemisphere and the changing nature of our relationship with the Latin Americans.[6]

THE BUSH APPROACH TO LATIN AMERICA

The election of George Bush as the forty-first president of the United States ushered in a host of new challenges for U.S. policy in Latin America. While the *contra* war was seemingly winding down, the revolutionary conflict in El Salvador was expanding and threatening to further test U.S. resolve. The war on drugs had reached a new plateau as campaign promises of tough action would be translated into specific policies. The debt crisis continued unabated, only this time joined by the twin specters of inflation and social disorder. Trade and aid policies related to the United States emerged as rallying cries for Latin American countries convinced that the United States had closed its door to their goods. And finally, relations with our closest neighbors, whether it be the increasingly divided Mexicans or the new huddled masses illegally entering our country from the Caribbean, posed new challenges for an administration seeking to solidify its southern border. Most observers felt that President Bush would take a more pragmatic, less ideological approach to U.S.–Latin American relations, but the potential for immediate crisis in the region was so great that many expected the new president would be tested early and forced to make critical decisions on how this country wanted to approach the problems of its neighbors to the south.[7]

The first test came in the form of a rigged election in Panama in 1989. Opposition candidates were denied victory in the presidential election by widespread fraud and voter intimidation. General Noriega, feeling confident and secure as the supreme leader of Panama, crushed the democratic movement in Panama despite condemnation from the Bush administration and most Latin American leaders. President Bush tried to rally the democratic opposition and sought to intimidate Noriega by sending 10,000 troops from the United States into the Canal Zone, but the wily dictator was able to weather the storm and again snub his nose at the United States.

The disappointment experienced by the Bush administration in its failure to dislodge Noriega was balanced somewhat by the successful transfer of power in El Salvador. After a second open election, El Salvador saw the office of the presidency shift from Napoleon Duarte's Christian Democrats to the ARENA party candidate, Alfredo Cristiani. Despite ARENA's reputation as a rightist vehicle for Roberto D'Aubuisson, Cristiani was able to separate himself from the extremists in his party and project a moderate image. Although the first months of his presidency were wracked by political assassination, U.S. policy makers were hopeful that Cristiani would be able to continue the process of democratization, initiate needed reforms, and fight the war against an increasingly bold rebel army. The tasks facing Cristiani were enormous, but with $1.5 million of U.S. aid per day coming into El Salvador, it was clear that the Bush administration was determined to see Cristiani succeed.

While attention focused on Panama and El Salvador, the Bush administration was working to achieve a solution to the troublesome *contra* war against Nicaragua. In March 1989 President Bush reached an accord with Congress that brought an end to the persistent wrangling over military assistance to the *contras*. In exchange for a congressional commitment to provide the *contras* with humanitarian assistance through the February 1990 presidential elections in Nicaragua, the Bush administration agreed to wind down the war and to encourage the *contras* to reenter Nicaraguan society.[8] The agreement was hailed as an example of bipartisan cooperation in foreign policy and a sign that the Bush administration was not going to pursue a military solution to the Sandinista revolution.

The encouraging developments in El Salvador and in the *contra* war provided only temporary relief from the spreading crisis in Latin America. The assassination of a leading presidential candidate in Colombia by the drug cartel initiated a major struggle between the government of Virgilio Barco and the Medellin drug lords. As the terrorism spread and the Colombian government vowed to reinstitute the policy of extraditing drug smugglers to the United States, the Bush administration decided that it was necessary to support the Barco government. As a result President bush pledged $65 million in military assistance to the Colombian government and praised President Barco for his courage in pursuing the drug lords. But as the United States delivered the helicopters and communications equipment that would strengthen the hand of the Colombian government, the drug cartel leaders stepped up their campaign of intimidation, killing judges, police officials, and innocent citizens. The war on drugs had entered an especially troubling period as the United States sought ways to assist Latin American governments that were so overwhelmed by the challenge from the drug smugglers that policy makers in this country wondered whether democratic leaders could effectively cope with the problem.[9]

While the drug war in Colombia tested the willingness of the Bush administration to use its resources to come to the aid of a neighboring democracy, an attempted coup against Manuel Noriega in the fall of 1989 became the first major foreign policy controversy faced by the new president. Dissident mid-level officers in the Panamanian Defense Force (PDF) burst into PDF headquarters and captured Noriega. The news of the capture caught the Bush administration by surprise and left it groping for more complete intelligence. Although the United States had pledged to bring Noriega to justice on drug-smuggling charges, its desire to go into the PDF compound and retrieve the Panamanian strongman became an issue. As the day wore on, Noriega's supporters in the PDF were able to free their leader and put down the coup attempt. When word of Noriega's temporary custody and the rumor that his captors were willing to hand him over to the United States became public, the Bush administration faced a storm of criticism for not acting quickly and forcefully to bring Noriega to justice.[10]

President Bush defended the handling of the Noriega affair by stating that lack of intelligence prohibited him from sending U.S. forces into the PDF headquarters, along with specific limitations in the Panama Canal Treaty that restricted the United States from participating in the internal affairs of Panama. Despite the reasoned statements of President bush, many critics in Congress and in the Republican party felt that the president missed an opportunity to score points in his war on drugs and to show the strength of the United States. Some of President Bush's supporters bemoaned the fact that Ronald Reagan would not have hesitated to go after Manuel Noriega, an observation that many felt summed up the difference between George Bush and his predecessor.

As 1989 came to a close the Bush administration was reminded that despite the positive developments in Eastern Europe and the growing rapprochement between the United States and the Soviet Union, the real trouble spots were in our own backyard. The process of negotiating an end to the civil war in El Salvador broke down amid a bold offensive of the leftist rebels against the capital city of San Salvador. After days of fighting, hundreds of deaths, and enormous human and economic dislocations, the rebels left the city. Although this urban offensive did not lead to a collapse of the Cristiani government, it proved that the Marxist guerrillas had not been defeated, and more importantly, that the process of peace would be long and difficult.[11]

The Bush administration was stunned by the rebel offensive and the execution of six Jesuit priests during the fighting, presumably by right-wing death squads. President Bush stood firm in his resolve to support the Cristiani government, but it was clear that the election had done little to solve the social roots of the revolution or bring the left and the right together. Furthermore, the rebel offensive was openly supported by Daniel Ortega, who boasted that he would continue to supply arms to the guerrillas and support the revolutionary process in Central America. These statements prompted Cristiani's government to break off ties with Nicaragua and send the Central American peace initiative into limbo. The only glimmer of hope came from the United Nations, which voted to send a peace-keeping mission to Central America in an effort to stabilize a volatile situation.

What started out in 1987 as a visionary experiment in Central American peace making seemed at the conclusion of 1989 to have completely collapsed as politics seemed to be overtaken by the extremes of right and left. The Bush administration, which had hoped that the problems in Central America would somehow disappear, was forced to recognize that not much had changed in the region despite elections and peace agreements. The only certainty was that the United States was becoming more deeply embroiled in the crisis and less able to resolve the problems that were creating the conflict.

As the fighting in El Salvador subsided and the five Central American presidents agreed to continue peace negotiations, President Bush's patience with the nonmilitary solutions to the Noriega narco-dictatorship came to an abrupt end. After a marine lieutenant was killed by PDF forces and other military personnel were beaten up, the president, in late December 1989, gave the go ahead to an invasion of Panama. In what was the largest military operation since the Vietnam war (More than 24,000 troops), U.S. armed units left their bases in the Canal Zone to capture Noriega and neutralize his supporters in the PDF. In a day of fierce fighting and extensive U.S. casualties, the U.S. forces were able to take control of the country and install the democratically elected president, Guillermo Endara. As for Noriega, he escaped capture and attempted a clandestine guerrilla operation against U.S. troops. The Bush administration offered a $1 million bounty for his capture and $150 reward for any PDF soldier who handed in his weapon.

After days on the run from U.S. troops, Manuel Noriega entered the Vatican embassy and asked for political asylum. The decision by Noriega to seek the protection of the Vatican further complicated the mission of the invasion as the United States was forced to pressure Rome to gain the release of the wily Panamanian leader.

The invasion of Panama by the Bush administration received initial support from Congress and the American people. The president's justification for the action in terms of the protection of American lives and support for democracy (along with the capture of Noriega) was viewed as appropriate. Latin American reaction, however, was quite different. The Bush administration was condemned for resorting to the traditional weapon of intervention and for its unwillingness to permit the Latin Americans to solve their own problems.

With Noriega out of the picture and a new government installed in Panama, concern shifted from the act of intervention to the issue of American occupation. Many observers felt that the Endara government would need not only extensive economic support from the United States but also a military "shield" to ward off disgruntled PDF forces. As with most U.S. interventions, the military phase in Panama was brief, while the solidification of new leadership and the rebuilding of the political system would take years.

While the first two years of the Bush presidency were marked by an aggressive military posture in the region, particularly in Central America, the advent of the 1990s brought a new sense of change as the forces of reconciliation, democratization, and cooperation were more pronounced. The key change came with the elections in Nicaragua. Pressured by the United States and the international community, the Sandinista government agreed to hold open and free elections in 1990. The Bush administration saw this as an opportunity to defeat the Marxist government and bring to power a government that was friendly to the United States. The Bush administration wasted little time in using its vast reservoir of resources to come to the assistance of the principal opposition candidate, Violeta Chamorro. During a rough and tumble campaign marked by violence, the United States pumped in an estimated $12 million of electoral assistance to Chamorro. The State Department, CIA, the National Endowment for Democracy, and a whole host of private consulting groups and election advisors came to the assistance of the opposition as it sought to get its message out to the Nicaraguan people.[12]

The assistance provided by the United States helped Violeta Chamorro to achieve a stunning victory over Daniel Ortega and the Sandinistas (she received 56 percent of the vote). The Chamorro victory was attributed to the growing dissatisfaction with the Sandinistas and the continuation of the *contra* war, but critics of the victory cite the involvement of the United States as the key ingredient.[13] Not only did the Bush administration bankroll Chamorro's candidacy but also Nicaraguans saw the election as a choice between either an end to the *contra* war and the U.S. embargo or a continuation of the socialist experiment with its shortages, inflation, and devastation. In the United States there was some dissatisfaction with the Bush administration's "electoral meddling" and its effort to "buy the election," but most in Congress felt that the assistance provided to Chamorro leveled the playing field and brought to power a friend of democracy and the United States. As a sign of its commitment to the new Chamorro government, the Bush administration pledged hundreds of millions of dollars in economic assistance (as of 1993 the total aid was $647 million) and quickly lifted the trade embargo.

The election of Violeta Chamorro was joined by a peace process in neighboring El Salvador that extricated the United States from years of huge economic and military assistance expenditures and frequent divisive debate over becoming bogged down in another jungle war. Taking its cue from Congress, which had little interest in continuing to support the military option in El Salvador or, for that matter, the Salvadoran generals, the Bush administration began what was termed a "winding down" of its aid commitment. From 1990 to 1992 aid to El Salvador dropped from approximately $450 million to less than $250 million. The pipeline, which had injected nearly $5 billion in economic and military assistance to El Salvador from 1980 to 1992, was beginning to run dry.[14]

The loss of interest in the Salvadoran civil war was not only economic. The public outcry in the United States over the slaying of the six Jesuit priests in 1989 and the failure of the government to bring the military men responsible to justice moved Congress to cut back military assistance and send a message that the United States would no longer tolerate a disregard for human rights and the rule of law. Also, by 1990, with the Soviet Union in collapse and Cuba no longer capable of financing revolution the leftists in El Salvador saw that their ability to sustain a protracted war would be impossible. The combination of congressional pressure on aid and the diminished threat of communism convinced the Bush administration that support for a peaceful resolution of the fighting was appropriate. The United States thus threw its support behind a UN–brokered peace agreement that was achieved on New Year's Eve 1991. The agreement ended twelve years of civil war, a war with 70,000 deaths, and costing billions of dollars in U.S. assistance. The war also shifted U.S. attention away from Central America leaving the nations of that region to their own designs in a world where communist expansionism had been replaced with talk of free trade zones and civilian democracies.[15]

The Bush administration's policy approach toward Latin America should not be defined solely in terms of its efforts to resolve the tensions in Central America or its invasion of Panama to remove Manuel Noriega. During the Bush presidency the United States made significant strides in its effort to expand trade and advance business opportunities in the hemisphere. The first step in this effort was the announcement in 1990 of the Enterprise for the Americas Initiative (EAI), which linked significant public sector debt reduction with increased aid for economic recovery and the promise of a trade zone that would encompass the entire western hemisphere. The EAI was well received throughout Latin America as leaders in the region felt the United States was finally interested in addressing their most pressing economic issues and willing to create a working regional partnership. The Bush administration backed up its claims of a new relationship with Latin America by forgiving significant public aid debts to countries like El Salvador and Bolivia and negotiating a series of framework agreements with Southern Cone countries to lay the groundwork for future trade negotiations and the eventual attainment of a region-wide trade zone.[16]

The Bush administration continued to press forward with its commitment to free trade with the successful negotiation and eventual signing of the North American Free Trade Agreement (NAFTA). In August 1992 President Bush announced that the United States, Canada, and Mexico had concluded negotiations on NAFTA. NAFTA created a more open trading relationship among the three countries as tariff barriers on thousands of goods were destined to be eliminated in stages over a fifteen-year period, investment opportunities would be enhanced as regulations and restrictions would be lifted, and intellectual property (copyrights, patents, computer software programs, and satellite transmissions) would be protected. President Bush hailed NAFTA stating that the three countries were embarking "on an extraordinary enterprise [that would create] the largest, richest and most productive market in the entire world: a $6 trillion market of 360 million people that stretches 5,000 miles from Alaska to the Yukon to the Yucatan Peninsula."[17]

NAFTA was presented as a historic milestone in what President Bush described as a New World Order and essential if the United States was to compete effectively with the Europeans (who in 1992 initiated their own free trade agreement) and the countries of the Pacific Rim. More than cast NAFTA in an international trading context, the Bush administration emphasized that the agreement would allow the United States to tap into a growing Mexican market. Carla Hills, the chief U.S. negotiator of NAFTA, listed a number of reasons why the agreement would have a positive impact on both the United States and Mexico:

The agreement would generate more than 600,000 new export oriented jobs as more goods are shipped to Mexico.

The agreement will help Mexico grow—seventy cents of each Mexican import dollar and fifteen cents of each additional dollar of Mexican income is spent on U.S. goods.

The agreement will allow many small and medium-sized businesses in the United States to benefit from lower tariff rates.

The agreement makes U.S. goods, in particular agricultural commodities, textiles, automotives and automotive parts, more competitive and enjoy greater access to the Mexican market.

The agreement opens new markets in Mexico for telecommunications, insurance, and financial services.

The agreement addresses the need for environmental clean up on the border with Mexico.

The agreement will allow the United States to tap into the Mexican economy, which is now the fastest growing export market for U.S. goods topping $40 billion in 1992.[18]

The fanfare and public pronouncements that accompanied NAFTA were met with a chorus of criticism, especially from unions and members of Congress who saw the agreement as a business ploy to shift manufacturing jobs to Mexico where taxes are low, environmental standards lax, and unions are weak. Congressman Richard Gephardt of Missouri, the House Democratic Majority Leader, became the major opponent of NAFTA citing the following reservations about the impact of the agreement on the U.S. economy:

Substandard environment conditions on both sides of the border will remain and get worse.

The incentives for American corporations to relocate to Mexico would increase with the loss of up to 550,000 jobs.

The agreement is insufficient in providing retraining for displaced workers.

Little provision is made in the agreement to build the infrastructure to sustain commerce with Mexico.

In the agreement the labor standards and working conditions affecting Mexican workers remain undisturbed.[19]

With the arguments for and against NAFTA set in place, politics and public opinion went into high gear. The issue clearly divided the political arena—Democrats versus Republicans, business versus labor, free traders versus protectionists—and forced the American public to reflect on the rapidly changing character of the domestic and international economy. NAFTA also became entangled in the 1992 presidential election in large part because of the entry of Ross Perot, the Texas billionaire, who ran on a platform of opposition to the agreement and who accused both President Bush and Democratic challenger Bill Clinton of embracing the concept of the global economy at the expense of the American worker. As the campaign moved forward it became increasingly clear that the debate over NAFTA encompassed more than the inclusion of a third world neighbor in a trading agreement; the United States was poised for a critical reevaluation of its economy and place in a new world.

George Bush lost the 1992 election to Bill Clinton with Ross Perot coming in a strong third. Election analysts cite the economic dislocations and the uncertainties created by the painful process of restructuring as contributing to Bush's defeat. But Bush's interest in foreign affairs at the expense of addressing domestic concerns also influenced voters who apparently wanted a change and a new direction. Although President Bush will be remembered most for his handling of the Persian Gulf War, his policies with respect to Latin America had a profound impact on the region and its future development. The invasion of Panama to remove Manuel Noriega, the winding down of the war in El Salvador, the transition to democratic rule in Nicaragua, the drug summits, the EAI, and NAFTA formed a substantial legacy and clearly were responsible for turning the region toward market principles and further solidifying democratic governance.

THE CLINTON APPROACH TO LATIN AMERICA

The election of Bill Clinton in 1992 not only brought a Democrat into the White House after twelve years of Republican rule but also initiated a thorough review of U.S. foreign policy, particularly in terms of the relationship of domestic economic conditions with the new global trade and investment environment. President Clinton quickly structured his administration to focus on policy issues, such as health care, education, and welfare reform. Foreign policy concerns took a back seat as the new president was averse to committing U.S. troops to localized "brushfire" wars in Somalia and ethnic strife in Bosnia-Herzegovina. The eventual removal of troops from Somalia and the interminable negotiations under UN and NATO auspices to find a solution to the fighting in the former Yugoslavia proved to many that the new president was unwilling to define the United States as a modern day policeman of the world. Although the Clinton administration was criticized for taking a hands-off policy toward the trouble spots in the less developed world and the former communist bloc, American public opinion reflected a mood akin to isolationism as attention was placed on restructuring the business community and the workplace, addressing serious social ills, and easing the country into a vastly changed international economy.

However, while the Clinton administration was reluctant to transform the United States into a military meddler it was more than eager to develop policies that advanced our standing in the global economy. President Clinton's interest in breaking down trade barriers, encouraging regional trading blocs, and expanding corporate investment around the world opened up new horizons in U.S. relations with Latin America. The centerpiece of the new economic ties between the United States and Latin America was the passage of NAFTA. Clinton recognized that passage of NAFTA would be perceived by the Latin Americans as proof that the United States was indeed committed to its claims of partnership and cooperation. In a real sense NAFTA was about not only opening trade with Mexico but also redefining inter-American relations.[20]

In his lobbying of Congress and the American people President Clinton, like George Bush, stressed the importance of NAFTA if the United States was to compete effectively in a global economy. Clinton, however, expressed major reservations about the impact of the treaty on the working men and women in the United States and the environmental safeguards that would be required to ensure compliance by the businesses that would locate across the border in Mexico. In his campaign for election Clinton promised that retraining of workers effected by NAFTA and side agreements on environmental issues would be a top priority. Nevertheless, Clinton clearly endorsed the treaty and vowed to work for its passage. As he said during the campaign, "We need not only to reduce the trade barriers, but to prepare our entire work force not only to compete in the global economy but to live with the changes in it and to make sure nobody gets left behind. I am convinced that the North American Free Trade Agreement will generate jobs and growth on both sides of the border if and only if it's part of a broad-based strategy, and if and only if we address the issues still to be addressed."[21]

Passage of NAFTA proved to be one of the most intense legislative confrontations in the history of Congress. Before the key vote was taken in the House of Representatives, the American people would see proponents and opponents of NAFTA give impassioned speeches on the benefits or drawbacks of including Mexico in the free trade agreement. The debate concentrated on the issue of jobs—whether the treaty would create new export jobs or escalate a movement of skilled jobs out of the United States—and wages—the $2.00 per day Mexican worker versus the $18.00 per hour American worker. There was also the famous debate between Vice President Gore and billionaire businessman Ross Perot, who championed the cause of those who felt the treaty would create a huge job loss to Mexico (the "giant sucking sound" of lost jobs). There was also the last minute lobbying and promises of President Clinton as he added perhaps as much as $1 billion in spending in districts of members of Congress who were wavering in their support of the treaty.[22]

In the end, NAFTA passed the House of Representatives by a comfortable margin of 234 to 200 as 132 Republicans joined the president in voting for the free trade agreement. President Clinton was buoyed up by the victory and proclaimed it "a defining moment for our nation." As for the opponents of NAFTA, especially the labor unions, there was anger over what they felt was a Democratic administration that had abandoned them in order to create a trade system that moved jobs south of the border to Mexico. Democratic House whip David Bonior, who led the fight against NAFTA, summed up the frustration of the unions over the vote: "The working people who stand against this treaty don't have degrees from Harvard. And most of them have never heard of Adam Smith. But they know when the deck is stacked against them. They know it's not fair to ask American workers to compete against Mexican workers who earn $1 an hour."[23]

As for the Mexicans, the vote in the House of Representatives was a validation of their movement away from a statist system that protected domestic industries to one that encouraged trade and investment. President Carlos Salinas was especially gratified because he advocated an opening of the Mexican economy and worked tirelessly to see NAFTA passed. The passage of NAFTA also was greeted with joy in the rest of Latin America as political leaders began developing strategies to convince the United States to move beyond Mexico and include other countries in a growing regional trade bloc. In anticipation of these strategies, immediately after the vote President Clinton called together leaders from Central America to advise them on the prospects for expanding the agreement while Vice President Gore, on a trip to Mexico to celebrate the vote, proposed a hemispheric summit (the first since 1967) that would undoubtedly concentrate on transforming NAFTA into a region-wide agreement.

The success of the NAFTA vote secured the concepts of free trade and regionalism, but the Clinton administration faced a new series of challenges as it sought to join economic partnership with democratic convergence. Early in his administration Clinton called on the Latin American countries to build a "Western Hemispheric Community of Democracies." There was much talk of cooperation with the Organization of American States (OAS) to ensure that authoritarian rule would not return to Latin America and to ensure protection of those who are victims of human rights abuse. With much of Latin America already in the hands of elected civilian leaders (except Cuba and Haiti), the call by Clinton to create not only an economic but also a political community was seen as attainable.

The effort to create "Community of Democracies" did achieve a measure of success in that the United States and the OAS were effective in forcing Guatemalan president Jose Serrano from assuming broad dictatorial powers and for marshalling support for his removal from office in what can best be described as a "democratic coup." The administration also worked quietly behind the scenes to convince the government of Peru's Alberto Fujimori to loosen the reins of martial law in that country and vigorously protested the attempted military overthrow of the Venezuelan government. In both cases the United States was seen in Latin America as properly using its influence—economic and diplomatic—to protect the rule of law and the wishes of the people.

However, the successes of the Clinton administration in Guatemala, Peru, and Venezuela were overshadowed by the intractable dilemma in Haiti where the military government refused to abide by the election of Jean-Bertrand Aristide. Ever since the coup against Aristide in 1992 the United States has been working to have the populist priest/president returned to power. When the military government of General Raoul Cedras, backed by the business elite, refused to recognize the legitimacy of the democratic election, the Clinton administration worked with the OAS to enforce an economic boycott of the country. The boycott did little to sway the generals (in large part because of smuggling from neighboring Dominican Republic), although conditions in the country deteriorated dramatically, especially for the millions of desperately poor peasants and urban dwellers.

The boycott did, however, bring the generals to the bargaining table. In 1993 on Governor's Island in New York City General Cedras and the representatives of President Aristide signed an agreement that returned the country to democratic rule. The joy brought about by the agreement was shortlived when it became clear that the generals were not willing to have their positions and their lives placed in jeopardy by the return of a leader who instilled such passion as Aristide. When a U.S. navy transport ship, the *Harlan County*, carrying observers and other administrative personnel to Port au Prince to implement the agreement, was not permitted to land because of a huge anti-American demonstration, the Clinton administration was forced to recognize that its ability to control events in Haiti was limited.

The refusal of the Haitian generals to abide by the Governor's Island agreement and the sign of a U.S. ship turning around in the face of protest appeared to immobilize the Clinton administration. Distracted by events in Bosnia, Russia, and the Middle East, the Clinton administration continued to enforce what was clearly a porous embargo and appeared unmoved by the deteriorating economic circumstances in Haiti and regular reports that the Haitian military was systematically killing opponents of the regime. As months passed with no change in the situation, Haitians in the United States, joined by leading members of the African-American community, pressured President Clinton to take further action against General Cedras. When Randall Robinson, an African-American activist, staged a hunger strike to call attention to the failed policy in Haiti, the Clinton administration began to renew its interest in returning Aristide to power.[24]

With critics of the administration stating that the president had no coherent foreign policy and on too many occasions made idle threats, Clinton ordered a more complete boycott of Haiti by convincing the Dominican Republic to close the border, cutting off flights to and from the country, and stopping the transfer of money to Haiti from the United States. The president also hinted that the United States would consider the use of force in order to remove the generals and return Aristide to power. Although a strong majority in Congress opposed the use of military intervention in Haiti and most Americans were unwilling to support another commitment to bring stability and reform to a third world nation, the Clinton administration was adamant in its determination to restore democracy to Haiti and perhaps flex its muscle as proof that the United States can sustain a commitment and influence the direction of affairs in the region closest to its border.

As a result of these contrary views the Haitian crisis became the focal point of a debate over Clinton's foreign policy. Lawrence Pezzullo, who was fired as the administration's advisor on Haiti, stated that the talk of military intervention was, "an act of great folly," and former National Security adviser, Brent Scowcroft, warned that a military intervention would result in "casualties and humiliations reminiscent of Somalia." Most of the critics were concerned that once in Haiti the United States would be forced to remain for months, even years, while it worked to restore order, rebuild the economy, and completely reconstitute the military, police, and other paramilitary forces.

Despite the reluctance on the part of the Clinton administration to use force to dislodge the Haitian military by fall 1994, there were few options left to the United States. In an eleventh hour surprise move President Clinton sent former President Jimmy Carter along with General Colin Powell and Senator Sam Nunn of Georgia to Haiti in an attempt to persuade General Cedras to relinquish power. After a marathon negotiation session and as the invasion forces were in the air on their way to Haiti, President Carter was able to arrange an agreement with the generals for their peaceful exit from power.

In September, as a last-ditch effort by the Clinton administration to have the Haitian military leave power and open the doors to President Aristide's return, former President Jimmy Carter, along with Colin Powell and Sam Nunn, were sent by President Clinton to negotiate a transition to democracy. After intense negotiations that only proved successful when word that U.S. invasion forces were in the air headed for Haiti, Cedras and his fellow generals agreed to a peaceful exit from power. The essentials of the Carter Accord are:

1. The purpose of this agreement is to foster peace in Haiti, to avoid violence and bloodshed, to promote freedom and democracy, and to forget a sustained and mutually beneficial relationship between the governments, people and institutions of Haiti and the United States.

2. To implement this agreement, the Haitian military and police forces will work in close cooperation with the US Military Mission. This cooperation, conducted with mutual respect, will last during the transitional period required for insuring vital institutions of the country.

3. In order to personally contribute to the success of this agreement, certain military officers of the Haitian armed forces are willing to consent to an early honorable retirement in accordance with UN Resolutions 917 and 940 when a general amnesty will be voted into law by the Haitian Parliament, or October 15, 1994, whichever is earlier. The parties to this agreement pledge to work with the Haitian Parliament to expedite this action. Their successors will be named according to the Haitian Constitution and existing military law.

4. The military activities of the US Military Mission will be coordinated with the Haitian military high command.

5. The economic embargo and the economic sanctions will be lifted without delay in accordance with relevant UN Resolutions and the need of the Haitian people will be met as quickly as possible.

6. The forthcoming legislative elections will be held in a free and democratic manner.

7. It is understood that the above agreement is condition on the approval of the civilian governments of the United States and Haiti.

With the Haitian generals' agreement, the U.S.–led multinational forces landed in Port au Prince and began the occupation of the country and the preparation for the return of President Aristide. Although President Clinton received heavy criticism for his decision to send troops to Haiti, the agreement worked out by Carter proved successful and Cedras, along with his family and associates, left for exile in Panama. The departure of Cedras paved the way for Aristide's triumphant return to power, but the U.S. military remained in the country well into 1995 in order to ensure that democracy was not threatened by anti-democratic elements. Although no U.S. personnel were killed during the occupation, called appropriately, Operation Uphold Democracy, the military were called upon to perform a number of difficult tasks, such as dismantling the military, police, and paramilitary forces and rebuilding a country that had been devastated by the embargo and years of corrupt management.

As the Haiti crisis moved out of the headlines the Clinton administration prepared for its much heralded Summit of the Americas in December 1994. President Clinton invited thirty-three heads of state from the hemisphere (minus Castro) to discuss a range of issues critical to the region beyond the year 2000. The presidents focused their attention primarily on the advancement of the hemispheric trade zone along with a series of so-called "action items" that included environmental cooperation, anti-corruption measures, narcotic trafficking and money laundering prevention, and numerous health and education initiatives. The summit was hailed by all as an example of the new-found spirit of cooperation present in the region. President Clinton called the summit "a watershed moment in the hemisphere" and pledged that the United States would work to achieve the trade zone by the year 2005. To prove the goodwill of the United States, President Clinton announced that he would forward legislation to include Chile as the next participant in NAFTA. The summit ended on an upbeat note as the presidents left Miami convinced that the region was headed for a new era and that the slogan of a "mature relationship" was indeed appropriate for U.S.–Latin American ties in the 1990s.[25]

President Clinton and 33 other presidents and prime ministers at the Summit of the Americas in Miami in December 1994 agreed to:

- Create a Free Trade Area of the Americas. It sets a deadline of 2005 to complete negotiations and calls for "substantial progress" by the end of this century.
- Expand the scope of existing trade agreements within the hemisphere, reconciling differences to create the larger free-trade zone.
- Keep the agreement consistent with the global trade pact known as the General Agreement on Tariffs and Trade. Erect no new barriers to trade.
- Phase out use of leaded gasoline.
- Fight corruption by developing reforms to make government operations open and accountable.
- Ratify a U.N. measure against drug trafficking and criminalize money laundering.
- Identify trafficking and money-laundering networks and seize assets.
- Secure the observance and promotion of worker rights as economic integration proceeds.
- Strengthen democracy by encouraging exchanges of election-related technologies and assist national electoral organizations upon request.

- Develop programs for the promotion and observance of human rights. Review and strengthen laws to protect rights of minorities and indigenous groups.
- Remedy inhumane conditions in prisons and lower the number of pretrial detainees.
- Promote the use of non-polluting energy technologies.
- Convene a meeting of ministers responsible for science and technology within a year.
- Stimulate tourism in the hemisphere.
- Guarantee universal access to quality primary education. Seek to attain by 2010 a primary-school completion rate of 100 percent and secondary-school enrollment rate of at least 75 percent.
- Develop programs to ensure access to basic health services.
- Address and reduce violence against women.
- Create a corps of "White Helmet" volunteers to help with natural disasters and emergencies, as well as social and developmental needs.
- Aim for conservation and sustainable use of biodiversity.
- Prioritize environmental issues in each country for possible international collaboration.

The NAFTA vote, the crisis in Haiti, and the Summit of the Americas were without question high profile foreign policy issues that helped shape U.S. relations with the hemisphere. However, despite the attention generated by these issues, the general consensus among those who monitor inter-American affairs was that the Clinton administration continued to view the region as having marginal influence on the course of U.S. foreign policy. As Peter Hakim of the Inter-American Dialogue states, "By and large senior policymakers stayed away from the region, and rarely mentioned it in their speeches."[26] The Clinton approach to Latin America may be remembered as one that started out with a homerun (NAFTA) and then sat back and played the game from a position of strength. Because NAFTA dramatically changed hemispheric relations and strengthened our standing with the Latin Americans, the Clinton administration felt that it could turn its attention elsewhere in the world, at least until a new crisis erupted in the region.

NOTES

1. U.S. Department of State, Bureau of Public Affairs, *Communist Interference in El Salvador*, no. 80.

2. Michael J. Kryzanek, "President Reagan's Caribbean Basin Formula," *AEI Foreign Policy and Defense Review* 4, no. 2: 29–36.

3. As reported in the *New York Times*, January 14, 1984.

4. Ibid.

5. See William Scott Malone, "How Not to Depose a Dictator," *Washington Post National Weekly Edition*, May 1–7, 1989, p. 23.

6.   See, for example, Margaret Daly Hayes, "The U.S. and Latin America: A Lost Decade," *Foreign Affairs: America and the World, 1988–1989* (Washington, D.C.: Council on Foreign Relations, 1989), pp. 180–198.

7.   See Richard C. Schroeder, "New Approach to Central America," *Editorial Research Reports*, May 5, 1989, pp. 246–259.

8.   For the text of the accord and President Bush's remarks concerning the accord see the Department of State *Bulletin*, June 1989, pp. 55–57.

9.   See Charles Rangel, "Yes, We Can Do Something for Colombia," *Washington Post* National Weekly Edition, September 4–10, 1989, p. 29.

10. See the *New York Times*, October 6–8, 1989, for the critiques of the Bush handling of the Noriega affair. In particular the critics of the administration stressed that the United States had no contingency plan in place when it heard that a coup attempt was imminent; it responded timidly when rebels asked the United States to block two roads that might be used by Noriega loyalists; and it allegedly turned down an overture from the rebels to turn Noriega over to U.S. authorities.

11. The Bush administration tried to put a positive face on the crisis. See the comments of Assistant Secretary of State for Inter-American Affairs Bernard Aronson on the rebel offensive and the stability of the Cristiani government in the *New York Times*, November 15, 1989, p. A 10.

12. See William I. Robinson, *A Faustian Bargain: U.S. Intervention in the Nicaraguan Election and American Foreign Policy in the Post–Cold War Era* (Boulder, Colo.: Westview Press, 1992).

13. Julia Preston, "The Defeat of the Sandinistas," *New York Review of Books*, April 12, 1990, pp. 25–26.

14. Douglas Farah, "The Lost Decade," *Washington Post Weekly*, June 14–20, 1993, in *Annual Editions, Latin America*, 6th ed., edited by Christian Soe. (Guilford, Conn.: Dushkin, 1994), pp. 180–183.

15. Douglas Farah, "Even in Peace, The Armies Remain Entrenched," *Washington Post Weekly*, June 14–20, 1993, in *Annual Editions, Latin America*, 6th ed., edited by Christian Soe. (Guilford, Conn.: Dushkin, 1994), pp. 189–193.

16. Remarks by President Bush to Business Community, White House, June 27, 1990, in Department of State, *Foreign Policy Bulletin*, September/October 1990, pp. 87–89.

17. Statement by President Bush in Department of State, *Foreign Policy Bulletin*, August 12, 1992, p. 77.

18. Statement by Carla Hills to Senate Finance Committee, September 8, 1992, in Department of State, *Foreign Policy Bulletin*, November/December 1992, pp. 24–28.

19. Remarks by Congressman Richard Gephardt in Department of State, *Foreign Policy Bulletin*, September 9, 1992, p. 28.

20. For an overview of the Clinton approach to Latin America see the remarks of Alexander Watson, "Key Issues in Inter-American Relations," address to the 1994 Miami Congressional Workshop on Hemispheric Political, Economic, and Security Affairs, Miami, January 7, 1994 in Department of State, *Dispatch*, January 17, 1994, pp. 21–26.

21. See Bill Clinton, "Expanding Trade and Creating American Jobs," speech delivered at North Carolina State University, October 4, 1992, in Department of State, *Foreign Policy Bulletin*, November/December 1992, pp. 37–43.

22. John Fenton, "Administration Pressed to Deal to Win NAFTA Converts," *Congressional Quarterly*, October 2, 1993, p. 2620.

23. John Fenton, "How Whips Walk a Tightrope in NAFTA Role Reversal," *Congressional Quarterly*, November 20, 1993, pp. 3184–3185.

24. See Pamela Constable, "Haiti: A Nation in Despair, a Policy Adrift," *Current History*, March 1994, pp. 108–114.

25.   Boston *Globe*, December 11, 1994, p. 22.
26.   Peter Hakim, "NAFTA . . . and After: A New Era for the U.S. and Latin America?" *Current History*, March 1994, p. 98.

Part II

ELEMENTS OF LATIN AMERICAN POLICY MAKING

5

Governmental Participants in Latin American Policy Making

In the more than 170 years of U.S.–Latin American relations one is struck by the fact that our policies were often the result of an intricate interplay of many individuals, institutions, and processes. Although Theodore Roosevelt may have "taken" the Panama Canal and Ronald Reagan showed little reluctance about giving the order to invade Grenada, those decisions were not made in isolation and certainly could not have been implemented without the support and assistance of other participants. The complex nature of U.S. foreign policy making is no accident, but is rather a reflection of our political system with its competing centers of power, complicated procedures for making public decisions, and spirit of democratic debate that often makes it difficult to attain a consensus.[1]

Examining the major participants in the formulation and implementation of U.S. policy toward Latin America, one is ultimately drawn to the tension between the president and the Congress. The adage "The president proposes and the Congress disposes" remains a valid description of the roles that these two power centers play in the making of public policy. Whether it be treaty ratifications, spending authorizations, or hearings to determine the proper direction of hemispheric relations, it is inevitable that both the president and the Congress will seek to place their mark on U.S. policy toward Latin America.

It is important to stress, however, that as this country's governing system developed, the process of making foreign policy included more than the interaction of presidential initiatives and congressional resolutions. A host of bureaucrats, advisors, intelligence specialists, and military strategists joined the ranks of participants. In addition, as U.S. ties to Latin America became more pervasive and included numerous programs to assist in the development of these nations, foreign policy was no longer concerned with issues of diplomatic recognition and geopolitical maneuvering. The U.S. relationship with Latin America has expanded to the point where this country's foreign operations in the

Southern Hemisphere include cultural exchanges, technology transfers, arms sales, commodity purchases, debt rescheduling, trade missions, and negotiations over issues ranging from drug trafficking to tuna fishing and illegal immigration.

The result of this expansion in the foreign policy arena is that the United States has become more specialized in its handling of Latin American affairs. A complete picture of our foreign policy apparatus would have to include a multiplicity of government agencies with responsibilities for furthering U.S. objectives in ways seemingly unrelated to the traditional practice of diplomacy. Moreover, the presence of this bureaucratic specialization has changed substantially the process of developing U.S. policy toward Latin America. Policy toward the hemisphere is not really "made" in the sense that it is possible to point to one individual or institution as the sole architect of a particular initiative or program. It would be more accurate to say that policy making *evolves* through a labyrinth of leaders and government agencies that shape, revise, and compromise a proposal in an effort to formulate a policy that can be supported both in government and among the U.S. populace. In many instances this diffusion in the policy-making apparatus makes coordination and cohesion most difficult as the various participants and agencies scramble to influence the decision-making process. This diffusion, like the tension between the president and Congress, is a basic component of the U.S. policy process.

Even though the U.S. foreign policy machinery, with its multiplicity of participants and its built-in checks and balances, may be confusing, this is not to say that this system is without direction or that it is impossible to place responsibility for decisions made and actions taken. The president remains the dominant force in the formulation, administration, and implementation of this country's policy toward Latin America. It is thus with the president that we should begin our examination of the governmental participants and their impact on U.S. policy in the hemisphere.

THE PRESIDENT AND LATIN AMERICAN POLICY

The president's role as the government official with the most influence on Latin American policy can be approached in two ways. First we examine the formal, constitutional powers that permit the chief executive to function as the primary representative of the United States in foreign policy matters. Second, we describe the more informal skills that are required for the president to lead the nation toward particular policy objectives. What it is important to recognize at the outset is that the president has a broad array of powers at his disposal that afford him a distinct advantage over his foreign policy competitors whether they be in the Congress, in the political parties, in the media, or in the vast reaches of public opinion. As we shall see, one of the major reasons why the United States has developed such an extensive history of diplomatic, military, and economic intervention in Latin America is that presidents have used their position at the pinnacle of foreign policy making to advance this country's interests in the hemisphere, sometimes without popular support and on occasion without even bothering to inform the Congress.

Formal Powers

The president's authority as the chief representative of the United States in international affairs stems from his power to make treaties with foreign governments as stated in Article II, Section 2 of the Constitution. But as with most powers granted to the president, treaty making is contingent upon some form of congressional involvement. In this case it is a two-thirds ratification vote by the Senate that turns the agreement between two nations into a binding document that is recognized as law. Involving the United States in a treaty with a foreign government is thus a two-step process of negotiation and ratification, with the executive branch undertaking the first step of negotiating an agreement and the Senate then determining whether it is willing to commit this country to the terms of the agreement. The shared responsibility in the formulation of a treaty has sparked controversy throughout U.S. diplomatic history, as presidents have bemoaned the Senate's interference in foreign policy making and have sought to ensure that agreements made between nations do not become captive to the partisan politics of the legislative branch.[2]

The Carter administration's struggle over the Panama Canal Treaty is an example of the executive-legislative tension that arises when the president negotiates and the legislature ratifies. The treaty between Panama and the United States was hailed by President Carter as a major breakthrough in inter-American relations. The administration used the treaty to show that it was willing to shed its image as a colonial power and accede to the demands of the Panamanians. The U.S. Senate, however, was interested less in the potential for better hemispheric relations and more in hemispheric security. The long and bitter ratification process eventually forced the president to accept several amendments in order to mollify conservative senators.

Although the treaty-making power of the president is often viewed as his premier foreign policy prerogative, much of this country's relations with its neighbors is conducted through executive agreement. Modern presidents, seeking to exercise their role in the area of foreign policy and to lessen the involvement of the Congress, have relied on the executive agreement as the most efficient means of advancing the interests of the United States. When a president signs an agreement with a foreign country, whether in the area of trade, aid, or military ties, the Congress expresses its position on the matter through debate or if applicable in deliberations associated with accompanying legislation or funding mechanisms. But unlike a treaty, an executive agreement does not allow the Congress (more specifically the Senate) the "advise and consent" power that can destroy or severely compromise the long negotiations between two countries.

There is an important addendum to the use of executive agreements that had particular relevance to U.S. trade relations with Latin America. In the process of approving the North American Free Trade Agreement (NAFTA) the Congress was bound by so-called fast track rules written to safeguard the complex negotiations that lead to international trade agreements. The rules state that Congress cannot amend a trade agreement and must vote within ninety days of receipt of the agreement. Congress has a limited opportunity to ensure that a trade agreement like NAFTA is in conformity with U.S. law and can make changes as long as those changes do not require renegotiation. As a result there was little room for Congress to alter the deal made with Canada and Mexico. The fast track rules clearly were a benefit to President Clinton when he sought approval of NAFTA, while Congress was permitted only the tough decision of saying yes or no. Many in Congress resented the limitations that fast track placed on them feeling that they could not adequately protect or advance the interests of their constituents and were confined to approving or rejecting an agreement that was not the product of an open and democratic process.

While there have been some serious confrontations between the executive and legislative branches as a result of treaties and executive agreements, it is in the area of the president's use of military force to advance U.S. interests that has caused the greatest constitutional and political controversy. The president is clearly recognized in the Constitution as the commander-in-chief of the armed forces, a title that has been viewed as his most important power in the field of foreign policy. A number of presidents have interpreted the commander-in-chief's power to justify sending U.S. troops to foreign countries and intervening in the internal affairs of neighboring nations. In some cases the president's actions were motivated by national security concerns, such as Franklin Roosevelt's decision to protect the hemisphere from the Nazis during World War II by creating a 300-mile zone and ordering the navy to "shoot on sight" any German submarines. Other military actions, though, were motivated more by desire for capitalist expansion (Taft's Dollar Diplomacy) or anti-communism (the Johnson intervention in the Dominican Republic). But for whatever reason, U.S. presidents have used the military as a proper means of furthering U.S. interests.

The broad interpretation of the president's military power as the commander-in-chief has prompted outcries from Congress over development of an "imperial" presidency and the unrestrained use of U.S. armed forces abroad. The controversy came to a head during the Nixon administration, when the United States was deeply involved in the Vietnam war. Congress, seeking to avoid any future Vietnam-like commitments made by the executive branch, passed the War Powers Resolution in 1973 over President Nixon's veto. The result was, first, an act that requires any president to report to Congress within forty-eight hours on any decision to commit U.S. troops outside the United States, and, if possible, to consult with Congress beforehand. Second, the act requires the president to terminate the use of armed force within sixty days if during that period Congress either has not declared war or has not given the president a thirty-day extension.[3]

Since its implementation, the War Powers Act has never been formally invoked and has diminished in influence as a control on the president's power as commander-in-chief. In the Grenada intervention the relative ease of the operation and the support given the United States by the Grenadian people and the neighboring island mini-states convinced legislators that invoking restrictive legislation was inappropriate. Critics of the invasion chided Congress for being carried away by the speed and success of the mission rather than by exercising their power under the law to require consultation before hand. But in light of the growing concern over communist expansionism in the region, the War Powers Act was not viewed as a critical ingredient in the political process of sending troops into combat. In the Panama intervention in 1989 there was more criticism in Congress of President Bush's reluctance to go after Manuel Noriega than concern over whether an intervention would trigger the War Powers Act.

The Grenada and Panama invasions may have quietly put the War Powers Act into the category of "inoperative." Although President Reagan was outspoken in his view that the act limited presidents from carrying out their function of commander-in-chief, most observers of executive-legislative relations felt at the time that the War Powers Act was a paper tiger that did not stop presidents from interjecting troops in foreign trouble spots and most likely would not in the future.[4] What has happened, however, in the making of foreign policy is that modern presidents are facing a Congress that has found other ways to challenge the powers assumed under the title commander-in-chief. The ability of Congress to marshal public opinion against a foreign policy initiative, the use of its power of appropriations in the area of aid and trade, and its growing interest in human rights issues have proven to be powerful counterweights to a chief executive intent on using military might as a tool of foreign policy.

President Clinton, for example, ran into heavy congressional opposition for even hinting about an invasion of Haiti. Democrats and Republicans united in their opposition to any armed intervention and forced the president to rethink the options available as this country sought to influence events in Haiti. Without even mentioning the War Powers Act, President Clinton was forced to function in a new foreign policy environment where the leeway and personal direction that a chief executive once had to use the military option has been replaced by a system that requires political consensus and, ultimately, citizen approval.

Despite the controversy surrounding its meaning and application, the War Powers Act has certainly forced presidents to consider congressional reaction to the use of military means in a crisis. Furthermore, modern day presidents must now recognize that the act invites greater public scrutiny of the foreign policy process. Because the Congress is a representative body and responds to public opinion, the president's decision to involve this country in some form of military action automatically increases public awareness.

Diplomatic recognition is another of the president's foreign policy powers. Quite often we associate the recognition power with the formal exchange of ambassadorial credentials, but recognition can be a potent weapon in the president's hands, especially when millions of dollars of economic and military assistance may be connected to a decision to establish formal ties with a new country or a new government. In inter-American relations, the recognition power has become crucial because many Latin American countries have experienced numerous changes in leadership over the years. On a number of occasions—for example, during the Chilean overthrow of Salvador Allende—military conspirators solicited the opinion of the Nixon administration on its plans for recognizing a new right-wing military government. When it was clear that the United States supported an overthrow and would look more favorably on a new pro-U.S. government, the military conspirators moved one step closer to staging the coup.[5] The prospect of U.S. recognition was not the key catalyst for the overthrow, but it gave additional incentive to the anti-Allende forces.

Breaking diplomatic relations can also be an influential foreign policy tool in the hands of the president. Severing ties between two nations is always viewed as a last resort and only occurs after a major dispute or a complete breakdown in relations. In U.S.–Latin American relations the breaking of diplomatic ties has even greater force than when applied to other countries. Because the United States is the dominant power in the hemisphere and is the chief source of trade and investment, a decision to recall an ambassador and break a long-standing relationship can have a devastating effect on a country's economy. The diplomatic fissure that developed between the United States and Cuba in 1960 had a serious effect on the Cuban economy, because Cuba's sugar exports were destined for U.S. refineries and its tourist hotels were populated by U.S. visitors. Ironically the diplomatic break probably helped to speed Castro's embrace of the Soviet Union, a move that points up the dangers that ending a relationship can bring.

Breaking diplomatic relations is often viewed as the ultimate sanction against a country, but a president can take steps short of breaking relations that often isolates a governing regime from the world community of nations. As mentioned earlier, President Clinton used a wide range of sanctions against the Haitian military government to weaken their resolve. These sanctions were put into place while the United States retained its embassy in Port au Prince and continued to negotiate with the government in an effort to achieve a peaceful resolution of the impasse.

During the 1980s in Nicaragua, the Sandinista government asked that U.S. Ambassador Richard Melton leave the country because it was alleged that he and members of his embassy staff were responsible for inciting antigovernment riots. Melton, a Reagan appointee with strong anti-Sandinista sentiments, used the incident to reinforce the administration's view that the Nicaraguan government cannot tolerate democratic practice. The controversy further strained U.S.–Nicaraguan relations and was criticized in Central America as an attempt by the United States to poison the peace process. The relevance of the diplomatic dispute, however, had more to do with the ways in which the diplomatic presence in a country can serve important political or ideological goals than with the activities of an ambassador or the internal posture of the host government.

One last issue related to the foreign policy power of the president is the matter of appointing and utilizing ambassadorial personnel. The recognition of a particular country also means that the United States will send ministers to represent our interests. The individuals chosen and the responsibilities they are given by the president can have a profound impact on the way the relationship develops. In our relationship with Latin America, many ambassadorial personnel have taken on the role of key advisors to national leaders and involved themselves in the day-to-day matters of policy making. John Bartlow Martin in the pre-civil war Dominican Republic, Turner Shelton in Somoza's Nicaragua, Thomas Pickering in revolutionary El Salvador, and Deane Hinton in post-invasion Panama are but a few of the ambassadors who have exerted enormous influence on the countries they were sent to as representatives. Even though these men operated far from Washington, the record shows that they were acting with the approval of the president and they kept in close contact with the White House and State Department before providing advice to government officials.

The involvement of U.S. ambassadorial personnel in the internal policy-making process has been the source of constant criticism from opponents of existing governments who allege that this country has overstepped the bounds of diplomatic propriety. Although a case can be made against this kind of "interventionist" diplomacy, it is important to remember that the substantial economic and military aid given many of these countries provides the United States with a powerful lever for expanding its influence and even dictating policy. Furthermore, the aggressive role played by some ambassadors in Latin America cannot be seen only as the result of ambition and diplomatic meddling. Because these ambassadors are the president's representatives, their actions point to the enormous influence that the chief executive can exert outside of the United States.

Informal Skills

As the modern presidency has evolved, more and more attention has been devoted to examining the management and promotion of U.S. foreign policy. Although the president's constitutional powers remain central to the execution of his role as the primary representative of the United States to the world, presidential scholars have shifted their attention to include the effect that presidential style, political leadership, and personnel administration have on the ultimate shape and character of the foreign policy. How a president performs in the arena of public decision making and what techniques he employs to achieve his objectives are now as closely analyzed as the decision itself.[6]

U.S. foreign policy often derives from presidential initiative. A president may be responding to a crisis or opening up a dialogue with an adversary. Whatever the stimulus, it is the president who points this country toward a particular policy and then uses his political skills to ensure that his vision of the national interest becomes accepted. But taking the initiative is not enough. A modern president must be able to sell his vision to the various constituencies that are a part of the policy-making process. Presidential foreign policy making requires the power of persuasion. The process of developing this country's response to events outside our borders has become so complex that a president must spend a good deal of his time convincing Congress, interest groups, the press, and of course the U.S. public that his policy is a correct one. The inability to effectively persuade the key players in the policy process can easily sidetrack or destroy a presidential initiative.[7]

President Lyndon Johnson was by most accounts the champion persuader of the legislative branch and used his considerable political influence, built up after years in Congress, to convince (and sometimes to intimidate) former colleagues to support his policies. President Jimmy Carter had the reputation of an ineffectual persuader who lost battles with Congress and the bureaucracy because of his failure to deal with the major participants in the policy process on a personal level. Carter was often portrayed as cold and unwilling to perform the more mundane courtesies that often win friends. Ronald Reagan was successful in promoting many of his foreign policy initiatives, not so much because he had the confidence of Congress, but because he seemed to have captured the mood of the American people and in the process had placed pressure on Congress to follow the lead of their constituents. Ronald Reagan was in the view of many observers the most adept "persuader" in the office in years. Reagan (who has been dubbed the Great Communicator by the media) relied heavily on his strong television presence to persuade Congress and the U.S. public that his campaign against communist expansion in Central America was essential for our national security. In fact, Reagan used television speeches to marshal support for his Central American policy to a greater extent than any past president seeking to advance a specific foreign policy initiative.

President Reagan's ability to communicate his foreign policy to the various constituents in the United States was not without its limitations. As president, Reagan had to be very careful not to misjudge the mood of the U.S. electorate and lead them toward a foreign policy goal that they were reluctant to support. For example, the president received considerable praise for his aid and democratization efforts in El Salvador. The U.S. public appeared convinced that it was in our national interest to provide economic assistance and guidance to neighboring countries beset by leftist revolution. But there was little support for the president's decision to mine the Nicaraguan harbors or assistance for the *contra* war. Public opinion polls have shown that the U.S. public viewed these actions as a threat to regional stability and a possible prelude to war. Furthermore, polls have also consistently shown that the U.S. populace had no desire to involve U.S. troops in Central America.[8] The lessons of Vietnam seem etched in the U.S. consciousness. In the formulation of his Central American policy Reagan was forced to realize that the American people were not willing to follow his lead. Despite a vigorous campaign over a number of years, Reagan at the end of his second term had largely abandoned his personal crusade against the Sandinistas primarily because support for war in Nicaragua had evaporated.

The two most recent presidents, George Bush and Bill Clinton are studies in contrast as far as their interest in foreign policy and their ability to advance their foreign policy agendas. Bush was the consummate foreign policy practitioner. Building on his wealth of experience at the United Nations, as ambassador to China, and as head of the Central Intelligence Agency (CIA), President Bush paid close attention to international trouble spots and sought to position the United States in the post–Cold War New World Order. In Latin America, President Bush regularly championed the causes of privatization, corporate investment, and free trade. He traveled to the region and developed good working relationships with many of the new civilian leaders. The two centerpieces of his Latin American policy, the Enterprise of the Americas Initiative and NAFTA, enhanced his stock in the hemisphere and in corporate boardrooms. Bush was also able to work well with Congress in winding down the war in Central America and in responding to the challenges from Panama's Noriega. President Bush was not thought of as a "great communicator," but his policy positions in the region were well received and his actions, although controversial, were supported in Congress and by the American people.

President Clinton, however, did not far as well as a foreign policy persuader. A combination of intense concern for domestic issues and an inability to adjust to the changing character of international power left the Clinton administration adrift in a sea of indecision. On issues such as the restoration of President Aristide in Haiti, the president appeared unsure and indecisive. The photo of the navy ship sailing away from the dock in Port au Prince became an image of Clinton's lack of resolve. Clinton did register a major victory on NAFTA, but that success was quickly overshadowed by the inability of the administration to influence events inside Haiti.

The Clinton administration was under constant attack by critics who felt he had no clear vision of how the United States would use its power to deal with problems in small third world nations like Haiti. Clinton's reputation as a weak foreign policy president was further damaged by his use of former President Jimmy Carter as a special envoy to North Korea and Haiti. Although Carter achieved success in resolving difficult and dangerous crises in these two countries, many in Washington felt that relying on someone from outside the administration proved the weakness of the Clinton team and the inability of the president to properly address foreign policy issues.[9]

Sometimes the president's persuasive skills have to be turned inward to settle disputes that may arise among his advisors. Presidents often serve as referees among competing teams of advisors who argue their cases before him. Although debate is a healthy part of policy making in a democracy, it can become so intense that the president is faced, not with advisors, but rather with adversarial camps that seek to outdo, frustrate, and defeat their competition. The most recent example of this factionalism occurred when Alexander Haig was President Reagan's secretary of state. Haig bemoaned the competition among various factions vying for the president's attention. Haig was constantly at odds with presidential advisors James Baker and Michael Deaver, who felt Haig's strident remarks and arrogance were hurting the president's image. Haig also competed with Secretary of Defense Caspar Weinberger, UN Ambassador Jeane Kirkpatrick, and National Security Advisor William Clark over the issue of who was going to control Central American policy formation.[10]   Although President Reagan tried on a number of occasions to mediate the dispute, in the end he saw Haig as a liability to his administration. President Reagan had a reputation for avoiding dismissal of his top advisors, but the constant friction and behind-the-scenes machinations caused by the Haig feuding forced the president to act and bring a modicum of stability to his foreign policy operation.

Later on in his second term, Reagan was accused of taking an opposite tack with his advisory staff. Evidence surfacing in the wake of the Iran-*contra* scandal pointed to a president who ignored the essential rule of foreign policy formulation and permitted his advisors to control the decision-making process without close presidential direction or intervention. There were indeed disputes in the administration over the issue of arms for hostages and the general conduct of the *contra* war, especially involving Secretary of State George Shultz, Defense Secretary Caspar Weinberger, National Security Advisor John Poindexter, and Assistant Secretary of State for Inter-American Affairs Elliott Abrams, but amid the flurry of opinions, options, and ideological positions Reagan appeared to be an ineffective manager of the disputes. Reagan's lack of interest in the internal disagreements over policy left the field open for individuals within his administration to take matters into their own hands and formulate decisions that would eventually come back to haunt the president.

President Clinton's management of the White House foreign policy team was marked not so much by internal disagreements between key players as general disorganization and lack of vision. On Haiti there were disagreements between civilian advisors and the military over whether to include invasion as an option and some nasty behind-the-scenes fights in the intelligence community concerning the mental state of President Aristide. But most of the analysis of President Clinton's advisory team centered on their inability to articulate how the United States should respond to internal civil disturbances, such as in Somalia, Bosnia, and Haiti. Some laid the blame on Secretary of State Warren Christopher who was seen as a weak voice in the administration. Others faulted the United States for relying too heavily on multilateral solutions involving the United Nations or the Organization of American States rather than charting its own independent course of action. Still others saw the Clinton administration as so focused on domestic issues that foreign policy debates were an afterthought. In fairness to the Clinton team, responding to trouble spots like Haiti did bring forth vigorous debate and conflict among staff members, but translating the results of the debate into substantive and sustained action seemed difficult to achieve.[11]

It is of course the president's responsibility to manage his corps of advisors and not permit personal or ideological disputes to influence the proper formulation of public policy. Unfortunately, although the president is a powerful decision maker, the presidency has become a complex organization that is filled with factions, temporary alliances, political convictions, and above all ambition. The policy that comes out of this maze is thus not really the president's but is the result of ideological commitment, internal dialogue, power struggles, and eventually compromise. A president who successfully masters this complex of advisors and opinions will have taken a major step toward placing an individual mark on foreign policy.

THE PRESIDENTIAL ADVISORY SYSTEM: THE STATE DEPARTMENT, THE NATIONAL SECURITY COUNCIL, AND THE CENTRAL INTELLIGENCE AGENCY

The president may possess the power to shape and direct foreign policy, but he must depend on the intelligence gathering, the analysis, and the on-site representation of professionals in the State Department, the National Security Council, and the CIA if he is to make decisions that are based on a full understanding of the issues at hand and the options available to him. These three agencies together form an advisory system for the president that provides him with the means not only to make sound policies but to execute those policies in an effective manner.

The State Department

The State Department is officially charged with representing the United States in the 155 countries where we have established diplomatic ties. Because of its presence in most of the world's nation-states, the State Department, and in particular the secretary of state, is in a unique position to advise the president on a broad range of foreign policy concerns. Using the wealth of information provided by the professional foreign service officers who are trained to monitor and report on internal political and economic events, the State Department can alert the president to potential trouble spots.

The State Department, like other large organizations, is a complex of specialized offices designed to address particular foreign policy problems or manage our relations with a specific country or region of the world. This bureaucratic structure of the State Department can be seen by examining the Latin American policy network, officially designated as the Bureau of Inter-American Affairs. The American Republics Area (ARA), which is one of five such geographic bureaus in the State Department, is a prime example of the specialized nature of policy making that has become commonplace in government. The management of U.S.–Latin American affairs requires that the chief Latin American official, the assistant secretary of state for inter-American affairs, coordinate a vast array of specific functions. ARA is composed of administrative deputies charged with responsibilities ranging from congressional liaison to implementation of NAFTA and regional concerns, such as narcotics, migration, and human rights. Below this deputy level are the highly specialized offices that concentrate on affairs in a major Latin American nation or in a subregion of the hemisphere, such as the Office of Mexican Affairs and the Office of Brazilian and Southern Cone Affairs. Tied into these specialized offices and forming another level are the country desks where foreign service officers manage information about each country in the region and report to superiors about political and economic trends.

The effectiveness of the reporting and analysis generated by the ARA depends upon the foreign service personnel who work in the embassies and consulates worldwide. It is the embassy staff, often called the country team, that not only represents the United States in formal intergovernmental exchanges but also administers development and aid programs, facilitates trade and investment arrangements, irons out visa and other travel problems, and in many countries works closely with the armed forces on security matters and arms procurement. The picture of a lonely foreign service officer manning a distant outpost for the United States is a far cry from the modern U.S. embassy, which is a multipurpose office designed to further a wide range of national objectives.

Figure 5.1, which describes the U.S. embassy in Venezuela, gives a clearer view of an embassy operation. The staff includes a wide range of specialists. Besides the foreign service personnel who perform administrative, visa, and reporting tasks, the Venezuelan embassy has specialists from the Agriculture and Commerce departments, the United States Information Agency, fifteen civilian and military employees from the Defense Department, and small groups of officials from the Drug Enforcement Agency, the Federal Aviation Administration, the Inter-American Geodetic Survey, and the Internal Revenue Service. Although the Venezuelan chart is a representative sample of a U.S. embassy operation, it is important to keep in mind that countries such as Brazil and Mexico have larger staffs that perform an even wider array of functions.

The hierarchical nature of the State Department and the complex character of its representational functions have created a major problem for presidents who often expect foreign service professionals to respond quickly to executive initiatives. Presidents have lamented the inability of the State Department to develop U.S. foreign policy according to administration directives. In some respects, the criticisms by past presidents are well founded because most career diplomats are not political appointees and tend to take a nonpartisan approach to their work. President Clinton was cognizant of the tension between career diplomats and political appointees when in 1993 he appointed three long-time State Department diplomats to ambassadorial positions in Nicaragua, Honduras, and Argentina. Nevertheless there continues to be ill will toward political appointees within the State Department, especially in the wake of the Reagan administration's "housecleaning" of Carter era Latin Americanists who were viewed by conservative Republicans as soft on communism. As one senior State Department official stated at the announcement of the Clinton appointments, "We're trying to end the cycle of political recriminations for those who served in the Latin American bureau."[12]

Figure 5.1
Members of the Staff of the U.S. Embassy in Venezuela

Chief of Mission
Ambassador
Personal Representative of the President

Deputy Chief of Mission
Minister-Counselor

-------- Country Team --------

Mission Unit	Agricultural Trade Office	Agricultural Counselor	Public Affairs Counselor	Commercial Counselor	Political Counselor	Economic Counselor	Administrative Counselor	Consul General	Defense Attache	Head Military Group (advisory)	Other Agencies Present
Home Agency	Agriculture	Agriculture	USIA	Commerce		Department of State			Defense	Defense	Drug Enforcement Agency Federal Aviation Administration Internal Revenue Service

U.S. Consulate in Maracaibo. U.S. staff 3 State 1 USIA

Source: U.S. Department of State.

But while Clinton sought to assuage State Department officials with his appointments, he created a firestorm of ill will with his use of Jimmy Carter as special representative to Haiti. Carter's success in mediating the dispute with the Haitian generals created a negative reaction in the State Department from career Latin American diplomats who felt the former president was moving in on their traditional turf. Carter, who had long battles with the State Department when he was president, stated that he found opposition to his Haiti mission, "illogical. . . . We've just had to accept the fact that there is this great reluctance, primarily concentrated in the State Department."[13]

But it is not only the political differences with the State Department that irritate presidents; it is also the fact that quite often foreign policy decisions have to be made quickly in order to respond to crises or to rapidly changing circumstances. The State Department, which has gained the name of Foggy Bottom (after the section of Washington where it is situated), has often been unable to move aggressively in the formulation and implementation of foreign policy decisions. In response to these criticisms foreign service officers point with pride to their role as objective analysts of world affairs and condemn presidential attempts to politicize their job. Needless to say, the resulting tension between presidential administrations and the State Department has on occasion made the operation of our foreign policy establishment more controversial than the policies.

The National Security Council

In 1947 the National Security Act established the National Security Council (NSC) as the highest executive branch entity "providing review of, guidance for and direction to the conduct of all national foreign intelligence and counter-intelligence activities." The NSC, which includes as statutory members the president, the vice-president, the secretaries of state and defense, and, as advisors, the director of the CIA and the chairman of the Joint Chiefs of Staff, has developed over the years into a key foreign policy agency. The national security assistant who in effect runs the NSC and its team of specialists commands a great deal of influence in the White House and can be the chief foreign policy advisor to the president. Henry Kissinger, for example, acting as President Nixon's national security advisor, expanded the role and influence of the position to the point where he dominated foreign policy development and completely overshadowed the secretary of state, William Rogers. In the Reagan White House, National Security Advisors Robert MacFarlane and John Poindexter wielded enormous power as the president chose to distance himself from the day-to-day activities of foreign policy. The involvement of MacFarlane and Poindexter in the Iran-*contra* scandal called into question the issue of who makes foreign policy and whether a body like the National Security

Council that is often shielded from public view should play such a dominant role in the formulation and implementation of this nation's relations with foreign governments. During the Bush and Clinton administrations there was less of the visible conflict and controversy that was present during the Reagan years but there were clear differences in personnel and approach, particularly with respect to inter-American affairs. President Bush chose as his national security advisor Brent Scowcroft, a former military officer who showed little interest in Latin America, except of course during the Panama invasion. President Clinton, however, appointed Anthony Lake, a man with academic credentials who had written a book about U.S. policy toward the Somoza regime in Nicaragua. Lake in turn appointed Richard Feinberg, a long-time Latin Americanist who also had academic credentials.

Although the NSC works primarily in the area of integrating intelligence reports and developing national security policy, the president has increasingly come to depend upon the NSC to take the lead in developing key foreign policy initiatives. Because the NSC advisor and his support staff are a mix of political appointees and career foreign service officers from the departments of State and Defense and the CIA, the president may, on occasion, find himself pulled in different directions by loyalists and careerists. This duality of approach to foreign policy making has caused friction, especially between the national security advisor and the secretary of state. Because both agencies and their leaders are vying for the attention of the president, there have been a number of heated conflicts over who controls the foreign policy turf in an administration.[14]

The conflict between the national security advisor and the secretary of state often diverts attention from the inner workings of the NSC and its impact on policy making. The NSC is organized along functional and regional lines. The Latin American region is one of six offices with a small staff of five. The Latin American staff funnels its analysis through larger review committees that meet regularly to address a broad range of intelligence matters, set priorities, and evaluate the quality of intelligence. But while the larger review committees are the heart of the NSC, other specialized committees can be formed. For example, during the development of U.S. policy toward Allende's Chile, Henry Kissinger formed what was termed the "40 Committee" (named after National Security memorandum no. 40), which made decisions on the use of covert activities in that country. The 40 Committee became the body that established the destabilization program against Allende. The State Department was often left in the dark as to what the Nixon administration was planning or doing in Chile, primarily because Kissinger was given the authority to manage the covert operations against the Allende regime, while Secretary of State Rogers played little if any role in the policy deliberations.

Because the NSC has grown not only in personnel but also in stature since 1947, the heightened compartmentalization of policy making as evidenced by the 40 Committee makes managing the foreign policy of the United States even more difficult. Not only can disputes arise between the national security advisor and the secretary of state over who makes foreign policy but factions within the NSC can work on their own to try and influence the direction of policy. There is always a possibility that a particular foreign policy may evolve without the president's having a firm command of the issues and the options. Even though these are in theory the president's men, a president who fails to inform himself of NSC operations can risk having his subordinates gain control of a key segment of the foreign policy process.

The Central Intelligence Agency

There is perhaps no agency of the U.S. government that elicits such suspicion and animosity as the CIA. Formed under the auspices of the same National Security Act that established the NSC, the CIA was charged with coordinating the nation's foreign intelligence operations. Since its founding the CIA has become an important participant in the formation and implementation of U.S. foreign policy. The intelligence that it provides the president and the NSC on particular countries, leaders, political parties, rebel groups, and social movements makes the CIA an invaluable part of the policy-making process.

Interestingly, the intelligence-gathering function of the CIA has never really created problems for the agency. Rather, it is its covert functions that have caused controversy both in the United States and abroad. To complement its intelligence role, the CIA has become involved in clandestine operations designed to create internal situations favorable to U.S. interests. These activities have in the past covered a wide range of tactics, including bribing opposition politicians, funding counterinsurgency rebels, and alleged assassination plots. Latin America has been especially vulnerable to CIA covert operations. As discussed earlier, the CIA directed the rebels who replaced the leftist Guatemalan government in 1954; it was involved in the failed Bay of Pigs invasion, the conspiracy to force Salvador Allende from power, and most recently the *contra* operation in Honduras.

Although these are the most well-known CIA operations, the covert arm of the agency can be found in most other Latin American countries. This is not to say that the CIA is actively seeking to replace existing leaders or weaken established governments, but it is involved in activities that are viewed as part of its intelligence-gathering function. Gaining influence in a key labor union, infiltrating a leftist political party, providing money to a pro–U.S. organization are all seen as essential operations if the agency is to succeed in its overall mission. CIA officials often state that their covert operations help to forestall or redirect internal forces in Latin American countries that could threaten U.S. interests. They contend that without the clandestine activity of the CIA the United States would lose a valuable means of ensuring that governments in the region remain pro–U.S.

The CIA's covert function has, not surprisingly, fostered criticism both in the United States and in Latin America. Many critics see these activities as unethical and as unnecessary meddling in the internal affairs of sovereign countries, while others stress the poor image that the CIA has developed for the United States, especially when it works to bring down or destabilize an existing regime.[15] As a result of this criticism, Congress and some recent presidents have worked to control the covert operations of the CIA. In 1974 Congress passed the Hughes-Ryan Amendment, which requires the president to notify the legislative branch when a covert action is being undertaken and certify its "importance to the national interests of the U.S." Also at this time the late Senator Frank Church of Idaho held hearings on the CIA's clandestine operations and exposed a number of its more questionable practices and missions. On the basis of these hearings, President Ford signed Executive Order #11905 in February 1976, which set guidelines for intelligence gathering and established an intelligence oversight mechanism. In May 1976 the Senate established the Select Committee on Intelligence to oversee the CIA. The House of Representatives followed suit in 1977. President Carter followed President Ford's lead by reorganizing the intelligence community in an effort to make it more responsive to the executive and permit greater presidential guidance of intelligence activities.

The initiatives of Ford and Carter were effective in placing controls on the CIA, but they created problems within the intelligence community. Career CIA agents felt that the United States could not compete effectively with the Soviet KGB in covert operations and was no longer able to influence the course of internal politics in other countries. When President Reagan entered office and appointed William Casey as head of the CIA, there was a marked turnaround in agency morale. Both the president and Casey were firm believers in the need for a vigorous CIA and were not bothered by the ethical and interventionist questions raised by the agency's critics. Perhaps the most vivid example of the resurgence of the CIA under the Reagan administration was the handling of Nicaraguan harbor mining by Casey. Despite set procedures for informing Congress of covert operations, Casey was less than candid in alerting the congressional committees charged with oversight. Once the mining operation was made known (some Congressmen found out in the newspapers) a flood of criticism followed from committee members who were outraged at the CIA's failure to follow the law. Although Casey apologized for the omission, it was clear that the Reagan administration encouraged covert operations and was not intimidated by the restraints established by its predecessors.[16]

Just as the Iran-*contra* affair contributed to a negative perception of the NSC, the CIA and Director Casey came in for even harsher criticism once Congress and the press began exploring the links between the agency and the *contra* rebels. As a result of testimony by CIA agents subpoenaed by various investigatory committees of Congress and a scathing biography of Director Casey by the *Washington Post*'s Bob Woodward, it became clear that despite congressional prohibitions against CIA involvement in supplying the *contras* with arms, the agency, at the alleged direction of Casey, engaged in a secret effort to fund the rebels. Furthermore, the CIA was also accused of tolerating the drug-dealing operations of *contra* leaders who used the profits from the sale of drugs to purchase arms and enrich themselves.

Although Casey died in the midst of the controversy surrounding the CIA-*contra* link, the attack on the agency continued. New allegations against the CIA arose in 1988, when Speaker of the House Jim Wright alleged that the CIA operatives had tried to develop a campaign of internal opposition in Nicaragua and had used agents to assist demonstrations "calculated to stimulate and provoke arrests." The announcement by Wright caused a storm of protest as the Reagan administration accused Wright of discussing covert operations and jeopardizing the lives of those Nicaraguans who were demonstrating against the Sandinista regime.

When George Bush became president he restored some strength to the CIA image. As a former director of the CIA, President Bush pledged to continue administration support for the work of the CIA and the value of sound intelligence. Yet despite the close ties between President Bush and the CIA, the intelligence community was not immune from criticism. The initial failure to remove Panamanian General Manual Noriega was in part blamed on faulty intelligence gathering and CIA Director William Webster's inability to participate with any degree of effectiveness in the deliberations that surrounded the attempted coup against Noriega. The key problem facing the CIA, however, was not so much intelligence gathering but the damage done to the CIA's reputation during the Casey years. That damage would be difficult to repair and would continue to foster the image of an intelligence agency that frequently skirts the Constitution in its attempt to influence events abroad.

With the onset of the Clinton administration the CIA entered a period of intense introspection as a budget conscious Congress and long-time critics of the agency pressured the new director, James Woolsey, to justify the huge outlay of funds for intelligence gathering and the necessity of maintaining a governmental bureaucracy that was instituted to fight the spread of communism in the post–Cold War world of communist collapse. As for the role of the CIA in Latin American affairs, the emphasis was definitely placed on intelligence gathering rather than on campaigns of destabilization. After the extensive role of the CIA in Central America during the Reagan years and the connection between the CIA and the drug empire of Manuel Noriega, the CIA appeared to take a low profile approach to events in the region. By 1994 the CIA was in full-fledged retreat with Clinton's appointee for director, James Woolsey, replaced after months of political wrangling by John Deutch.[17]

THE ROLE OF THE CONGRESS

So far the U.S. policy-making machinery has been viewed from the perspective of the executive branch. But as Clinton Rossiter, a leading expert on the presidency, states, "No important policy, domestic or foreign, can be pursued for long by even the most forceful president unless Congress comes to his support with laws and money."[18] As we shall see, in the realm of foreign policy making, and in particular with recent Latin American policy development, the Congress is playing an increasingly important role as a critic of the administration and as a powerful counterforce to administration initiatives in the region. After a period during which the legislative branch languished under the "imperial" presidencies of Johnson and Nixon, the Congress of the 1980s sought to expand its involvement in the foreign policy arena. Congress's enactment of strong human rights laws directly affected longstanding relationships with many Latin American dictatorships, along with debates in both the Senate and the House over the proper methods of responding to the spread of communism and over economic and military aid to this region. In the 1990s the Congress has been less focused on the political issues of the region choosing to concentrate on the impact of NAFTA and burgeoning private sector development in the region that is being spurred by U.S. investment. The turmoil in Haiti, however, has once again forced Congress to review presidential policies toward the region and address old issues of inter-American relations such as intervention, democratization, and human rights.

The assertiveness of the Congress and its willingness to challenge the president in foreign policy development has made the Senate and House targets for groups that wish to influence our relations with Latin America. In Congress, presidential initiatives toward the hemisphere can be sidetracked or at least compromised. Thus, groups that heretofore have been unable to gain access to policy-making circles in the executive branch are now looking to the Congress as an advocate for their positions. Human rights organizations, labor unions, peace advocates, Hispanic-American groups, trade associations and corporate lobbyists, and others are now regularly approaching the Congress to present their grievances and to suggest remedies.

The result of Congress's increased involvement in the foreign policy process is more frequent confrontations between the president and the legislative branch. In the 1980s the battleground between the legislature and the executive involved aid to the *contra* rebels. The critical confrontation between a president determined to place increased military pressure on the Sandinista government and a Congress reluctant to make commitments that seemed reminiscent of the Vietnam war era came in 1986 over the $100 million *contra* aid package submitted to the legislature by President Reagan.

In an initial test vote on the $100 million request in March 1986 the House, on a vote of 210 to 222, rejected the proposed appropriation. The House defeat of the measure capped a flurry of lobbying efforts by the president to sway undecided legislators and to marshal public opinion in favor of the *contra* aid package. The efforts by the president may have failed to garner the required number of votes, but it did reveal the intensity with which the administration viewed the *contra* aid issue. President Reagan promised that he would be back and would again take his case to the halls of Congress and to the American people.

While the House was narrowly rejecting the aid proposal the Senate gave the president a victory (53 to 47) on *contra* aid, although the senators insisted, through a number of amendments attached to the vote, that the administration pursue all avenues toward a negotiated settlement of the conflict. Support in the Senate was a reflection not only of a more conservative composition among the membership but also of the deep divisions within Congress over how to respond to the presence of a new Marxist government in the hemisphere. Furthermore, the Senate vote was taken at a time when the Sandinistas decided to invade neighboring Honduras in an attempt to destroy the *contra* base camps.

As promised by President Reagan, the divided Congress was not permitted to rest on the issue of *contra* aid, because the administration again introduced an assistance package that included monies for weapons. The second round of House debate on the aid was a complicated net of parliamentary procedure and partisan politics as the Democratic leadership tied the aid package to a supplemental appropriations bill that the president vowed he would veto. The Republicans, angered by the Democratic attempt to scuttle the aid by forcing a presidential veto, surprised the membership by voting to withhold *contra* aid, thereby throwing the whole legislative process into chaos. The Republican strategy was to prevent the Democratic-controlled House from considering another anti-*contra* aid vote that was certain to pass. The so-called parliamentary suicide vote delayed a vote on the *contra* aid for months, but it sent a message to the Democrats that the Republicans would do almost anything to achieve their objectives in funding the rebel army.

Although the Republican strategy delayed the *contra* aid bill until June 1986, the outcome of the third debate on the issue was favorable to the president. By a vote of 221 to 209, the House approved military aid to the *contras*. Again, President Reagan pulled out all the stops as he sought to convince two dozen undecided congressmen of the need to provide military aid to the *contras* as a means of guaranteeing serious negotiations. The bill passed by the House also provided $300 million in economic aid to the democratic nations in the region and, perhaps most important, permitted the CIA to once again administer the assistance. Liberals in Congress lamented the loss and warned of a new "proxy war" against the Sandinistas. The Republicans and the president naturally were elated over the victory and promised that the assistance would force the Nicaraguans to come to the bargaining table and make real concessions.

The House victory for President Reagan, however, did not end the saga of *contra* aid. Because the *contra* aid was attached to a new military construction appropriation the Senate had to vote again on the issue. Even though the Senate seemed more predisposed to support the $100 million aid package, liberal senators planned a filibuster of the measure as a last-ditch attempt to stop the president. The plan to talk the aid proposal to death, however, was short-lived as a vote of closure ended debate and set the stage for a 54 to 46 vote in favor of *contra* aid. In the debate the Senate grappled with the long-term implications of *contra* aid. Democrats stated that the $100 million was but a first installment of what would become a multibillion dollar Vietnam-like involvement. Republicans retorted that aiding the *contras* was better than having to send U.S. troops to the region to offset the spread of communism in the hemisphere.

Despite the difference between liberals and conservatives, Democrats and Republicans, in the Congress, President Reagan gained the victory on *contra* aid that had eluded him for so many years. The joy of victory was brief, because the Iran-*contra* scandal soured members of Congress on aid to the rebels. President Reagan backed off his plan to seek $270 million in new *contra* aid and had to settle for a series of minor humanitarian aid packages totaling approximately $20 million in 1987. Then, in a key vote in February 1988, the House shifted gears again and rejected by a vote of 211 to 219 Reagan's new request of $36.25 million for military and nonmilitary assistance. The rejection of the aid request coupled with the ongoing peace process in Central America ended, at least for the Reagan administration, the battle over *contra* aid. With the *contras* unable to achieve any major victories, continued allegations of misdeeds by *contra* leaders, and the growing hope that the Central Americans might be able to generate a successful peace process, Congress seemed fearful of spending money on a lost cause. President Reagan was forced to accept the fact that the only aid that would be made available by Congress would be to wind down the war, relocate the rebels, and ensure a minimal level of maintenance while the negotiation process continued. A listing of the *contra* aid appropriations from 1982 to 1990 is provided in Table 5.1.

The wrangling over the *contra* aid package accents the importance that the appropriations process can have on the formulation and

Table 5.1

Aid Authorizations to the *Contras*, Fiscal Years 1982–90

Year	Amount (in millions of dollars)	Type of Authorization
1982	29.0	CIA covert aid authorized by President Reagan
1983	29.0	CIA covert aid
1984	24.0	Covert aid, under the first "Boland Amendment"
1985	—	The Boland Amendment prohibits U.S. aid
1986	27.0	Non-military aid administered by the State Department
1987	100.0	CIA and Defense Department military and non-military aid approved by Congress
1988	25.8	Non-military aid administered by the Agency for International Development (AID)
1989	27.1	Non-military aid administered by AID
1990	49.7	Non-military aid administered by AID
Total	311.7	Direct U.S. government aid to the *contras*
	40.3	Non–U.S. government aid (private donations, Iran arms sales, and contributions from other nations)
Total	352.0	

Source: Compiled from congressional sources.

execution of U.S. foreign policy. Congress was determined to use the power of the purse to place its mark on the Central American policy of the administration, and in a sense to become a co-participant with the president in directing our future activities in this vital region. Its ability to eventually curtail the *contra* lethal aid shows the effect that concerted opposition to a presidential policy can have in the Congress.[19]

Also important to remember is that although the Congress is an institution of rules, structured committees, and hierarchical lines of authority, it is clear that frequently personal rather than procedural or organizational factors carry the day. The legislative debate over the president's aid requests also called in to question the value of partisan affiliations when they run up against ideological commitments. Congress may be a highly partisan institution, but foreign policy issues are often not as susceptible to the rigors of party discipline. The issue of aid appropriations was fought among congresspeople who feared communism, abhorred repression, supported the process of democratization, or worried about the prospect of U.S. intervention. Partisan politics did play a role in each debate, especially in the House of Representatives, but there was enough erosion of party allegiance on both sides to show that when an emotional issue is put to the vote, loyalty to the party standard weakens significantly and conscience takes over.[20]

What is perhaps most interesting about the *contra* aid battle was the impact of personalities on the process and the extent to which events outside the United States changed legislative positions. A phone call by the president to an undecided legislator, visits by delegations of *contra* leaders to the halls of Congress, the forcefulness of deeply committed liberals and conservatives to block a vote or to add an amendment were critical elements in the legislative legacy of *contra* aid. On the other hand, the unrelenting Marxist rhetoric of Daniel Ortega, the invasion of Honduras by the Sandinistas, and the regular efforts to flaunt the Nicaraguan-Soviet connection did more to shift the votes of fence-straddling congresspeople than any reasoned argument from an administration policy maker.

It is essential to point out that the president, when he marshals the considerable power of his office and effectively presents his case, as he did in 1986, can be an almost unbeatable opponent. This small case study of Congress at work in the foreign policy field shows that a president who utilizes his lobbying skills, his party alliances, and his opportunities to generate favorable public opinion can overcome vast numbers of legislative opponents. The president is by no means invulnerable to legislative action, but he still has the edge when it comes to directing this country's foreign policy. Many legislators are simply reluctant to restrain the president from carrying out his constitutionally mandated duties in the area of foreign policy. A wise president, however, will recognize that this congressional deference has its limits and can easily be transformed into determined opposition. In the case of *contra* aid, Congress simply lost confidence in the rebels and in an administration that appeared willing to circumvent the Constitution in order to advance its foreign policy objectives. Gaining support for a program and acquiring the necessary funding is often a product of trust in those who you must deal with and belief in the prospects of success. In terms of *contra* aid, Congress, after numerous battles with the president and enormous pressure from constituents and special interests, came to the conclusion that there was a better way to spend U.S. tax dollars than on a proxy army with few victories and little popular support.

The premier executive-legislative showdown of the 1990s that also called upon the major players in both branches of government to utilize their skills of persuasion, power politics, and coalition building was over the passage of NAFTA. Just like the *contra* appropriation debates and votes tested President Reagan's ability to bend Congress to his will, NAFTA required President Clinton to convince a majority in the House (where the key vote occurred) that a free trade agreement, which would likely cause the loss of jobs in the United States and would substantially restructure the domestic economy, was in the long-term interests of this country.

Although the proponents and opponents of NAFTA had been presenting their arguments concerning the accord ever since President Bush signed the document in 1992, the critical step in the process of approving NAFTA was the bill implementing the legislation. With the vote in the House scheduled for November 17, 1993, the Clinton White House engaged in a flurry of activity designed to convince uncommitted representatives that NAFTA would be the right step for the United States. The administration introduced a worker retraining bill designed to assuage the concerns of labor and opened a free trade bazaar on the White House lawn to show the impact that expanded trade with Mexico would bring.

These public actions were also accompanied by backstage maneuverings by the Clinton administration to convince reluctant members of Congress from southern and western states, such as Louisiana, Florida, and California, who were concerned that trade in agricultural commodities with Mexico would have a deleterious impact on their constituents. The Clinton administration's most vexing problem, however, was in convincing pro-labor representatives, many of whom were Democrats, that a vote for NAFTA would eventually mean greater prosperity and more jobs, even though in the short run there would be job dislocation. The AFL-CIO waged a vigorous campaign in industrial states reminding representatives that over 500,000 jobs had already moved to the Mexican *maquiladora* region and that more would follow, especially as a result of a manufacturing wage of $2.17 per hour in Mexico compared to $15.45 per hour in the United States. From the union perspective NAFTA would only benefit the large multinationals while jeopardizing the security of the American worker. As Richard Donahue of the AFL-CIO stated in testimony before Congress, "The North American Free Trade Agreement from start to finish is nothing more than the latest version of Reagan-Bush trickle-down economics and an enlargement of the interests of U.S. and Canada-based multinational corporations, to the detriment of the U.S. worker."[21]

As the date for the vote approached the Clinton administration pulled out all stops to gain the support of uncommitted representatives who numbered approximately thirty. These thirty representatives were pushed and pulled by a president who said that his credibility as a trade negotiator would be damaged if NAFTA failed and by Democratic leaders like House Majority Leader Dick Gephardt of Missouri who led the fight to stop the accord and stated that he "has never seen a political issue with such intensity as NAFTA." Slowly the White House claimed that it was making inroads among the 30, but still was 10 votes short of the 218 necessary for victory. The admission by the White House gave strength to the opponents of NAFTA who felt that the fear of job loss and the restructuring of the U.S. economy were convincing members of Congress to cast a negative vote.[22]

Also adding to the political mix was the highly visible efforts of Ross Perot who was a staunch opponent of NAFTA. Perot criticized the agreement on the grounds that it would take jobs away from the large industrial centers of the United States and place them in the *maquiladora* zones in Mexico where multinational corporations could get increased profits because of the low wage and tax environment there. The Perot challenge to NAFTA reached its zenith in a live television debate with Vice-president Al Gore a few days before the crucial vote. Most observers of the debate felt that the vice-president carried the day by calling into question Perot's own involvement in a free trade zone area in Texas that was built to take advantage of markets in Mexico. Gore also gave Perot a picture of Depression era senators Hawley and Smoot who were responsible for protectionist legislation that many economists believe contributed to the severe drop in the U.S. economy in the early 1930s. The poor showing of Ross Perot appeared to give the Clinton administration the public opinion boost it needed as it got ready for the crucial vote in the House.[23]

When the House met on November 17 to vote on NAFTA the Clinton strategy for victory surprisingly depended upon the vote of the Republican membership. With the president losing traditional Democratic support due to heavy union pressure, the pro–free trade and pro-business Republicans were counted upon to provide the administration with the margin of victory. As the votes were cast, however, it became clear that the president had worked the phones successfully and had forged a bipartisan coalition to defeat the opponents of NAFTA. The final vote for the accord was 234 to 200, but the real margin of victory was contained in the Republican tally of 132 to 43. President Clinton's Democrats only supplied 102 votes for NAFTA in what was viewed as a stinging rebuke of the president's trade policies and his acceptance of the price that had to be paid in order to enter into the global marketplace.

The victory in the House was not achieved without some last minute deal-making in order to satisfy legislators worried about the impact of free trade with Mexico. Members of the Florida delegation gave their approval of NAFTA only after President Clinton agreed to tougher safeguards for tomato growers in the event that Mexican tomatoes flood the U.S. market. One congressman from New York held out his vote until the president approved a Small Business Administration loan program to assist workers displaced by NAFTA. Critics of the horse-trading estimated that the cost of the last minute agreements to sway votes approached $1 billion with the majority of the promises going to states that border Mexico and would likely feel an immediate impact from NAFTA.[24]

The NAFTA victory boosted the confidence of President Clinton and gave him the support he felt he needed to hammer out agreements with other trading partners, such as the Japanese. As for the Latin Americans, the news of the vote was received with a sigh of relief and the recognition that their economies would be changed dramatically in the coming years. The end to trade barriers in Mexico, and eventually throughout the region, would not only allow the Latin Americans to increase their trade but would see more and more goods and services from the United States. With the United States selling Mexico over $33 billion worth of goods in 1991 before NAFTA, proponents of the accord were convinced that its passage would mean a continued acceleration of the trade. U.S. companies, from Reebok, which was interested in shortening its shipping time by relocating some operations from Asia to Mexico, to AT&T, which saw the agreement as enhancing its chances of entering the burgeoning Mexican telecommunications market, greeted NAFTA enthusiastically.

The passage of NAFTA by the House (and later the Senate in a much less contentious atmosphere) again reinforces the importance of adroit presidential persuasion and coalition building. Although there were marked differences between the *contra* debate and the NAFTA vote, the central role of the president working the Congress on behalf of his legislation and his beliefs provides a clear example of how public policy is made. What is interesting, however, in comparing the Reagan *contra* legislation with the Clinton NAFTA legislation is how much the world had changed in ten years and how the votes reflected that change. With the *contra* votes the debates were over familiar Cold War containment policies, admittedly dressed up differently, but basically no different from many others since World War II. With NAFTA, though, the vote was over the economic future of the United States in a vastly changed world community. In both cases the stakes were high, and the voices raised were filled with passion. But in a world where communism had collapsed, Congress was faced with not an enemy but a challenge wrapped in an opportunity—how to enter the global economy and profit from it without damaging the domestic employment base. The uncertainty of what lay ahead in the global economy and increased trade with Mexico made NAFTA a decision with profound and long-term implications.

OTHER GOVERNMENTAL PARTICIPANTS IN FOREIGN POLICY MAKING

The study of U.S. foreign policy making has often concentrated on the more obvious institutional participants: the president, the State Department, and the Congress. But as the United States has expanded its international trade, increased its development-assistance commitments, strengthened its information and cultural exchange programs, and continued to upgrade its defense posture, the number of participants and their impact on the conduct of foreign policy making has grown significantly. Again using Latin America as our field of study, let us examine some of these other governmental participants.

The Agency for International
Development and the Peace Corps

The Agency for International Development (AID) is responsible for U.S. foreign economic aid programs in the form of loans, grants, and technical assistance. AID, the chief development agency of the U.S. government, is charged with assisting the poorer countries of the world to raise their living standards and improve the quality of life. AID missions are active in most of the seventy-six countries receiving bilateral economic aid from the United States. In Latin America AID has permanent representation in each of the Central American countries as well as in Jamaica, Haiti, the Dominican Republic, Guyana, Ecuador, Bolivia, and Paraguay. Although AID programs cover a wide range of activities in Latin America, agency officials are primarily involved in agriculture, health care, education, and specific technical projects such as irrigation and road construction. Quite often AID officials will work closely with experts from other agencies such as the Department of Agriculture or the Department of Education to administer a particular program or complete a project.

In recent years AID has changed its mission in order to respond to new developmental challenges and tighter budgets. In President Clinton's FY 1995 international affairs budget, the restructuring of AID is evident in the type of programs it offers. In the budget authorization of $20 billion AID is involved in a number of areas that have direct impact on Latin America. The most important areas are in promoting U.S. prosperity through trade, investment, and employment; building democracy; promoting sustainable development; and providing humanitarian assistance. Of special interest for the region is AID's Countries in Transition program, which in recent years means assistance to strengthen the administration of justice, consolidation of democratic reforms, and institution-building. Also of importance are programs under the title of promoting sustainable development, such as new initiatives to deal with the spread of HIV/AIDS and the reduction of threats to the environment, particularly biodiversity and ozone depletion, which are especially troubling to Latin Americans.[25]

A vital part of the U.S. presence in Latin America and elsewhere in the Third World is the Peace Corps. Founded by President Kennedy, the Peace Corps today has close to 7,000 volunteers in 95 countries. Peace Corps volunteers in the 1990s are primarily technicians—carpenters agronomists, veterinarians, wildlife experts—who can provide a country with the expertise that will assist the development process in a small village or an outlying region. Latin America has always welcomed Peace Corps volunteers. During the early 1960s the Alliance for Progress program and the Peace Corps worked well together as examples of U.S. commitment to reform rather than revolution. Since those days Peace Corps volunteers can be found in most of the Caribbean ministates, in

Central America, and also Ecuador, Chile, and Paraguay. As a companion agency to the Peace Corps in Latin America is the Inter-American Foundation, which provides grants to private, grass-roots organizations to foster self-sufficiency through credit, technical assistance, training, and marketing services.

Trade Promotion and Investment Assistance

The United States has long been an active promoter of increased trade with Latin America. But to maintain that position the United States has developed a number of government entities and programs with the responsibility of stimulating trade in the region. The Commerce Department's Bureau of International Economic Policy has a large office for Mexican trade and one for the rest of Latin America. The Agriculture Department also has a foreign agricultural service that promotes trade in U.S. commodities. Also AID has gained responsibility for administering the Trade and Development Agency that assists in creating opportunities for American companies involved in the infrastructure and industrial sectors in Third World countries. These agencies often work through export-development offices that have been started in a number of Latin American cities, such as Mexico City; São Paulo, Brazil; and Caracas, Venezuela, and in Miami (which serves as the locus for Caribbean trade). The Miami office is especially active with its yearly trade convention that brings Caribbean officials and U.S. investors together to discuss the latest issues in trade and business. These offices and the programs they offer provide the United States with field representation that assists private companies in gaining access to Latin American markets and calming their fears about investing and doing business in the region.

Also invaluable to the private corporation seeking to develop a Latin American market is the Overseas Private Investment Corporation (OPIC). Established during the Nixon administration, OPIC provides qualified investors with political risk insurance, financial assistance, and investment counseling. Because OPIC's main concern is with helping to stimulate investment in the Third World, the knowledge that the U.S. government is not only backing their efforts but insuring them against the disruption of political unrest has encouraged reluctant businesses to expand their operations. The combined efforts of OPIC and the Export-Import Bank, which, as mentioned earlier, facilitates the financing of U.S. imports and exports and helps U.S. businesses to sell their goods abroad, provide the corporate sector with support services that ease their entry into the Latin American market.

Information and Cultural Exchange Centers

One of the more active government agencies in recent years is the United States Information Agency (USIA). Known abroad as the United States Information Service, this agency is responsible for educational and cultural exchange programs and for the dissemination of news and information about the United States. At U.S. embassies many of these duties are handled by the public affairs officer, but in some countries the work of the embassy is supplemented by the development of "American Centers," which may include libraries, exhibit halls, lecture facilities, and movie theaters. There are American Centers in Mexico, Panama, the Dominican Republic, Ecuador, Trinidad and Tobago, Guyana, Brazil, Argentina, and Uruguay. An integral part of the information-dissemination program of the United States Information Service is the international broadcasting system. The primary vehicle for the transmission of the news is the Voice of America (VOA), which sends U.S. programming all over the world. In Latin America the VOA broadcasts are now over eighty hours per week with either English language, Spanish, or Portuguese programming. VOA, like AID, was the target of budget cuts in President Reagan's second term. Broadcasts worldwide were cut by 10 percent and two programs that have benefited Latin Americans—the International Youth Exchange Program and the International Visitors Program—were reduced.[26] During the Clinton presidency the USIA underwent a massive restructuring effort to strengthen its reference and outreach services and to streamline its electronic news and policy information capabilities. The restructuring was undertaken to allow USIA to benefit from the state of the art electronic advances now emerging and to end costly duplication of international broadcasting.

The Drug Enforcement Agency

A fairly recent addition to the complement of U.S. personnel in Latin America is officers of the Drug Enforcement Agency (DEA). In the war on drugs the DEA agents are the frontline troops representing the United States in countries such as Colombia, Mexico, Bolivia, and Peru. Working with their counterparts in Latin America, DEA agents attempt to stem the flow of drugs that enter the United States from their source. The work of the DEA in Latin America is both frustrating and dangerous. Rampant corruption among government officials in many countries and the violent world of drug lords make the work of the DEA extremely difficult. The torture and execution of DEA agent Enrique Camarena in Mexico in 1985 highlighted the dangerous world of drug control. The death of Camarena and the subsequent stalled investigations into his murder created a period of tension between the United States and

Mexico over what U.S. leaders felt was footdragging by Mexican criminal justice officials.[27]

Because drug trafficking has now become a multibillion dollar industry, DEA agents have increased their presence in the region. On one occasion in 1986 DEA agents joined U.S. military personnel in staging a series of drug raids in Bolivia to destroy cocaine labs. Despite the heightened presence of DEA agents in Latin America and numerous high-profile programs, the job of combating drugs at the source is becoming nearly impossible. Besides corrupt officials and powerful drug organizations, DEA officials are increasingly facing governments that are too weak or afraid to cooperate and populations that see the drug kingpins as folk heroes. In Colombia, for example, the DEA agents stationed there have been particularly disturbed over the inability of the government to put an end to the drug cartels of Medellin and Cali. On numerous occasions U.S. drug operations have been compromised by leaks within the security forces of the government. Also a problem for the DEA is Colombian nationalism, which is accented whenever U.S. drug agents appear to overstep the legal or political boundaries in their zeal to arrest drug smugglers or destroy their base of operations. In the face of such enormous obstacles many DEA personnel feel they are fighting a losing war. Many Latin Americans are convinced that the U.S. approach to drug smuggling, which accents interdiction, is hopelessly flawed and that the United States should shift toward policies that strengthen the legal economy of the drug-producing nations.[28]

Military Mission

No discussion of this nation's foreign policy machinery would be complete without mentioning the armed forces. Although we often think of the military as agents of civilian foreign policy makers whose principal job is to protect this country, it is important to know that the military can be an influential participant in the policy deliberations that affect other countries. Pentagon officials and U.S. military officials in the field can play a significant role in charting future policy. Because presidents and top White House aides depend on reports from military commanders, their opinions and recommendations can be critical.

Top-level military officials are but the tip of the iceberg when discussing the influence of the armed forces in foreign policy making. As the chart of the U.S. embassy staff in Venezuela presented earlier (Figure 5.1) shows, the defense attaché and the head of a military advisory group are prominent members of the U.S. mission. In fact most Latin American embassy representatives from the four branches of the armed forces can be found functioning in advisory capacities. The title military attaché or military advisor covers a wide range of duties, from reporting on military affairs in a host country to training local units in the techniques of warfare, to serving as uniformed salesmen for U.S.

weaponry. In whatever capacity, the officers perform a valuable foreign policy function, especially since Latin America has a strong tradition of military rule. With the chances of a civilian president being replaced by a member of the local officer corps at least a possibility in most Latin American countries, it is essential that the embassy have competent military attachés who can develop close ties to these potential leaders.

With the emergence of viable democratic government in most of the Latin American nations and the subsequent decline of military influence the United States has deemphasized its substantial commitment to bolstering the armed forces in the region. Where the United States was once pumping billions of dollars in military assistance into countries like El Salvador and Honduras, the pipeline has dried up substantially with foreign assistance now going to democratic institution building. Where this country had over 11,000 troops stationed in Central America, the exit of the United States from Panama and the end of the civil war in El Salvador have meant sharp declines in manpower. (Strangely, the United States still retains its presence at the Palmerola base in Honduras where 1,200 U.S. troops rotate through the facility in connection with tracking drug smuggling at an estimated cost of over $50 million a year.) Where the United States viewed the military as a staunch opponent of communism in Latin America, the State Department and the Pentagon are now touting the armed forces as protectors of democracy.

It must be emphasized that the United States has not abandoned the Latin American military. There is still a good market for U.S. defense contractors who are interested in selling the Latin Americans aircraft, ships, and modern radar and communications equipment. The U.S. anti-narcotics campaigns in Colombia, Peru, and Bolivia, for example, work closely with the armed forces in the ongoing war on drugs and provide them with the training and weapons necessary to counteract the substantial private armies of the drug lords. The United States also continues its officer training programs at the U.S. Army School of the Americas at Fort Benning, Georgia, which, since it was established in 1946, has trained thousands of Latin American officers in professional military operations.

The School of the Americas was brought to the attention of Congress and the American people in 1994 when Congressman Joseph Kennedy of Massachusetts introduced legislation to abolish the school. Kennedy's argument against the continuation of the school was in his opinion the school's poor record of inculcating democratic values in the Latin American officers who attend the training program. Kennedy listed examples of graduates from Peru, Colombia, Honduras, Guatemala, and El Salvador who were implicated or convicted of human rights abuses. In particular Kennedy cited that two of the three army officers named in the 1980 murder of Archbishop Romero and nineteen of the twenty-six named as participants in the 1989 murders of the six Jesuit priests were graduates of the School of the Americas. In Kennedy's words, "Continued operation of the School of the Americas, with its history and tradition of abusive graduates, stands as a barrier to establishing a new and constructive relationship with Latin American militaries after the Cold War. And it continues to associate the United States with those abuses." But despite the forcefulness of Kennedy's argument the House refused by a vote of 256 to 174 to abolish the school with the majority convinced that more good than bad was achieved in training the officers to become democratic professionals.[29]

In the coming years the relationship between the United States and the Latin American military will continue to undergo a transition. The Southern Command, which is responsible for U.S. military operations in the hemisphere, was removed from its base in Panama and shifted to Miami. The role of the Latin American military in the war on drugs will undergo review as the Clinton administration wrestles with the best strategy for stemming the tide of illegal drugs into this country. The use of sanction and force against authoritarian regimes will remain a vexing problem, especially since the Pentagon and many in Congress are leery of interjecting U.S. troops to bring stability or enhance the environment for democratic governance.

Although the U.S. military presence in Central America is cause for alarm among those who fear the prospect of a slow march into another Vietnam, the role of the military in Latin America received the greatest attention when the issue of how best to fight drug smuggling was raised. When President Bush announced his war on drugs in the fall of 1989, the question arose regarding whether the administration should use the armed forces as a new weapon of interdiction. Liberals in Congress pressed the administration on the use of the military, stating that if this was indeed a true war, then troops must be used to combat the endless stream of drugs entering the United States. The military, for its part, was opposed to the transformation of its traditional mission of defending the country and had extensive support for this position from such key legislators as Senator Sam Nunn of Georgia. Nevertheless, the role of the U.S. armed forces had in part already been transformed with the establishment, prior to President Bush's speech, of two military task forces to detect and monitor the flow of drugs into the United States. The formation of the task forces signaled that the military may be expanding its role from defending the nation from its enemies to protecting its citizens from drug smugglers.[30]

NOTES

1.   See Roger Hilsman, "Policy-Making is Politics," in Charles W. Kegley, Jr. and Eugene R. Wittkopf, eds., *Perspectives on American Foreign Policy* (New York: St. Martin's, 1983), pp. 250–59.

2.   Thomas E. Cronin, in his article "A Resurgent Congress and the Imperial Presidents," *Political Science Quarterly* 95 (Summer 1980): 209–37, makes an analysis of the more recent tensions between Congress and the presidency.

3.   See George McKenna's discussion of the War Powers Resolution in his *Constitution: That Delicate Balance* (New York: Random House, 1984), pp. 45–57.

4.   See Kenneth Sharpe, "The Post-Vietnam Formula Under Siege: The Imperial Presidency and Central America," *Political Science Quarterly* 102, no. 4 (1987): 549–69.

5.   Seymour Hersh, *The Price of Power: Kissinger in the Nixon White House* (New York: Summit Books, 1983), pp. 273–96.

6.   Margaret C. Hermann, "Explaining Foreign Policy Behavior Using the Personal Characteristics of Political Leaders," *International Studies Quarterly* 24 (1980): 7–13.

7.   The classic study of presidential persuasion is Richard Neustadt's *Presidential Power* (New York: John Wiley, 1980).

8.   The most recent poll on U.S. attitudes toward Central America can be found in the Gallup Report 266, November 1987.

9.   Murray Kempton, "The Carter Mission," *New York Review of Books*, October 20, 1994, p. 71.

10.   See a discussion of the infighting within the Reagan administration in Barry Rubin, "Reagan Administration Policy Making and Central America," in Robert S. Leiken, ed., *Central America: Anatomy of Conflict* (New York: Pergamon, 1984), pp. 299–318.

11.   For an insider's discussion of the White House planning of the Haiti invasion see Ann Devroy, "Hostage to Haiti," *Washington Post Weekly Edition*, September 26–October 2, 1994, pp. 6–7. For a critique of Clinton foreign policy in Latin America and the Clinton foreign policy team see Howard Wiarda, *Democracy and Its Discontents* (Lanham, Md.: Rowman and Littlefield, forthcoming).

12.   Steven Holmes, "Envoy's Appointment Seen as Bid to Boost Foreign Service Morale," *New York Times*, March 27, 1993.

13.   Curtis Wilkie, "Ties Strained for Carter, State Department," Boston *Globe*, September 24, 1994.

14.   See I. M. Destler, "The Rise of the National Security Assistant 1961–1981," in Hugh Heclo and Lester Salamon, eds., *The Illusion of Presidential Government* (Boulder, Colo.: Westview Press, 1981), pp. 263–85. See also Loch K. Johnson, "Covert Action and Accountability: Decision-Making for America's Secret War," *International Studies Quarterly* 33, no. 1 (1989): 81–116.

15.   A congressional assessment of the CIA operations in Central America was published in 1982 that addresses many of these issues: "U.S. Intelligence Performance on Central America: Achievements and Selected Instances of Concern," Staff Report Sub-Committee on Oversight and Evaluation, Permanent Select Committee on Intelligence (September 22, 1982).

16.   "House Select Committee on Intelligence Requiring CIA to Inform Congress of Covert Activities," *New York Times*, April 5, 1984.

17.   See Walter Pincus, "Woolsey's Departure is Symptomatic of a Troubled Legacy," *Washington Post Weekly Edition*, January 2–8, 1995, pp. 31–32.

18.   Clinton Rossiter, "President and Congress in the 1960s," in Cyril Roseman et al., eds., *Dimensions of Political Analysis* (Englewood Cliffs, N.J.: Prentice Hall, 1964), p. 34.

19.   For a more detailed discussion of the *contra* votes see *Congressional Quarterly Almanac*, pp. 112–35. See also Cynthia J. Arnson, *Crossroads: Congress, The Reagan Administration and Central America* (New York: Pantheon Books, 1989).

20.   I. M. Destler, "The Elusive Consensus: Congress and Central America," in *Central America: Anatomy of Conflict*, edited by Robert Leiken, pp. 319–36 (New York: Pergamon Press, 1984).

21.   Statement of Thomas R. Donahue to Congress, September 22, 1992, Department of State, *Foreign Policy Bulletin*, November/December 1992, pp. 35–36.

22.   "As NAFTA Countdown Begins, Wheeling, Dealing Intensifies," *Congressional Quarterly*, November 13, 1993, pp. 3104–6.

23.   "Perot Gores His Own Ox in Debate," *Congressional Quarterly*, November 13, 1993, p. 3105.

24.   "Decisive Vote Brings Down Trade Walls with Mexico," *Congressional Quarterly*, November 20, 1993, pp. 3174–79.

25.   See "FY 1995 International Affairs Budget: A New Outlook and New Priorities," Department of State *Dispatch*, February 1994, pp. 3–4.

26.   *Fundamentals of U.S. Foreign Policy* (Washington, D.C.: U.S Department of State, March 1988), p. 94.

27.   See *Congressional Quarterly*, April 16, 1988, p. 998.

28.   See Gustavo A. Gorriti, "How to Fight the Drug War," *The Atlantic*, July 1989, pp. 70–76.

29.   See Bob Hohler, "House Rejects Bid to Close Army School," Boston *Globe*, May 21, 1994, p. 3.

30.   "House and Senate Approve Defense Budget of $450 Million to Fight Drug Wars," Boston *Globe*, September 4, 1989, p. 1.

6

Nongovernmental Participants in Latin American Policy Making

One of the U.S. political system's strengths is that it has always provided an opportunity for citizens with similar interests and opinions to form groups and petition government. Since the days of James Madison's defense of "factions" in Federalist Paper 10, the United States has viewed interest groups not only as organs of representation but as an effective means of influencing public policy formation. Today interest groups are an important part of the political process and they join with political parties as key conduits of public opinion. Interest groups have become so common on the national scene that there are few recognized organizations or causes that do not maintain offices in Washington in order to be near the nerve center of public policy making.

Although interest groups have been a prominent part of the governing process on the domestic scene, only recently has group activity in the foreign policy field experienced a dramatic growth spurt. Corporations, banks, arms merchants, and commodity traders have long been active in trying to influence U.S. foreign policy, primarily because they often serve as unofficial representatives of the United States in other countries. But only since World War II, and particularly since the Vietnam war, have a wide range of reformist, religious, and issue-oriented organizations joined the ranks of active interest groups seeking to gain access to governmental decision-making circles.

The explosion of interest-group activity has caused problems in formulating and implementing this country's foreign policy. Foreign policy making has now become so thoroughly democratized that it is no longer the sole domain of the president, Congress, and the State Department. Policy initiatives may emanate from these institutions, but along the way numerous interests seek to influence the final outcome. This eagerness to play a role in the foreign policy realm may make for a more democratic decision, but it also creates a policy that may be hopelessly compromised, unnecessarily delayed, and often played out in public forums rather than the quiet confines of diplomatic discussion.[1]

Latin American policy making has not been exempt from this interplay of interest groups and governmental institutions. A wide range of these nongovernmental participants have over the years formed a Latin American lobbying system. In the 1980s this system was made up of trade associations anxious to have government develop policies that open up new markets; human rights groups committed to using government as a means of pressuring foreign regimes to abide by the rule of law; agents of Latin American countries hopeful that the United States will follow a course of action beneficial to their own government; and labor unions seeking to protect jobs from foreign competition. Together these Latin American lobbyists provide a rich cross section of U.S. political life and, as can be expected, represent widely divergent views on the proper conduct of U.S. policy in the hemisphere.

THE BUSINESS LOBBY

The relationship between government and the corporate sector in Latin American policy development has long been recognized as critical. With hundreds of U.S. business firms investing over $89 billion in Latin America (1992 figures) and contributing significantly to the economic growth and modernization of almost every country in the region, the opinions and positions of corporate executives cannot easily be ignored by government decision makers. What is even more important about the connection between government and business in Latin American policy process is the organizational scope and strength of the corporate lobbying community. In addition to the lobbying efforts of individual companies, a number of major associations represent the interests of the business sector at large. These associations carry a great deal of weight as representatives of the business position toward key issues of Latin American policy.

The Council of the Americas

The Council of the Americas (COA), the primary associational lobby for business activity in Latin America, is the brainchild of David Rockefeller, the former chief of the Chase Manhattan Bank. The COA is supported by over 225 businesses that together control 90 percent of the U.S. equity in Latin America. Some of the top executives in the United States serve on its sixty-five–member board of directors and its administrative staff is considered to be the largest and perhaps most professional of the groups active in Latin American lobbying. Its 1992 budget of $2.75 million is the largest of any group seeking to advance interests in the hemisphere. But, as Lars Schoultz states in his analysis of the COA, the council's "major strength lies in its ability to link executives of member corporations and foreign policy makers of the highest levels of government."[2] COA pioneered this type of direct lobbying and has used personal friendships developed with government leaders as a powerful means of making its voice heard.

The COA also relies on its reputation for expertise in Latin American affairs to convince governmental leaders to adopt probusiness policies. In fact many presidents have relied upon the COA for advice on Latin American policy issues, such as trade enhancement, technology transfer, energy exploration, and investment opportunity. The major publication of the council, *Washington Report*, receives wide circulation in business and government circles and serves as a forum for new ideas and initiatives concerning the hemisphere.[3] The COA has become such a respected agent of the business community that it often works closely with an administration in formulating policy (especially if that administration is Republican). This ready access and reputation for expertise has made the COA a key lobbying force in Washington and the envy of other groups anxious to wield such influence.

The Association of American Chambers of Commerce in Latin America

Also of importance in the lobbying efforts of the business community is the role played by the Association of American Chambers of Commerce in Latin America (AACCLA). Founded in 1967, the AACCLA is a subsidiary of the American Chamber of Commerce and concentrates its lobbying in the areas of trade expansion and foreign investment for U.S. companies already active in Latin America or contemplating a move into the Latin American market. The AACCLA is made up of sixteen chambers that are headquartered in the major capitals of Latin America. In the last few years the AACCLA has been most concerned with lobbying in Congress to relax trade barriers between Latin American countries and for an expansion of Export-Import Bank loans to the region as one means of heightening the volume of trade. One study of business interests concerned with Latin America characterized the AACCLA as, "the most active business lobby intervening directly with Congress and the president with regard to U.S. Latin American relations." Although it cannot compete with the COA in terms of staff and reputation, the AACCLA is fast becoming a valuable additional voice for the Latin American business lobby and one that can claim to represent the views of corporate subscribers directly involved in the day-to-day problems of conducting business in Latin America.

The Caribbean and Latin American Action

One of the more recent additions to the business lobby for Latin America is the Caribbean/Latin American Action (C/LAA). Born out of the Reagan administration's Caribbean Basin Initiative, C/LAA has grown quickly into an organization that seeks to follow through on the president's charge to expand the U.S. business presence in the circum-Caribbean region. C/LAA was instrumental in helping to draft the Caribbean Basin Initiative and worked vigorously to ensure its passage. Its list of members includes many of the chief multinational corporations active in the region including United Brands, Tesoro Petroleum, R.J. Reynolds Industries, and Johnson & Johnson. David Rockefeller is a trustee of C/LAA and a strong advocate of President Reagan's Caribbean Basin Initiative.[4]

Like the other business groups, C/LAA holds seminars and conferences on investment opportunities, testifies before Congress on key policy issues, and presents position papers on pending legislation or executive initiatives. It has also developed new programs, such as a cooperative effort that links U.S. cities with Caribbean and Central American countries in an attempt to increase investment and encourage U.S. business access to the region. Despite its relatively recent emergence as a probusiness lobby, C/LAA also holds a yearly conference in Miami designed to bring together business and government leaders from the United States and the Caribbean Basin. In recent years C/LAA has been in the forefront of efforts to expand NAFTA to the countries of the Caribbean, Venezuela, and Colombia. It also lobbied for the Cuban Democracy Act of 1992 and was an outspoken critic of the Clinton administration's Haitian economic boycott on the grounds that it would destroy the small U.S. assembly industries in that country.

The Role of Key Multinationals in Latin American Policy Making

Individual corporations also play a key role in the formation of U.S. policy toward Latin America. Besides these umbrella associations, most major multinationals also maintain their own lobbyists and lobbying agenda because many times legislation or administrative action may affect a particular corporate investment. Although many Latin American issues and concerns may lead corporations to mount major lobbying campaigns, the example of International Telephone and Telegraph (ITT) in Chile suggests the impact that one company can have on U.S. policy.

In the late 1960s ITT had a considerable investment in the Chilean economy; it owned the nation's telephone system as well as a number of chemical and pharmaceutical factories and extensive real estate. When the election of socialist Salvador Allende became a real possibility in 1970, ITT, led by its chairman, Harold Geneen, pressed the Central Intelligence Agency (CIA) to join with the company to stop Allende's election by providing financial assistance to his electoral opponents. After a number of high-level contacts between ITT and the CIA, in which former CIA director John McCone (an ITT board member) acted as a go-between, the agency, then under the direction of Richard Helms, declined to become involved. The decision not to accept ITT's offer was made primarily because the U.S. ambassador to Chile, Edward Korry, was vehemently opposed to such covert government-business alliances.

ITT, however, did not cease its efforts to stop Allende. Chairman Geneen met with the CIA's clandestine operations chief for Latin America and offered to make a "substantial" contribution to the campaign for Jorge Alessandri, the conservative candidate for president. Despite official CIA disapproval, ITT on its own provided $350,000 in covert political assistance to Alessandri. Later on an internal review committee of ITT also found that under Geneen's order monies were funneled to the conservative newspaper *El Mercurio* to help in its public relations campaign against Allende. In 1970 ITT gave the newspaper $100,000 and in 1972 another $125,000.[5]

The lobbying campaign of ITT and its chairman, Harold Geneen, is not representative of the manner in which most U.S. corporations seek to influence U.S. policy or affect the internal politics of countries where they have lucrative investments. In fact other companies active in Chile at the time, such as General Motors, Ford, and IBM, were reluctant to become involved in economic pressure against Allende. Most multinationals expressed displeasure over Allende's policies and quietly supported the Nixon administration's destabilizing program, but the covert government-business connection proposed by Geneen was considered a "renegade" operation. What the ITT case does show, however, is how a major corporation can, if it wants to, use its resources, its connections, and its reputation to pressure government to act on its behalf. The access and influence exist for major companies if they wish to use it. Government may not always follow their policy suggestions, but most major companies certainly can get a foot in the door.

Much has changed for the U.S. business community since the days of ITT in Chile. In the era of free trade and privatization Latin American nations are much more receptive to multinationals and have dismantled restrictive measures designed to limit ownership and profits. As a result of this probusiness climate U.S. multinationals have flooded the Latin American market. Corporations from Pizza Hut, which has a strategy designed to open 400 restaurants by the year 2000, to General Motors, which is now the largest employer in Mexico, to the venerable Coca-Cola, which, as in the past, is everywhere in Latin America, are finding that expanding their operations in the hemisphere is smart business. Everyday in Washington or New York or Miami seminars are being held to introduce potential U.S. investors to Latin America and to encourage them to look to the hemisphere rather than to Asia or Eastern Europe when considering expanding their operations. In many respects the U.S. multinational presence in Latin America is reminiscent of the early twentieth century when major U.S. interests were welcomed to the region and were encouraged to use their capital and expertise to strengthen and modernize the economies of the host country. In a relatively short period of time U.S. multinationals have gone from the prime example of the ugly American to a key partner in regional development.[6]

Also of growing popularity as a means of changing the traditional corporate-host country relationship in Latin America is the formation, particularly in the Caribbean Basin, of duty-free industrial zones. Designed primarily to attract smaller companies or subsidiaries of larger corporations, the duty-free zones have become very attractive to U.S. businesses because they offer liberal tax benefits and lease arrangements. These duty-free zones, in countries like the Dominican Republic, Haiti, Barbados, and Jamaica, have become centers of extensive economic activity as U.S. firms seek to bring down costs. Unfortunately, what may benefit Latin America has created problems in the United States as corporate investment in duty-free zones is frequently criticized by labor leaders for taking work out of this country in order to save on labor costs and tax obligations.

THE BANKS

While the multinationals have redefined their involvement in Latin American economies (or in a number of cases have pulled up stakes and sought opportunities elsewhere), U.S. banks have become highly visible institutions in the region and the focus of intense policy debates. The importance of U.S. banks in Latin America is directly related to the enormous debt problem. During the 1970s, when petrodollars from inflated oil prices were entering U.S. banks, major banking institutions such as Chase Manhattan, Citibank, Manufacturers Hanover, and the Bank of Boston developed liberal loan policies and actively encouraged Latin American countries to borrow extensively for modernization projects. With demand heightening in Latin America for both expensive infrastructure facilities and social welfare programs, the Latin Americans were only too anxious to borrow from the U.S. banks. However, when the oil boom turned to the oil bust and a worldwide recession settled in, countries like Mexico, Brazil, Venezuela, and Argentina had accumulated huge debt obligations to U.S. banks.

Although the debt crisis threatened the very economic foundations of many Latin American countries, U.S. banks were also hit hard as country after country in the region either demanded a rescheduling of debt payments, proposed reduced compliance with the banks, or in some cases skirted perilously close to default. As a result of the angry reaction from the Latin Americans to meeting debt payment deadlines and intervention from the Reagan administration in the form of the so-called Baker Plan in 1985, which offered new proposals for solving the debt crisis, U.S. banks have been working diligently to address the debt problem. The Baker Plan, which coupled more loans with a request that

Latin American countries privatize their economies and begin dismantling their huge state enterprises, never really gained much steam and was criticized by Latin American nations as a new form of U.S. intervention.

With the onset of the Bush administration the accent was on trying to develop programs that partially forgave the debt. The Bush debt plan, often called the Brady Initiative (after Treasury Secretary Nicholas Brady) was generally viewed as more promising because the Latin Americans were adamant that debt forgiveness was essential if their economies were to rebound from years of recession. By the conclusion of 1989 the Bush administration had successfully negotiated two debt reduction deals: one with Mexico and one with Costa Rica. Although the agreement with Mexico was considered a landmark move to forgive large portions of debt while at the same time providing new international loans, the Latin Americans continued to express dismay that the United States and the private banks were not moving quickly enough to solve the debt crisis.[7]

While the Bush administration dealt with the realities of increasing Latin American debt, some U.S. banks simply wrote off part of the debt as a loss, while others developed complicated programs to have Latin American countries pay back the loans at reduced rates or sell the debt to third parties. Despite these efforts at reform the debt keeps piling up (there is an estimated 10 percent increase in interest charges yearly on the $400 billion debt obligation) and the banks continue to look for ways to manage a financial crisis that does not seem capable of resolution. The Clinton administration came into office with a view that the best answer for the Latin American debt problem was for the countries to grow out of their obligations by moving quickly and decisively toward free market practices. Clinton officials also stressed that keeping long-term interest rates low was a critical ingredient as even modest decreases in rates could reduce obligations by billions. The answer to the debt crisis may be in resurgent Latin American economies, but even then the nations of this region will remain dependent on outside sources of development capital. It thus appears that U.S. banks will remain critical actors in the policy process of Latin America for some time to come.

THE HUMAN RIGHTS LOBBY

One of the best examples of how interest-group activity in foreign policy development has increased in recent years is the number of human rights organizations that are now recognized participants in the areas of foreign assistance programing, human rights monitoring, and the relationship between U.S. policy and the democratization process in Latin American. Founded during the Nixon-Kissinger-Ford era, when this country worked closely with authoritarian regimes, these organizations are dedicated to a foreign policy founded on moral principles and are supportive of governments that follow the rule of the law. Human rights organizations have been especially active in Latin American affairs, and during the Carter presidency they attained a number of legislative and administrative victories, either cutting off aid to right-wing dictatorships or placing the United States on record as opposed to repression. Since the Carter years there have been peaks and valleys in terms of the U.S. commitment toward human rights in Latin America as evidenced by the go-slow posture toward the repressive military in El Salvador during the Reagan and Bush presidencies and the outspoken criticism of the Clinton administration toward the brutal regime in Haiti. But no matter what emphasis presidential administrations placed on human rights, various organizations have remained vigilant and outspoken in defense of those who have been abused, tortured, or murdered for political reasons.

The Washington Office on Latin America

One of the most visible human rights organizations currently working to curtail repression in Latin America is the Washington Office on Latin America (WOLA). Founded in 1974 by an amalgam of diverse religious organizations, WOLA regularly publishes a newsletter that is distributed widely throughout the United States and sponsors numerous seminars led by human rights activists from throughout Latin America. The newsletter and the gathering of data on human rights abuses are WOLA's primary tools, because one of the major roadblocks in the fight against repressive governments is proof that massacres, disappearances, and torture have occurred.[8] WOLA has also become a vigorous lobbyist with numerous contacts among liberal legislators who support human rights issues, such as Senator Edward Kennedy of Massachusetts and Senator Tom Harkin of Iowa. During the Carter administration, WOLA was viewed by many observers as the group to contact for the most reliable information and the most professional understanding of the intricacies of the policy process. But when the Reagan administration entered office, WOLA encountered difficulty in gaining access to policy discussions in the State Department and had less success in championing the cause of human rights as the focus in the 1980s turned toward containing communism. In the later years of the Reagan administration and in the Bush presidency WOLA was forced to function in a policy atmosphere that accented democratization in Latin America (support for elections and institution building) but not human rights monitoring. The Clinton presidency has reinvigorated WOLA but the failure of the administration to bring a quick end to the Haitian human rights tragedy convinced organization leaders that a sympathetic ear in the White House does not necessarily translate into positive results.

Amnesty International

A human rights organization with a much wider scope of interest is Amnesty International (AI). AI is headquartered in London and opened its Washington office in 1976. Probably the most prestigious of the human rights organizations, AI is primarily concerned with data collection and public awareness of human rights abuse. Because of its international reputation (including a Nobel Peace Prize), AI is viewed by many human rights advocates in Washington as the most authoritative source of information on the status of dissenters and political activists. Its 1973 report entitled *Amnesty International's Report on Torture* focused on a number of Latin American countries—specifically Chile, Uruguay, and Argentina—for human rights abuses. AI was also one of the leaders in developing a campaign of worldwide pressure on the Argentine government to curtail it "dirty war" against leftist opposition

In 1984, AI published a scathing report on human rights violations in El Salvador. Timed to come out during the inauguration festivities for President José Napoleon Duarte, the report cast doubt on the new president's ability to end the years of political murders, which AI estimated at 40,000.[9] In order to begin to restore personal rights and legality, the report stated that major changes would have to occur not only at the highest level of the military but also in the courts and among the local police.

As the turmoil in Central America intensified and authoritarian or weak democratic governments sought to control the political process, AI broadened its efforts to report on human rights abuse in the region. Its yearly human rights assessment, coupled with a number of critical studies of officially sanctioned repression in countries like Peru, Mexico, and Colombia, mistreatment of political prisoners in Cuba and Nicaragua, rural violence against peasants in Brazil, and disappearances of opposition leaders in Chile, have alerted the world to the continuing failure of governments to respect basic human rights.

One identifying characteristic of AI is its worldwide reputation and visibility because it has been willing to engage in high profile events to attract attention to particular human rights conditions. For example, its rock concert in Santiago, Chile, in the waning days of the Pinochet regime brought international stars, such as Sting and New Kids on the Block, to the country in an attempt to rally young people against the regime. AI has also taken the lead in developing and distributing a wide range of videos depicting the horrors of repression in Latin America and other parts of the world that are increasingly finding their way into a vast organizational structure on college campuses. These more contemporary tools of promoting human rights will likely keep AI in the forefront of the movement to strengthen democracy in Latin America and the rest of the world.

Church Lobbies

Religious organizations not only sponsor groups like the WOLA but also conduct their own information gathering and lobbying operations. Because many of these religious organizations are involved in missionary work in Latin America and, as in the case of the Catholic Church, have lost scores of priests, nuns, and lay ministers, they are increasingly active in the human rights movement. The National Council of Churches, which represents a number of Protestant denominations, was one of the first organizations to denounce right-wing repression in Latin America. The Office of International Justice and Peace of the United States Catholic Conference has also been quite active and was a vigorous critic of the Reagan administration's laxity in pushing for an early trial and conviction of those responsible for the murder of four U.S. churchwomen in El Salvador.

Individual Catholic orders, such as the Jesuits and the Maryknolls, have also joined in the lobbying efforts against current U.S. policy in Central America. The Maryknoll order in particular were among the most vocal critics of Reagan policy, and its priests, sisters, and brothers are some of the most politically active missionaries in Latin America, with some even joining guerrilla groups. Although Latin America is a predominantly Catholic region, other denominations can be found working there and involving themselves in the human rights struggle. The Mennonite Church, the Church of Jesus Christ of Latter-day Saints (Mormon), and the Church of the Brethren are but some of the missionary groups that have joined in lobbying efforts to influence U.S. human rights policy.

However, not all religious institutions are connected with the human rights lobby. Fundamentalist Christian organizations, such as Reverend Jerry Falwell's Baptist ministry, Reverend Pat Robertson of the nationally televised "700 Club," and evangelist Jimmy Swaggart, have all traveled to Latin America (Swaggart even preached the gospel in Marxist Nicaragua), established missionary organizations there, and have publicly lent their support to conservative groups and military officials active in anti-communist politics. Falwell, for example, backed General Rios Montt of Guatemala in his successful coup attempt primarily because of Montt's virulent anti-communism and also because the general was a born-again Christian. The active support of many U.S. fundamentalist preachers for conservative forces in Latin America does not mean that these ministers endorse the human rights abuses of right-wing regimes but, rather, that they are more concerned with stopping the spread of communism in Central America and are convinced that a strong military presence is necessary to achieve that goal. Also, these fundamentalist groups are opposed to the supporters, primarily in the Catholic Church, of what has come to be called Liberation Theology, which mixes the gospel of Christ with an active and sometimes violent struggle to achieve human rights. To the fundamentalist, the Christian religion is to be spread to the people and not used as a means of bringing about social and political change.

Other Members of the Human Rights Lobby

Several less prominent groups are also working to influence U.S. policy. Organizations such as Americas Watch have emerged as vigorous monitors of human rights abuse in Latin America. Based in New York City, Americas Watch gained a reputation for calling attention to the Indian massacres in Guatemala. During the civil war in El Salvador, Americas Watch was outspoken in its criticism of the rightist regime, especially during the period after the execution of the six Jesuit priests in 1989 and in the documentation of the killings in remote villages by U.S.-trained elite military units of the Salvadoran military.[10] Also gaining attention in recent years for its dedication to human rights monitoring is the Lawyer's Committee for Human Rights. This organization has been active not only in calling attention to human rights abuse but in using its expertise to seek damages from those responsible for torture and death and to deny access to the United States to those linked to human rights violations. Joseph Eldridge, a long-time advocate for human rights in Latin America and former director of WOLA, is the Washington director of the Lawyer's Committee for Human Rights. Mention must also be made of the Quaker-based Friends Committee on National Legislation (an original backer of the Harkin Amendment, which denied economic aid to countries with gross violations of human rights) and the International Commission of Jurists (one of the first groups to alert the U.S. public through a massive newspaper campaign to the extensive human rights abuses in Chile), which continue to press the government for a strong human rights policy toward Latin America. Besides saving lives, these groups aim to gain enough influence in government so that human rights concerns become a common ingredient in foreign policy development. So far it has been an uphill battle with many disappointments, but the number of groups joining the human rights lobby attests to their resolve and their belief that moral principles have a place in the conduct of U.S. foreign policy.

AGENTS OF LATIN AMERICAN GOVERNMENTS

Diplomats and U.S.–based agents of Latin American countries also play an important role in the policy process. Traditionally, diplomatic representatives of foreign countries are frontline lobbyists who advocate their government's position at the highest levels. With ready access to State Department officials, and in many instances the National Security Council, these diplomats can have a powerful impact on policy, especially if the country they represent is on good terms with the United States or is seen as a strategic economic ally.

Although the lobbying agendas of Latin American countries vary based on their domestic political circumstances and regional issues, embassy staffs have in recent years been most concerned with levels of economic and military assistance, possible reductions in commodity quotas, surcharges on exports bound for the United States, and government policies that allow for greater entry of foreign goods into this country. Small, poverty-stricken countries like the Dominican Republic have been working through official channels for years to pressure the United States to increase its quota of sugar while battling domestic sugar-beet producers who do not want the U.S. market flooded with foreign sugar. Likewise, major industrial giants like Brazil have been active (and largely successful) in lowering the surcharge on shoes entering the United States, a very sensitive issue because the shoe industry in this country has entered a serious decline primarily because of cheaper foreign-made footwear.[11]

In addition to their own diplomats, many Latin American nations also use paid agents, either U.S. law officers, advertising firms, or private individuals with experience in Latin American affairs. In particular, countries with a negative image in the United States, such as Guatemala and Chile, or those with their very existence at stake, such as Somoza's Nicaragua in the late 1970s, depend upon extra diplomatic assistance to ensure a constant flow of aid or a continuation of official U.S. support. The task of these agents is not only to gain influence within the executive branch or among congressional leaders but also to present through various media a favorable picture of life in the country that is paying for their services. Purchasing newspaper ads, promoting television interviews with key government officials, providing tourist vacations for influential reporters, and developing newsletters that extol the virtues of visiting or investing in the country are but some of the techniques used by these agents.

Because private U.S. representatives of Latin American governments operate as lobbyists in the executive and legislative branches and negotiate contracts that are often substantial, the United States requires that these agents register with the Justice Department under the Foreign Agents Registration Act and report semiannually on their activities. The Foreign Agents Registration Act requirement, however, is often seen in Latin America as a formality of doing business rather than as a check on questionable or unethical lobbying practices. On occasion, these agents overstep the bounds of legality in their lobbying efforts, but Latin American governments often insist that advertising agencies or consulting firms do not embarrass them by breaking the law.

Despite the legal and practical restrictions placed on this type of lobbying, agents of Latin American governments can mount aggressive and costly campaigns on behalf of their clients. Perhaps the best example is the case of Nicaraguan dictator Anastasio Somoza and his attempt to assure the continued flow of U.S. assistance in the face of mounting administrative and congressional opposition to his regime. As documented by Lars Schoultz, the Nicaraguan government spent over $570,000 between 1975 and 1977 on public relations because the Somoza regime wanted to develop a more favorable image of Nicaragua and its president. Complementing his effort was the work done by two Washington attorneys, William Cramer and Fred Korth, who agreed, for a hefty retainer, to contact government officials on behalf of the Nicaraguan government. As the support for Somoza waned in Congress, the Nicaraguan dictator intensified his lobbying campaign, paying Cramer $150,000 in 1978 to pressure representatives and to from new lobbying organizations such as the Nicaraguan-American Trade Council to enhance further the image of Nicaragua.[12]

One of Cramer's primary lobbying tactics was to utilize his past membership in Congress. Through personal contacts, telegrams, and a barrage of pro-Somoza information, Cramer sought to convince his former colleagues that failing to back the Nicaraguan president and provide his government with aid would be a major strategic mistake and a betrayal of one of the staunchest allies of the United States. While Cramer was conducting his congressional lobbying campaign, the other attorney, Fred Korth, was concentrating on convincing key representatives such as Charles Wilson of Texas that it was dangerous not to support Somoza. The personal relationship between Korth and Wilson paid off as the influential Democratic leader championed the fight to restore $3.1 million in military aid to Nicaragua.

Whereas Cramer and Korth were active during the waning years of the Carter administration trying to improve the image of the Somoza regime, the work of foreign agents during the Reagan years was directed mainly at counteracting unfavorable impressions of authoritarian leaders and regimes connected to drug smuggling. These were the years that Central American generals hired Washington public relations firms to clean up their image in order to open up military sales or to stall congressional investigations. Members of George Bush's campaign staff were accused of working to enhance the reputation of the Bahamas and its prime minister Linden Pindling at a time when Pindling was under suspicion of receiving drug payoffs in return for allowing the Bahamas to be used as a shipment point for the drug trade. The public relations contract with the Washington firm of Black, Monafort and Stone showed the importance that Latin American governments place on presenting a favorable image in Washington. In this case of image building, however, the Bush campaign was embarrassed that those close to the Republican candidate for president would accept a contract with someone whose reputation was suspect.

The Clinton administration was not immune to controversy connected to high priced agents of Latin American governments. Secretary of Commerce Ron Brown had a bumpy road to confirmation in 1993 in large part because he received a $12,500 per month lobbying fee from 1982–86 from Haiti's dictator, Jean-Claude Duvalier. During the lengthy and contentious NAFTA debate Mexican officials spent millions of dollars trying to gain passage of the trade agreement even though President Clinton, during the campaign, criticized the involvement of foreign agents in the domestic political process. One independent study of the lobbying effort stated, "In the context of lobbying by foreign interests on a specific issue, Mexico has mounted the most expensive, elaborate campaign ever conducted in the United States by a foreign government."[13]

Despite the fact that lobbying efforts on behalf of Latin American governments and leaders can on occasion reveal the seamier side of image building, the use of paid agents to promote a regime and lobby for its interests is now a common means of influencing Latin American policy. As long as image making, information dissemination, and personal contact remain vital components of the lobbying process, foreign governments will supplement their diplomatic efforts with other professional assistance.

THE *CONTRA* LOBBY

One of the most controversial lobbying efforts to influence the U.S. policy on Latin America was the work of conservatives anxious to maintain the flow of military supplies to the *contra* rebels. In the face of congressional restrictions on lethal assistance to the *contras*, private programs to aid the rebels began in 1984 when conservative fund-raiser Carl R. Channel collected millions of dollars from private citizens. Although the fund-raising of Channel was eventually exposed as fraudulent (Channel pleaded guilty to mail fraud in 1987), the private assistance programs on behalf of the *contras* continued.

At the height of the congressional debates over *contra* aid in 1987 and 1988 organizations, such as Citizens for Reagan and the Council for Inter-American Security, used direct mailings and relentless pressure on members of Congress to advance the administration's *contra* aid package. Citizens for Reagan sent out Nicaraguan Action Kits containing bumper stickers ("Free Nicaragua"); postcards showing Daniel Ortega, Fidel Castro, and Muammar Khadafi together; and other visual reminders of the left-wing bent of the Sandinistas. The Council for Inter-American Security also relied heavily on public relations ploys and offers to present the slide show used by Lt. Col. Oliver North to prove the Sandinista expansionist intentions to their contributors.

But once Congress rejected military aid, *contra* supporters shifted their emphasis toward campaigns that solicited humanitarian aid for the rebels. Organizations such as the Nicaraguan Resistance-USA and the Nicaragua Resistance Educational Foundation acquired tax-exempt status and began soliciting funds for food, medicine, and clothing so that, according to the statement from Nicaraguan Resistance-USA, "the pro-Sandinista liberals in Congress must not be allowed to destroy the Nicaraguan Resistance."[14]

Because the Bush administration showed little interest in continuing U.S. involvement in Central America and the internal situation in Nicaragua and El Salvador changed, the *contra* lobby faded from the scene. Today the *contra* lobby has been replaced by what is commonly called the Central American lobby, a loose grouping of organizations interested in pursuing human rights claims against governments, attracting trade and investment opportunities to the region, and building social and political institutions. The diversity of interests in Central America in the 1990s is a testament to how quickly the region changed from the days in which the *contras* occupied center stage in the U.S. political process.

THE CUBA LOBBY

While the *contra* lobby is no longer a factor in the U.S. political process, it has been replaced by an equally powerful and passionate movement. The Cuba lobby, which has as its primary goal the removal of Fidel Castro and communism from Cuba, has been an integral part of U.S. policy in the hemisphere ever since the revolution that overthrew U.S.–backed Fulgencio Batista in 1959. In the early years of Castro's rule anti-communist Cubans who fled to Florida organized paramilitary groups, such as Alpha 66, and trained for the day when they would be permitted to liberate their homeland. But when the Bay of Pigs invasion failed and Castro consolidated his power, Cubans in the United States turned their attention toward other methods of weakening the regime while placing unrelenting pressure on Washington policy makers to further isolate the Havana regime.

With the victory of Ronald Reagan in 1980 Cuban-Americans saw the opportunity to intensify their efforts to shift U.S. policy away from the accommodationist mode taken by the Ford and Carter administrations to one of hard-nosed isolation. With Reagan focused on anti-communism in the hemisphere and Secretary of State Alexander Haig stating that the United States would "go to the source" of revolution in the region, Cuban-Americans moved quickly to advance their agenda. At the center of the efforts to isolate Castro's Cuba was the Cuban American National Foundation (CANF) and its controversial leader Jorge Mas Canosa, a participant in the Bay of Pigs invasion and dedicated anti-communist. Mas Canosa has transformed CANF into a major player in the foreign policy scene in Washington. He has been described as a well-connected voice for a democratic Cuba and a relentless force for bringing an end to the Castro regime.

CANF's major contribution to its cause was its successful lobbying effort on behalf of the Cuban Democracy Act of 1992, which tightened trade ties with Cuba and sent a clear signal to Castro that the United States was not interested in normalizing relations with Havana. CANF was able to pressure President Clinton to withdraw the name of Mario Baeza, a New York lawyer of Cuban descent, from consideration as the Assistant Secretary of Inter-American Affairs, in large part because Mas Canosa felt Baeza would not bring a strong enough anti-Castro voice to the policy process. CANF has also been successful in stalling efforts by the Congress to end the TV Marti program, which beams television programs to Cuba from a base in Florida. Although Castro jams most of the programs and viewing is limited to early morning hours by those Cubans with access to satellite dishes, CANF has been able to keep this costly anti-Castro program alive.[15]

Mas Canosa and CANF continue to pressure Washington policy makers even though the heady days of support from Reagan, Bush, Oliver North, and Jeane Kirkpatrick are over. As David Dent says in his detailed analysis of the interest group techniques of the Cuba lobby, "The Cuba Lobby continues to exercise power over Cuba policy in Washington, with PAC contributions to candidates (both Republicans and Democrats) sympathetic to CANF's goals and objectives and personal links to the White House through Clinton's relatives in Miami."[16] It is expected that the Cuba lobby will continue to be a force to reckon with in U.S. policy circles. Groups like CANF are well funded by the Miami exile community; they publish anti-Castro literature and distribute it widely; they have become effective supporters of candidates for Congress who carry their message; and they are not reluctant to intimidate those who would propose policies that accent normalization of relations. Despite the fact that Fidel Castro is increasingly showing signs of opening up his country and reentering the world community of nations, the Cuba lobby is moving in the opposite direction as it works to isolate and, if possible, remove the dictator from power.

THE LABOR LOBBY

The role of U.S. labor and labor unions in the development of U.S. policy toward Latin America may not be readily apparent, because workers' issues have traditionally been viewed as domestic rather than international in nature. Yet U.S. workers, and in particular U.S. unions, have long taken an interest in government policies toward Latin America. The major union confederation in the United States, the AFL-CIO, publishes a yearly statement of principles and positions that outlines not only its "bread and butter" economic concerns but also its stance on a number of foreign policy issues. As might be expected, the

AFL-CIO has been most active as a foreign policy lobbyist on issues that
have an impact on the job market in the United States. For instance,
legislation to stop illegal immigration into this country has been a top
priority for labor. Union officials claim that unemployment would drop
by 30 to 40 percent if our borders were better patrolled and businesses
were prosecuted for hiring illegals. Also the AFL-CIO has been consistent through Democratic and Republican administrations in its
opposition to free trade policies that jeopardize domestic employment.
Some of the leading proponents of protectionist trade legislation in this
country belong to the U.S. labor movement. Finally, the AFL-CIO has
been a frequent critic of investment policies promoted by federal agencies, such as the Export-Import Bank and the Overseas Private Investment Council, which encourage U.S. businesses to shift their operations
to Latin America where labor costs are cheaper. Labor leaders point out
that although such investment may be good for business and for the
economy of the host country, it reduces the job opportunities of the U.S.
worker.[17]

Although the AFL-CIO and its member unions focus their efforts on
government policies that affect the job market, it is possible to see the
labor lobby at work in areas such as enhancing the union movement in
Latin America. Since the cold war era of the 1950s, the AFL-CIO has
worked to support, both financially and through training programs,
labor unions and labor union leaders who were committed to forming
democratic and pro–U.S. organizations. During the Reagan administration the AFL-CIO joined with the U.S. Chamber of Commerce to help
initiate the National Endowment for Democracy, a program designed to
assist the growth of democracy and pluralism in Latin America. Many
of the program's participants are current or future labor leaders who it
is hoped will return to their country imbued with the spirit of democratic principles.

Working closely with the AFL-CIO in the unionization of Latin
America is the American Institute for Free Labor Development
(AIFLD). Founded in 1960 with a $20,000 grant from the AFL-CIO,
AIFLD has been the leading force in training Latin American labor
leaders. Since its inception AIFLD has worked closely with the United
States and is now a familiar participant in U.S. aid programs in Latin
America. At present AIFLD receives almost all of its funds from federal
budget allocations, although there is some foundation support. Staff
members concentrate their education and organization efforts on in-
country seminars or conferences at the George Meaney Center of Labor
Studies in Silver Spring, Maryland. Thousands of union leaders have
been trained in organization techniques, collective bargaining, financing, and industrial relations. The institute also funds a number of
grammar schools, clinics, and community centers in Latin America.

The most striking characteristic of AIFLD is its strong anti-communist posture, which is the reason for its long involvement in official

U.S. programs. Long-time executive director of AIFLD, William Doherty, was accused by many Latin American leftists of developing the institute into a covert arm of the CIA responsible for inciting labor unrest against socialist governments, such as the Goulart regime in Brazil in 1964 and the government of the Marxist Cheddi Jagan in Guyana in the 1960s. Recently AIFLD was closely involved with the State Department, National Endowment for Democracy, and the CIA in weakening support for the Sandinista movement in the critical 1990 presidential elections. This involvement renewed calls for an end of AIFLD's involvement in issues related to U.S. foreign policy in Latin America. Although U.S. union leaders disagree as to whether the AFL-CIO should continue to support the work of AIFLD, the linkage between these two organizations remains solid. The prevailing position among union officials is that promoting prodemocratic unionism and "assisting" the U.S. government in combating left-wing infiltration of the Latin American working class serves as a counterforce to the extensive network of communist union organizers in the hemisphere.[18]

Although U.S. union leaders disagree as to whether the labor movement should support the political activities of AIFLD, there is general agreement that a need exists to build strong democratic labor organizations in Latin America. As a result AIFLD appears to have shed its image as an anti-communist arm of the U.S. government. Today AIFLD concentrates on institution-building in the hemisphere and keeps a wary eye out for union-busting techniques in the duty-free zones of the Caribbean and Central America and the *maquiladoras* of Mexico.

Latin America is not often thought of as a region where union activity plays a critical part in internal politics. But both the AFL-CIO and AIFLD are convinced that the U.S. labor movement must foster pro–U.S. attitudes among the workers. Because working-class opposition to existing governments is at the root of leftist revolution, labor confederations like the AFL-CIO are increasingly conscious of their responsibility to contribute to a favorable union climate in these countries, while AIFLD is committed to ensuring that labor leaders who hold democratic values are given an opportunity to rise to positions of power within their country.

THE ROLE OF NEWSPAPERS, TELEVISION, AND THINK TANKS

While the four groups just discussed act as lobbyists for interests related to Latin American affairs, newspapers, television networks, and academic think tanks participate in the policy process primarily as opinion shapers. Although these institutions cannot be considered interest groups per se, there is no doubt that by presenting the news, broadcasting programs, and engaging in research, newspapers, television, and think tanks are powerful agents of influence. Foreign policy decision makers have consistently maintained close ties with reporters, anchorpersons, and academic scholars as a way of gaining a sense of public opinion, generating grassroots support for specific initiatives, or obtaining a different perspective on a public policy. As a result the relationship between government and these three kinds of institutions has grown significantly as administrative and congressional leaders alike have come to see the benefits that can be attained by utilizing the services and the vast potential for public opinion formation that newspapers, television, and think tanks can provide.

Newspapers and Latin American Policy

The role of U.S. newspapers in U.S. policy development toward the hemisphere is a long and colorful one, dating back to the yellow journalism days around the turn of the century, when the Hearst papers reflected the rising tide of nationalism and consciousness of international power that accompanied this country's expansionist policies in Latin America. In many instances newspapers were responsible for galvanizing public opinion and for pressing presidential administrations to adopt policies that they were not always prepared to follow.

Today U.S. newspapers are much less involved in the kind of rabble-rousing and jingoism that characterized newspaper publication at the turn of the century, but that does not mean that newspapers have ceased trying to influence public opinion or sway executive or legislative decision making. Major newspapers such as the New York *Times*, the Washington *Post*, the Boston *Globe*, the Chicago *Tribune*, and the Los Angeles *Times*, along with the news services, all employ reporters who cover Latin America regularly and have in a number of cases become expert analysts of U.S. policy in the region.

The power of the press, however, comes not only from its reporting and analysis of events in Latin America but also from the editorial position taken on key issues of U.S. relations in the hemisphere. With readerships in the hundreds of thousands, newspapers like the New York *Times* and the Washington *Post* can have a major impact on a particular government policy. Furthermore, newspapers are read not only by the average U.S. citizen but also by administration officials, members of Congress, and other participants in the policy process. An editorial position for or against a particular policy can influence the course of a debate within the circle of decision makers. Public policy is certainly not a captive of the press, but many of the policy debates are fought on the pages of major newspapers and these reports become the backdrop against which public opinion is formed. The press in past years was instrumental in shaping public opinion against the U.S. involvement in Vietnam. The press in the 1980s faced a key challenge with respect to this country's involvement in Central America. Although editorial positions and the presentation of the news on Central America varies from paper to paper and from region to region, the reporting on right-wing death squads, conservative intransigence to fundamental reforms, and the military success of the guerrillas has been at least partly responsible for public opposition to further U.S. commitments in this region.[19] The Reagan administration's occasional hostility toward influential newspapers that criticized the government's approach to this region showed the president's concern for the ability of the press to limit his power to control the foreign policy process in this country. Despite the periodic blasts at the press, Reagan knew that his foreign policy decisions would continue to be scrutinized by newspaper reporters and editors and evaluated by the U.S. public.

In the 1990s the press was immersed in the issues of free trade and immigration. The NAFTA debate in 1993 was covered in detail as reporters and editors attempted to explain the complex and on occasion arcane characteristics of breaking down tariff barriers. The issue of job loss, particularly in the industrial centers of the country, created deep fissures within newspaper editorial boards as the long-term benefits of free trade collided with the short-term pain from unemployment. In those states that were affected by the flow of illegal immigration, newspapers also struggled with the dilemma of this country's traditional open door policy and the domestic pressures to rein in the flood of migrants to our shores. Editorial by-lines and letters to the editor reflected the deep-seated fissures in public opinion about immigration. In both cases, however, the newspapers served as essential forums for contrasting views and allowed complex issues to be explained in ways that television could not.

Television Networks and Latin American Policy

Perhaps the most powerful institution influencing public policy in the United States today is television. Through the medium of television the U.S. public can sit at home and observe the implementation of foreign policy decisions. It can see an election in El Salvador, a revolution in Nicaragua, and an invasion in Panama. The images of Latin American policy at work that television presents to the U.S. public can be a boon to an administration policy or they can undermine its promotion and justification. The Reagan administration, for example, criticized the frequent televised stories that showed in vivid detail the atrocities committed by Salvadoran death squads. For an administration seeking to promote El Salvador as an emerging democracy, the pictures of bullet-ridden peasants made it difficult to convince the U.S. public and Congress to continue supporting existing policy. During the Clinton administration television served up heart-wrenching images of Haitian boat people and in the process made even more difficult the government's task of making foreign policy decisions in an impassioned and neutral manner.

The power of television in the foreign policy arena was tested, and some say compromised, when the Reagan administration refused to allow network coverage of the Grenada invasion. Citing security concerns, the administration agreed with the Defense Department that television crews would hamper the operation. The television networks were outraged by this censorship (the first such censorship of wartime coverage since the Civil War), but were obliged to follow the guidelines set by the administration. Critics of the Reagan decision to limit television coverage argued that the administration was worried about the potentially negative domestic reaction to the invasion. Strangely, the administration, after it became aware of the Grenadian's support for the U.S. armed forces, permitted extensive coverage of the post-invasion clean-up, in which painted walls hailed the United States with slogans such as "God Bless Ronald Reagan."

But where the government can limit access to television coverage of war and deny newspeople the ability to evaluate a military expedition, government officials can use television as a means of presenting their views, justifying their policies, and on occasion enhancing their image. One of the most memorable episodes of "television politics" or "television policy making" in recent memory was the nine-minute interview-exchange between Dan Rather of CBS and Vice President George Bush in 1988 over the Iran-*contra* scandal. Vice President Bush consented to be interviewed by Rather to clarify his involvement in the *contra* arms sales. Once the live interchange began, Bush and Rather got into a no-holds-barred media confrontation that left viewers stunned. Bush repeatedly denied his knowledge of the arms sales, while Rather attempted to link the vice president to the illegal policy decisions. The confrontation was a powerful event that further established television not only as the premier source of information and analysis in our society but as an institution that has become an additional check on executive power.

With nearly every household in the United States owning a television and with the U.S. populace increasingly relying on video sources for information, network news programs and documentaries will continue to shape public opinion. The government will also continue to devise strategies that help it use television to promote or justify its policies. It will be the responsibility of the U.S. populace to recognize the advantages of television as a means of information gathering, while also seeing the dangers that can arise when government or the networks seek to manage the news or package it in a misleading way.

Think Tanks and Latin American Policy

Academicians, whether in the university or in privately endowed think tanks, have long been interested in Latin America and the Latin American policy of the United States. No other part of the world, except perhaps Western Europe, has gained as much scholarly attention as Latin America. Latin American specialists are found in most major universities and colleges, Latin American studies concentrations are quite common as academic disciplines, and doctoral dissertations on Latin American issues remain popular topics for graduate students. In the policy area, though, it is the private think tanks that are most active in seeking to influence the decision-making process through their research, publications, seminars, public forums, and other informational enterprises.

Because government has increasingly approached think tanks for consultation and support, these institutions have assumed an ideological bent, with Republicans and Democrats, liberals and conservatives, aligning themselves with specific think tank operations. On the conservative side, both the Reagan and Bush administrations developed close ties with the Hoover Institution at Stanford University, the American Enterprise Institute, and the Heritage Foundation, which evolved as the primary source of think tank policy analysis for Republicans. On the liberal side, the Council of Hemispheric Affairs and its director, Larry Birns, is an important voice, while the more leftist Institute for Policy Studies can be counted on to take highly visible positions against the presence of multinationals in Latin America. Although not a think tank, the Latin American Studies Association, the principal academic organization for the region, has a clear liberal proclivity and has in the past taken positions in support of revolutionary governments. The center of the ideological spectrum is jointly occupied by the Brookings Institution, the Foreign Policy Research Institute, and the Council on Foreign Relations. The Council on Foreign Relations, which is centered in New York, publishes the prestigious journal *Foreign Affairs*.

These and other smaller think tanks help fill the growing need for government to rely on outside expert opinion in the formulation of public policy. Even though government has a talented corps of experienced career diplomats and analysts, the thirst for "second opinions" is so great that the professional think tank has become a permanent fixture in foreign policy formulation. To some this explosion of experts and expertise may serve to cloud an issue rather than clear the air, but in the current policy system think tank analysis has become an essential requisite of policy making. More important, it has become part of partisan politics, with one party using its experts to challenge the interpretations of the other party's experts. There is no doubt that the think tanks make valuable contributions to the analysis and debate on current policy, but they are also living proof of how specialized and intricate the foreign policy process has become.

THE U.S. POPULACE AND LATIN AMERICAN POLICY

The U.S. populace is not often thought of as an interest group because it is not a formal organization and rarely acts as a unified lobbying force. Historically the U.S. public has often articulated opinions about Latin American affairs from a narrow, stereotypical perspective. To many Americans life in the region to their south is dominated by soccer, sandy beaches, and breakfast commodities like coffee, sugar, and bananas. But when properly focused or when a crisis arises, the opinions of the U.S. public and actions in support of or in opposition to the government can have a powerful impact on the direction of hemispheric policy. The U.S. citizenry's participation in matters of foreign policy has primarily been as a sounding board for administration initiatives. Modern presidents have become diligent poll watchers to see how a particular policy is "playing" in various parts of the country or among various subgroups of the U.S. electorate. A negative public reaction to an administration policy can be a powerful check and may force the government to reevaluate if not rescind its action.

U.S. public opinion, however, cannot be seen as a consistent means of influencing foreign policy makers. Quite often public opinion polls show either widespread ambivalence on a particular issue or ignorance of the policy alternative being debated. The U.S. populace has traditionally placed greater emphasis on domestic concerns and has left foreign policy up to the president; thus, the public too often is ill prepared for or uninterested in influencing policy. The U.S. public in general may possess some broad opinions such as an aversion to war or a fear of communist expansionism, but the people are reluctant to apply those feelings to individual situations. People's aversion to immerse themselves in questions of foreign policy usually allows the president a bit of breathing room in the formulation of his position, sometimes just enough time to push the policy through before public opinion coheres.

Studies of U.S. policy development during our involvement in Central America reveal these problems of ambivalence, ignorance, and reluctance to move beyond general principles to specific application. Everett Carl Ladd, in a study of public attitudes on Central America, found the U.S. public "woefully uninformed" about Central America but nevertheless committed to supporting a U.S. policy aimed at containing what the people felt was a communist threat to our national security.[20] Other studies by pollsters such as George Gallup show that the U.S. public is basically cautious about a major commitment in El Salvador. When asked the specific question of whether U.S. troops should be sent to Central America to stop the spread of communism, the answer was a resounding "no."[21] This dual fear of communism and of possible entry into war mirrors the growing debate in Congress over the correct approach to the instability in this vital region. Because the people are ambivalent about what this country's policy in Central America should be, it is no surprise that the legislators who represent the people are themselves divided.

The unwillingness of the American people to support Reagan administration policy in Central America led some of the president's advisors to develop programs designed to sway public opinion, even if questionable and illegal methods were used. In a report in 1988 made to the House Foreign Affairs Committee it was revealed that the CIA in union with the National Security Council and a little-known agency of the State Department developed and implemented "a domestic propaganda campaign designed to win public support for U.S. policy in Central America," The program, which sought to place favorable articles in newspapers, arrange interviews with *contra* spokesmen, place large numbers of government-sponsored materials in college libraries, and send advocates of administration policy on speaking tours, created a stir in Washington because the CIA is prohibited from involvement in domestic affairs and the individuals who ran the program kept it secret from Congress.[22]

More recently, the link between public opinion formation and Latin American policy has been critical. In both the NAFTA debate and the Haitian crisis the Clinton administration and its opponents used a wide range of strategies to shape opinion and to influence executive and legislative decision makers. The NAFTA debate was a public opinion showcase as television commercials, newspaper advertisements, interest group demonstrations, the Gore-Perot debate, and a plethora of direct-mail initiatives sought to sway Americans. In Haiti, the suggestion by the Clinton administration that it was contemplating an invasion of the country revealed a solid opposition to the use of military force. Members of Congress opposed to the invasion drummed up public opinion to send a clear signal to the president that any decision to use the military would not be met by support from the American people. The adroit use of public opinion data and vigorous public criticism of the president's suggestion that invasion was an option served to limit the administration's options and strengthen the resolve of the Haitian generals.[23]

Despite shifts in policy positions and frequent inattention, it is important not to underplay the power of the people of the United States in foreign policy matters. Even though the American people are largely uninformed, they often react to policy rather than take the initiative, and in many instances they do not have firm or consistent positions. In our democratic form of government the views of the public cannot be ignored for long. Presidents may be able to shape opinion and Congress may choose to vote its conscience on foreign policy issues, but when the voice of the people speaks out clearly, the government must listen. Admittedly, problems can arise when the people take an active role in the foreign policy process, especially in the midst of war or in delicate or controversial negotiations. However, these risks are outweighed by the benefits that accrue to the country whose policies are backed by popular support.

NOTES

1.   Bernard C. Cohen, "The Influence of Special-Interest Groups and Mass Media on Security Police in the United States," in Charles W. Kegley and Eugene R. Wittkopf, eds., *Perspectives on American Foreign Policy* (New York: St. Martin's, 1983), pp. 222–41.

2.   Lars Schoultz, *Human   Rights and United States Policy Toward Latin American* (Princeton: Princeton University Press, 1981), p. 67.

3.   See the Council of the Americas, *Annual Report, 1994.* Americas Society, Inc., 680 Park Avenue, New York, New York 10021.

4.   *C/CCA Action*, the bimonthly publication of the organization published a list of its corporate contributors and board members in its November-December 1982 issue.

5.   Seymour Hersh, "The Price of Power: Kissinger, Nixon and Chile," *The Atlantic*, December 1982, pp. 38–39.

6.   Nathanial Nash, "Corporations Rush into Latin America," *New York Times*, April 11, 1993, p. 1.

7.   For a good summary of the Brady Plan and the issue of Latin American debt see "New Initiatives on Latin American Debt—Summary Report," The Second Harvard Conference, Institute of Politics, John F. Kennedy School of Government, Harvard University, May 15–16, 1989.

8.   For example, WOLA published a special update on repression in Guatemala that sought to document the extent of right-wing terror. See "Guatemala: The Roots of Revolution," *WOLA Special Update*, February 1983, p. 1.

9.   See *Christian Century* 101 (May 30, 1984): 569.

10.   See Americas Watch, *Peru Under Fire: Human Rights Since the Return to Democracy* (New Haven, Conn.: Yale University Press, 1992).

11.   See Albert Fishlow, "Flying Down to Rio: Perspectives on U.S./Brazilian Relations," *Foreign Affairs* 57 (Winter 1978–79): 387–405.

12.   Schoultz, *Human Rights*, pp. 58–64.

13.   Bob Davis, "Mexico Mounts a Massive Lobbying Campaign to Sell North American Accord in U.S.," *The Wall Street Journal*, May 20, 1993, p. A18.

14.   For a more complete discussion of the pro-*contra* groups see John Felton, "Contra Aid Entangled in Regional Politics," *Congressional Quarterly*, July 30, 1988, pp. 2084–85.

15.   CANF publishes a series of pamphlets outlining its position. See for example, Cuban American National Foundation, *U.S. Policy and the Future of Cuba: The Cuban Democracy Act and U.S. Travel to Cuba* (Miami, Fla.: Cuban American National Foundation, 1993).

16.   David Dent, "Interest Groups," in David Dent, ed., *Handbook of U.S. Latin American Policymaking* (Westport, Conn.: Greenwood, forthcoming).

17.   See a symposium of experts on labor entitled "Labor's International Role," *Foreign Policy* 26 (Spring 1977): 204–46.

18.   For a critical look at AIFLD's operations in Latin America see Penny Lernous, *Cry of the People* (London: Penguin Books, 1982), pp. 211–13.

19.   Mark Falcoff, "The Apple of Discord: Central America in U.S. Domestic Politics," in Howard Wiarda, ed., *Rift and Revolution: The Central American Imbroglio* (Washington, D.C.: American Enterprise Institute for Public Policy Research, 1984), pp. 360–81.

20.   See "U.S. Public Not in Support of Troops in Central America," *Times of the Americas*, October 26, 1983, p. 1.

21.   *Gallup Report 216*, September 1983, pp. 5–8.

22.   "U.S. Officials Speculate on Outcome of Haitian Election," Boston *Globe*, January 17, 1988, p. 2.

23.   See R. W. Apple's column on the Clinton Haiti policy, New York *Times*, September 17, 1994, p. A1. See also the reporting of President Clinton's speech to the American people, New York *Times*, September 16, 1994, p. A1.

7

Shaping U.S.–Latin American Policy: The Human Element

So far we have approached the formulation of policy toward Latin America in a traditional way. We have focused our attention on the major participants in the policy process: the institutions, the officials, and the interest groups. This approach, however, can be too limited in that it only emphasizes the structure of policy making and the actions of the key players. To complete the picture of the policy process, we must examine a number of additional factors that are often critical in shaping U.S. relations with Latin America.

As we will see, foreign policy making is more than the result of presidential initiatives, legislative debates, State Department diplomacy, and interest-group lobbying. The contemporary policy process is also affected by such factors as the unique personal characteristics of the president, the limitations of the intelligence and advisory system, the political maneuverings and machinations of electoral politics, the quality of bureaucratic performance, and the internal policy conditions within the Latin American states where policy is being implemented. Government proposals for the hemisphere may not be affected by every one of these factors, but when we examine the full range of inter-American relations it becomes clear that policy making is a far more complex process than it appears.

These added features also serve to remind us that there is a human element in making governmental decisions. U.S. policy toward Latin America has often been portrayed in a rather cold, formalistic manner, with the accent on key votes, aid authorizations, weapons procurement, and manpower commitments. This chapter shows that policy making is also the result of personality traits, group dynamics, electoral politics, organizational management, and the Latin American ambiance.

PRESIDENTIAL CHARACTER

In an ideal world, government decision makers would always formulate and implement policies with objectivity, a thorough examination of the issues at hand, and a careful determination of the proper course of action to follow. But even though presidential administrations can be seen adhering to what Graham Allison calls the Rational Actor model of decision making, human factors can easily influence the level of rationality and produce policy decisions that are more the reflection of the president himself than of sound deliberations.[1] The fact that presidents and other major policy makers have made decisions that were guided by pressures to accent certain personality traits or were molded by past experiences has prompted a number of studies seeking to decipher the relationship between the mind of the decision makers and the decisions they make. James David Barber's highly influential book *The Presidential Character* examines the personalities of modern day presidents and analyzes how their psychological profiles may have affected their performance during crisis.[2]

For example, Barber argues that through John Kennedy's handling of the Cuban Missile Crisis in 1962 the young president sought to change his image as an inexperienced and vacillating chief executive. Despite the natural apprehension that Kennedy must have experienced during this period, the president was determined to show the U.S. populace (and certainly Soviet premier Nikita Khrushchev) that he could act decisively and with a toughness that had not always been readily apparent. Barber also praises Kennedy's capacity for control and caution in the midst of the world's first major nuclear confrontation. Agreeing with presidential scholar Richard Neustadt, Barber claims that Kennedy "mistrusted passion" and therefore brought an analytical and deliberate approach to the crisis that not only lessened the tensions but permitted the Soviets to remove the missiles without the appearance of capitulation.[3]

Juxtaposed to the generally positive analysis of John Kennedy's leadership personality is much of the work done with respect to President Richard Nixon. Nixon's involvement in Watergate and his resignation from the presidency prompted many scholars and journalists to investigate his psychological makeup and determine to what extent it influenced his actions. Most studies of this type conclude that Nixon was a loner who often relished his privacy and sought to cut himself off from competing sources of information or criticism.[4] His hostility toward the press and to what he viewed as his enemies in the Washington establishment forced him further and further into isolation and led him to rely on trusted aides who either skirted the law or engaged in outright violations. During the Watergate crisis, Nixon, rather than follow an accommodationist stance and work to avoid further confrontation through bargaining and compromise, sought to take on his adversaries and "stonewall" them.

The reliance on psychological analysis in the study of presidential decision making is part of a growing body of research that is commonly described as psychohistory. Psychohistorians examine the personality development of major policy makers because they believe that decisions usually reflect people's values, attitudes, idiosyncracies, and memories. Because psychohistory appeals to those who feel that decisions are no more than the result of a person's lifetime experience, there has been a tremendous push to "psyche out" current presidents and attribute their actions to some character trait or flaw.

To more orthodox students of government, psychohistory research and analysis merely deflects attention away from interaction of the president, Congress, bureaucracy, and interest groups as crucial ingredients to public policy formation. Despite the criticism, however, psychohistory has become an integral part of explaining the "why" of decision making. The more we know about the policy-making process, the more obvious it becomes that the people who make decisions bring their past, their egos, and their beliefs with them and cannot easily separate their personality traits from the purely objective deliberations that are required in developing government policy.

Another important personal factor in the decision-making process is what can be called leadership style. Every individual who comes into a position of governmental authority develops a distinctive manner of dealing with his or her aides, the Congress, and the U.S. public. Components of leadership style include the amount of time given to active involvement in policy deliberation, the propensity to delegate authority, the capacity to deal effectively with political adversaries, and the image that the leader wants to convey to the general public. Leadership style has often been equated with those unique behavior patterns that differentiate one leader from another, but it also can be an important contributing factor in the management and promotion of public policies.

Nowhere is the impact of leadership style more in evidence than in the contrast between the administration of Jimmy Carter and Ronald Reagan. President Carter can best be described as an "immersive" chief executive; he made it his practice to become personally involved in the details of government policy making. Carter, perhaps because of his engineering background, paid more attention to the development of new programs and initiatives than to the political and bureaucratic lobbying that was required to ensure their success. Few would criticize Carter for his energy as president, but many join James Fallows in describing the Carter presidency as "passionless" and lacking the ability to persuade legislative opponents or stimulate the thinking of the U.S. public.[5] History may look favorably on President Carter's Latin American policy, especially his negotiation of the Panama Canal Treaty and his commitment to introducing moral principles into our foreign policy, but in the 1980 election, the U.S. voters rejected a president who gave the appearance of weakness and failed to develop a leadership style that captured the nation's attention.

Ronald Reagan, on the other hand, entered office with a different view of how a chief executive should operate. Acting more as a chairman of the board, Reagan chose to delegate a great deal of policy-making authority to subordinates and concerned himself with using his fine communication skills to advocate his brand of conservative philosophy. Reagan preferred to avoid the internal debates over the specifics of a particular policy and instead used his keen political sense to influence Congress and the U.S. populace to support his policies. Although Reagan often left himself open to criticism from those who describe him as unconcerned about the details of major policies, the president was in most cases able to survive these attacks by relying on his fine rapport with the people.

The American public's patience with President Reagan's casual leadership style was tested during the Iran-*contra* scandal, when the president revealed an inability to remember key meetings in which the arms-for-hostages policies were discussed. Many Americans wanted to know why their president was not involved in such critical decisions or permitted underlings to direct foreign policy initiatives. Yet when the Iran-*contra* controversy faded from public view, the protests of the president's style of decision making faded as well. The American public seemed to have accepted the fact that their president was not one who bothered with the day-to-day details of key foreign policy issues, but rather allowed those around him a great deal of leeway in developing public policy.

Where the differences in leadership style between Carter and Reagan were pronounced and reflected contrary views on the role of the president in the decision-making process, the differences between Presidents Bush and Clinton were more a result of personal interest and the changing nature of international politics. George Bush was without question a president who relished involvement in foreign policy. His background in government service gave him a unique preparation for guiding the external affairs of the United States. Throughout his administration Bush focused on foreign affairs and in particular paid close attention to affairs in the hemisphere. Although the record shows that Bush's approach to Latin America was influenced less by moral principles than economic pragmatism, his style of leadership was marked by a firm commitment to free elections and free trade. The Bush White House was viewed by many as conducting its Latin American policy with an aggressive single-mindedness that stemmed from an unabashed belief in the American system.

The Clinton approach to Latin American policy making was erratic. There were no major trips to the region and few memorable speeches. There was of course the North American Free Trade Agreement (which was negotiated by Bush) and the Summit of the Americas (which was more form than substance), but both of these initiatives were framed by President Clinton more in terms of their domestic impact than as a comprehensive policy for the region. When faced with a purely Latin American political issue, such as the Haitian crisis, the Clinton White House often appeared immobilized, unable to respond effectively to events. Much of the problem for the poor foreign policy record of the administration in places like Haiti was traced to Clinton's inexperience in international affairs, his penchant for changing policy direction, and his unwillingness to sacrifice the domestic focus of his presidency. If Carter was immersive, Reagan inattentive, and Bush aggressive, President Clinton's leadership style in foreign policy can best be described as distracted.[6]

PRESIDENTIAL GROUP DYNAMICS

One of the presidency's long-established myths is that the man who occupies the White House is the principal architect of public policy. This view no longer fits the reality of a decision-making system where appointed advisors hold enormous influence. In the modern presidency, bright minds and savvy politicos provide the chief executive, not only with advice and counsel, but with new proposals and policy directives. In this system the president has come to act more and more as a coordinator of the advice that is brought before him and a final arbiter of the disputes that often arise among his closest aides.

Because of the demands placed on the president and the increasing complexity of issues in our country and the world, the advisory system will undoubtedly remain and perhaps even expand. Yet despite its importance to sound policy formation and the advantage of bringing some of this country's most talented individuals to Washington, there are nevertheless a number of dangers inherent in the advisory system that can lead to faulty decisions and ultimately jeopardize the president and the country.

Basic to any good decision-making process are sound data and unbiased intelligence gathering. But the information upon which public policy formation is based is rarely value free or resistant to bureaucratic management. Unfortunately, just as the same statistics can be used to reach two seemingly opposite conclusions, intelligence data in the hands of advisors wishing to prove their analyses correct can misrepresent reality. Advisors to key decision makers need not lie to their superiors by providing false information; they just selectively pick and choose data that substantiate their case. As a result, a president or secretary of state with only a general knowledge of the issue at hand could easily agree to a policy proposal that turns out to be ineffective or even disastrous. The Vietnam war provides some of the most glaring examples of data misrepresentation by military intelligence officers and upper-echelon State Department officials anxious to please their superiors or to support a prevailing theory about the conduct of the war.

In recent Latin American policy making some of the most serious intelligence debates concerned the issues of verifying Sandinista arms shipments to the Salvadoran rebels and the capability of the *contra* rebels to mount successful military campaigns against the Nicaraguans. The Reagan administration long sought to prove that Nicaragua served as a conduit for Cuban and Soviet arms shipments to the Salvadoran rebels. Using everything from foot patrols and radar sweeps to sophisticated high-altitude photography, the administration tried to convince the Congress and the public that the revolution in El Salvador was part of a communist effort to subvert the region. The problem was that convincing evidence and hard data (what some congresspersons refer to as the "smoking gun") eluded the intelligence gatherers. Even when the Reagan administration finally presented its long-awaited report on arms trafficking in Central America in August 1984, many critics remained apprehensive because the government refused (or was unable) to provide specific intelligence information that documented the flow of weapons. Except for some pictures of suspicious-looking crates on Salvadoran beaches and third-hand statements of Nicaraguan defectors, the long-sought link with Cuba and the Soviets remained circumstantial.[7] Luckily for the Reagan administration, the efforts to prove Sandinista revolutionary expansionism was aided by Nicaraguan leader Daniel Ortega, who on a number of occasions in 1986 and 1987 publicly boasted about the arms transfers to the Salvadoran rebels and the commitment of the Sandinista government to Marxist revolution.

Once the administration was able to develop a link between Nicaragua and revolution in El Salvador it was faced with an intelligence debate over the fighting capability of the *contra* rebels. Assessments from State Department officials like Elliott Abrams, who hailed the rebels as an increasingly effective fighting force, clashed with professional military analysis and congressional investigations that pointed to a ragtag army with no base of popular support and only minimal capability to challenge the Sandinista armed forces. The intelligence debate over the ability of the *contras* to wage war against the Sandinistas was at the core of the congressional dispute over lethal aid and the value of pursuing a negotiated settlement of the war. In many respects the intelligence debate reminded some of the early Vietnam war days, when administration officials stated that additional increments of aid would surely transform the South Vietnamese army and bring the communist Vietcong to their knees. Those in Congress who successfully defeated *contra* aid used intelligence reports critical of the rebels to show that "just a little more" aid might trap the United States in a protracted jungle war akin to Vietnam.

An entirely different type of intelligence debate ensued during the Clinton presidency over the character and mental condition of deposed Haitian president Jean-Bertrand Aristide. Senator Jesse Helms of North Carolina, citing Central Intelligence Agency (CIA) psychological profiles, described Aristide as having a history of emotional problems. In Helms's view returning Aristide to Haiti would only rekindle attacks on the business class and put into power a leader of questionable emotional stability who would sanction new attacks. For a few weeks in 1994 Washington was abuzz with conjecture over whether the Clinton administration was making a serious error in backing Aristide. Supporters of Aristide immediately rejected Helms's charges as false and discounted the profiles as an attempt by some in the CIA to paint Aristide as an unbalanced leader who was not worthy of regaining the presidency of Haiti. The so-called "whispering campaign" against Haiti was quickly rejected by the Clinton administration as a political ploy designed to slow the efforts to restore an elected president but it did point out potential impact that intelligence information, whether accurate or fictional, can have on the policy process.[8]

Another pitfall connected to the use of intelligence data in policy formulation concerns the actual format for arriving at a decision. Specifically, to what extent are advisors permitted to express dissenting or contrary views to the president and, as a corollary, how willing are these advisors to become captives of their desire to tell the president what they think he wants to hear? The Rational Actor model mentioned earlier suggests that the decision makers arrive at a final position after all sides of the issue have been explored and all opinions have been solicited. Fortunately for U.S. policy, this model has been followed quite regularly by top decision makers, but there have been instances where presidents have closed the circle of advisors to ensure a certain policy conclusion or created an advisory system in which aides suffer from what Irving Janis calls "group think," commonly known as a propensity to act as presidential yes-men and give advice that supports the chief executive's views.[9] Again, the administrations of Lyndon Johnson and Richard Nixon are often cited as examples of advisory systems that valued loyalty rather than honesty and sought to manage or suppress the channels of dissent.

The most widely documented example of an effective procedure for decision making was the White House deliberations during the Cuban Missile Crisis. President John Kennedy ordered the formation of a policy group called the Executive Committee of the National Security Council (EXCOM) and charged it with the task of making a "prompt and intensive survey of the dangers and all possible courses of action." The EXCOM group included Attorney General Robert Kennedy, Secretary of State Dean Rusk, Secretary of Defense Robert McNamara, Director of the CIA John McCone, Secretary of the Treasury Douglas Dillon, Special Assistant for National Security Affairs McGeorge Bundy, Special

Counsel Theodore Sorensen, Undersecretary of State U. Alexis Johnson, Assistant Secretary of State Edwin Martin, Soviet expert Llewellyn Thompson, Deputy Secretary of Defense Roswell Gilpatric, Assistant Secretary of Defense Paul Nitze, and Chairman of the Joint Chiefs of Staff Maxwell Taylor.[10]

To ensure that the advisors would not be intimidated by his presence, Kennedy purposely left these men on their own and openly encouraged their debate of the various alternatives. No option was thought unacceptable for discussion, no one whose opinion was thought useful was denied access to the group. As for the president, he served as a kind of sounding board for the various options that emerged from a series of subgroups that formed within the EXCOM. The final decision was, of course, President Kennedy's (with significant brotherly pressure from Robert Kennedy), but the process itself was candid, objective, and based on a trust in the benefits of soliciting a wide spectrum of advice.[11] In the thirty years since the Cuban Missile Crisis the EXCOM method of decision making has served as a model for other presidents who seek to establish an advisory system that provides a full range of policy options and does not become a mirror of perceived presidential wishes.

Recent presidential administrations have shown signs that they have learned from the mistakes of the Johnson and Nixon eras and are actively seeking to create advisory systems that are open and committed to a thorough discussion of policy issues. In the case of President Carter, his desire to follow a strictly democratic decision-making format and to increase the participants in the consultative process worked on occasion to the detriment of efficient policy formulation, because the president gave the appearance of uncertainty and vacillation when faced with a critical issue. Although the Reagan White House did not suffer from these periodic bouts of immobility, it faced other problems that accompany democratic decision making. In particular President Reagan, especially in the area of Central American policy formation, presided over an advisory system that was often torn by ideological, political, or personal disputes. But unlike the Kennedy EXCOM, the policy disputes in the Reagan administration left the impression of internal disorganization and petty feuding.

During the Bush presidency the issue of conflict within the advisory system was over the tricky question of when to use military force in Panama. Secretary of State James Baker, Secretary of Defense Dick Chaney, National Security Advisor Brent Scowcroft, and Chairman of the Joint Chiefs of Staff Colin Powell are portrayed by Bob Woodward in *The Commanders* as divided and wavering, especially when informed of an internal coup attempt by a disgruntled member of Noriega's inner circle of military officers. In part because of fear of backing an unknown and also concern over the domestic and regional response, the Bush White House concluded that support for the coup was not the proper course of action. When the coup effort failed and Noriega became even more emboldened in his attacks on the United States, the press and some in Congress castigated the decision-making process of the foreign policy team for vacillating and being timid when offered an opportunity to remove a leader that it had stated must go.[12]

The criticism faced by the Bush foreign policy team appeared to strengthen its resolve. With the president clearly stating his intention to bring Noriega to justice, his advisors put to rest their concern over the use of force and formulated an invasion plan designed to remove the Panamanian dictator from power. But even with a unified team and careful planning, the Panama invasion almost failed to achieve its main objective of capturing Manuel Noriega. Intelligence as to the likely whereabouts of Noriega as the invasion commenced proved unreliable. For days the Panamanian leader led the U.S. invasion force on a country-wide chase from safehouse to safehouse until Noriega entered the Papal Nuncio's residence and eventually agreed to surrender.

Although reliable and objective intelligence data remain the heart and soul of sound foreign policy decision making, one cannot ignore the fact that presidents and advisors can often be swayed toward a specific policy option simply because it is familiar or easy to comprehend and fits nicely into their own personal worldview. As Barbara Kellerman points out regarding this quite common characteristic of decision making:

In a crisis situation, the decision maker simply cannot identify and evaluate all the potentially favorable and unfavorable consequences of all the feasible courses of action. The more general inclination, therefore, is to restrict the quest for information to a relatively small number of variables, and to associate but a single outcome with each of the available alternatives.[13]

By restricting the options and relying upon familiar patterns presidents and advisory staff may ease the burden of decision making, because it is easier to set policy from a base of traditional guideposts than it is to engage in untested and unfamiliar analysis. Although relying on the familiar is quite normal and occurs in our own daily decision-making routine, there is a danger of accepting stereotypical or outdated conceptions of reality, a practice that can lead to faulty and ineffective public policy.

For example, one of the most consistent sources of conflict in foreign policy has been our attitude toward communism. Debates have ranged regularly over whether a president and his advisors have properly assessed the motives or actions of Marxist revolutionaries. Lyndon Johnson in the 1965 intervention of the Dominican Republic came to his decision largely on the basis of his fear of a second Cuba. Despite little evidence that the uprising would transform the Dominican Republic into a revolutionary state, Johnson chose to stick with his ingrained perception that the unrest would eventually lead to a spread of communism in the Caribbean. So too with President Reagan's decision to invade Grenada. Although the sending of U.S. troops to the tiny island was billed as a rescue mission of medical students, the president saw the instability there as an opportunity to once gain foil the advance of communism. There was scant debate over whether the leftists in Grenada posed a threat to U.S. interests; rather, the decision to invade was made within firmly entrenched anti-communist guidelines.

In post–Cold War Latin America defining policy objectives, particularly in the area of military intervention, have become more complex and ultimately more frustrating as ideological adversaries and strategic threats are redefined. The Clinton administration, for example, in its decision to invade Haiti relied on democratization and humanitarian objectives in its public justification for using military force. Many in Congress and the American public were not convinced about the decision to invade and registered their complaints based on traditional national security objectives. Their view was that the use of military force should only become an option when a clear threat to the security of the United States existed. But in this new world order, where traditional adversaries are disappearing, while new problems and concerns are appearing with dizzying regularity, the arguments for and against intervention are being recast in a different light. For U.S. policy makers the 1990s may be a time in which hemispheric relations are not only focused on issues such as trade and investment but also reflect a critical tug of war over when and why to use force.[14]

POLITICAL REALITIES AND ELECTORAL CHOICES

Public policy formation is first and foremost a political process. Partisan politics and particularly electioneering have a considerable impact on the final shape of policy primarily because the determination of this country's positions and actions toward the hemisphere is often played out in public forums and is affected by citizen reactions to foreign policy decisions. Because key policy makers such as the president and members of Congress are subject to regular elections and view themselves largely as the voice of the people in government, public policy cannot help but be influenced by the political environment.

Unfortunately, the U.S. political system does not function with great efficiency because of its large, complex, open, and most of all democratic composition. What makes it work, however, is the recognition among key participants in the executive and legislative branches that policy must of necessity benefit from good faith bargaining, compromise, and an ever-watchful eye on the electorate. Few presidential foreign policy initiatives are transformed into legislative action without being examined, not only in terms of their value as future U.S. policy, but also as to whether they will survive the rigors of an inevitable partisan debate in Congress and be accepted by the people "back home." Presidents and legislators can ignore the political dangers inherent in public policy formation and follow their conscience or their ideological principles, but the prospects for legislative effectiveness are greatly diminished and the electoral repercussions can be devastating.

In the area of Latin American policy making, a few examples of the influence that partisan and electoral politics can have on the outcome of a presidential initiative come to mind. The first concerns the fiscal 1985 round of aid debates and votes on aid to El Salvador. It will be recalled from Chapter 4 that President Reagan had an extremely difficult time convincing Congress of the need for so-called urgent aid for war-torn El Salvador. Liberals in the Democrat-controlled House put up a strong opposition, only to lose key authorization votes by narrow margins. The mood in the House was an angry one, with those who opposed the president's policy adamant in their belief that their policy prescriptions would eventually carry the day.

By late summer of 1984 the politics of the El Salvador aid debate had changed dramatically. The election of José Napoleon Duarte and the reduction in the level of civilian repression convinced many members of Congress that President Reagan was indeed correct in his approach to curbing the revolution. With El Salvador seemingly reinvigorated by its newly found democracy, few members of Congress were willing to vote against a policy that appeared to be working. Moreover, with national elections in the United States but a few months away, most congresspersons were wary of going back to the electorate to answer questions on why they voted against money for a friendly democracy. The prospect of being linked with "selling out" El Salvador and being at least partially responsible for "losing" the country should leftist insurgents prove victorious prompted many in Congress to revise their earlier stand against additional aid.[15]

In a key vote on August 10 the Congress approved by a wide margin an additional $70 million in military aid for El Salvador for the fiscal year that would end on September 30. Also in August the House Appropriations Subcommittee on Foreign Operations approved $123.25 million in military aid for El Salvador for fiscal 1985; that figure was a mere $9.25 million less than what President Reagan had requested. The House subcommittee, which in the past had been a staunch opponent of additional military aid to El Salvador, was reluctant to deny the Duarte government aid at this crucial juncture in its development. Subcommittee chairman Clarence Long stated that his support of the aid request was based on a personal plea from President Duarte. Long's agreement seemed to lessen the partisan wrangling and paved the way for the authorization.

The success in attaining the supplemental aid and the breakthrough in the Long subcommittee signaled that the mood in Congress had changed. As Republican representative Lee Hamilton from Indiana stated, "There's been pretty much of an agreement that we should support the Duarte government." Hamilton's viewpoint was echoed by Democratic majority leader Jim Wright who said, "It seems to me very important that we give a firm and wholehearted commitment, not an equivocal commitment to El Salvador."[16] Comments such as these and the voting shift toward aid for El Salvador reveal the changeable nature of politics and the effect that this change can have on public policy. Because elected officials must be guided not only by the national interest but by their own political interest, policy debates often exhibit the tension between doing what is wise or moral and doing what is practical and prudent. In the case of aid to El Salvador many legislators placed their reservations behind them and opted for a policy that they viewed as politically acceptable and electorally smart.

Electoral considerations also can play a role in determining the future direction of public policy. The whole question of U.S. interests in the Caribbean Basin, for instance, was a prominent source of debate material during the 1984 presidential election campaign. Both political parties and their candidates addressed the issue of communist-inspired revolution in the hemisphere and the proper response that should be made to that threat. In the 1984 campaign Ronald Reagan was running again on his platform of staunch opposition to communist expansionism, particularly in the Western Hemisphere. Walter Mondale, however, was presenting himself and his Democratic party as more cautious and responsible than the incumbent president. Mondale reminded his audiences of heightened military involvement in the region and our consistent support of governments who blatantly ignore the principles of democracy.

President Reagan was put on the defensive during the final days of the campaign when a CIA-sponsored handbook used to advise *contra* rebels on guerrilla techniques suggested that Sandinista officials and supporters should be "neutralized" (commonly thought to mean assassinated) as a means of furthering the insurgency effort. The Mondale camp used the handbook and its support of "neutralizing" the opposition as a further example of U.S. interference in the internal affairs of another country. At the second presidential debate, Mondale and the president exchanged sharp views on who was responsible for the handbook and whether the United States advocated a policy of so-called neutralization. The president promised to investigate the handbook issue further and after the debate stated that he felt the problem was one of faulty translation from English to Spanish. The official policy, according to Reagan, was that this country seeks the "removal" of Sandinista leadership from office, but in no way advocates assassination.

The CIA handbook issue may have reinforced the fears of those who were opposed to covert activities in Nicaragua, but overall Central American policy never really became a critical concern of the U.S. electorate in 1984. Rather, the views of the average voter on issue such as national pride, military strength, anti-communism, and a resurgence of U.S. influence in the world became more important than the ethical or national security questions involved with our presence in Central America. Furthermore, Ronald Reagan's landslide victory in the presidential election in which he won in forty-nine of fifty states and swamped Walter Mondale in the popular vote by 18 percentage points was interpreted by many analysts as a mandate for the president to pursue his free-market policies on the domestic scene and his aggressive anti-communism in foreign affairs.

Interestingly, the 1988 campaign for president hardly touched on the issue of Central America and the *contra* war. By the time George Bush and Michael Dukakis were debating foreign policy issues, the war in Central America was off center stage. Bush and Dukakis skirted the issue of *contra* aid or Soviet influence in the region. Both men, perhaps sensing that the war in Central America was not the issue to mount a national campaign on, returned to pocketbook issues and debates over symbols such as the Pledge of Allegiance.

After the Republican victory, President Bush continued to downplay the *contra* war and put off any immediate commitment to attempt a refinancing of the rebels. Bush took office with a less ideological bent than his predecessor and a greater willingness to seek negotiated settlements of regional disputes. The twin dilemmas of budget and trade deficits that faced the new president seemed to convince him that there would be little sentiment in the country to fund a proxy war or to become embroiled in a national debate over the proper use of U.S. military power.

The campaign of 1992 between George Bush and Bill Clinton continued the downside of attention toward hemispheric relations as the two candidates addressed domestic concerns. Despite President Bush's penchant for stressing foreign policy over domestic policy, challenger Clinton was able to dominate the issue agenda with his calls for economic revitalization and social reform. Even the mention of the North American Free Trade Agreement with Mexico was cast in the light of domestic jobs and long-term growth and not as an opening to regional trade and the development of neighboring economies. Both candidates were sensitive to the issues of Castro's Cuba and Haitian boat people, but these were peripheral concerns in a campaign where the public wanted answers on health care, taxes, and the budget deficit. The contest between Bush and Clinton revealed the extent to which the years of intense concentration on revolution and communist expansionism during the Reagan presidency had been replaced by a period in which Latin American affairs were seen more in terms of global issues and business opportunities.

THE IMPLEMENTERS

The noted political scientist Karl Deutsch once described the impact of the bureaucratic establishment on the policy-making process in this way: "If a policy is to work or if a leader or party is to have real power, it must have the support of a body of administrative personnel that is loyal and competent to give effect to its order."[17] Deutsch's observation points up the critical role played by the implementers of public policy. Once a policy has survived the political jockeying between the president and Congress, its success is in the hands of nonelected bureaucrats who have the opportunity to shape the decision in terms of its delivery and administration.

One of the most troublesome problems connected with bureaucratic implementation lies in ensuring that the policy initiated by the president and agreed to by the Congress is the policy that is applied in the field. It is a long way from Washington to the embassies in Latin America, and this distance has occasionally contributed to bureaucratic reinterpretation of administration objectives or, worse yet, outright opposition to established policy. Despite sophisticated communication with field offices and frequent visits back to the states by embassy personnel, policy implementation, like executive decision making and legislative deliberation, is subject to the human element. Bureaucrats, especially those who hold career rather than political appointive posts, may view administration directives as shortsighted or inappropriate for the country in which they serve and then use their position either to reshape the policy or sabotage it. As Deutsch says, "while politics, leaders and parties change, bureaucrats remain. Bureaucracy may be an unmovable anvil that wears out many hammers of reform. If a new policy is to be implemented, can the old bureaucracy be expected to administer it?"[18]

Although U.S. policy in Latin America is implemented every day, in most instances with efficiency, professionalism, and a spirit of co-operation, occasionally the administrative structure breaks down and exhibits signs of disloyalty, incompetence, and improper management of this coutry's interests. In the case of the Alliance for Progress programs, most observers felt that government agencies, like the Agency for International Development, were simply overburdened by the explosion of new initiatives and the injection of hundreds of millions of dollars into the foreign-assistance pipeline. The result was often poor planning, infighting among competing and overlapping bureaucracies, and general mismanagement. Although there were many successes during the Alliance years, there could have been many more if the bureaucratic establishment had adjusted more quickly to the new programs and worked more effectively with the labyrinth of agencies that participated in this enormous foreign-aid enterprise.[19]

A different bureaucratic problem occurred during the Dominican intervention of 1965. As documented by Abraham Lowenthal, U.S. policy during this period was seriously flawed primarily because the participants in the decision-making chain of command were deficient in their reporting, their negotiating skills, and their overall representation of the U.S. position. Because of a combination of personal ambition, ideological proclivities, and just plain incompetence, a complete and fair picture of what was happening in the Dominican civil war was never presented to President Johnson. The result was that the U.S. intervention not only could have been avoided but the U.S. troops probably quashed a rebellion that was destined to bring forth a government of liberal democracy and firm constitutionality, not communism. But as Lowenthal says of the performance of the U.S. embassy personnel and that of the State Department in Washington:

The foreign policy making process is political, not scientific, and personal judgements and preferences are often at its heart. Individuals with different conceptions of personal, organizational and national goals struggle to make their views prevail. By pulling and hauling in different directions, they often produce results different from what any of them intend.[20]

Perhaps the most startling example of the inherent problems in bureaucratic implementation of public policy can be found during the Nixon administration and its handling of the Chilean destabilization of the Allende regime. Although we have already touched on this episode in our historical review, what has not been made clear is the internal machinations that occurred among key policy makers in the White House, the CIA, the State Department, and the U.S. embassy in Santiago. The performance of participants in Chilean destabilization, whether as decision makers or as policy implementers, reveals the problems that can develop when a deep division exists between officials in Washington and diplomatic representatives in the field.

The most serious problem in the bureaucratic chain of command during this period was the antagonisms that surfaced between Secretary of State Henry Kissinger and the U.S. ambassador to Chile, Edward Korry, over the extensive covert CIA activities that were conducted without Korry's knowledge or support. The rift between Kissinger and Korry developed because of the ambassador's refusal to endorse and help implement a Chilean military coup to prevent the inauguration of Salvador Allende in 1970, a position initially favored by Kissinger. The level of acrimony became so intense that the Nixon administration began working around the ambassador and increasingly relied upon CIA operatives to search for Chileans willing to participate in a coup attempt.

The personal division between Washington and the U.S. embassy, coupled with the "end run" being staged by the CIA, created a bureaucratic atmosphere filled with tension, uncertainty, and mistrust. Policy implementation in Chile centered on strategies to circumvent the ambassador or lay blame for failure rather than on effective means of stopping the Allende presidency. Because the bureaucratic team was in disarray, policy toward the Allende regime became disjointed, with the administration scrambling about looking for potential supporters of a coup, while its ambassador worked vigorously to suppress the military option.[21]

Salvador Allende survived the White House attempts to prevent his inauguration, but the U.S. bureaucratic network that formed to curtail his ascendency to power was in shambles. Ambassador Korry was replaced, the CIA mission to Chile was reorganized, and the so-called Track II policy of encouraging a military coup was downgraded in favor of more intensive economic and diplomatic pressure. As for President Nixon and Secretary of State Kissinger, they eventually saw the demise of the Chilean leader in 1973, but their handling of the anti-Allende campaign in 1970–71 serves as a reminder of how the administration of foreign policy can suffer when decision makers and bureaucratic implementers work at cross purposes.

During the Reagan years the bureaucratic issues were primarily in the areas of oversight and accountability. With hundreds of millions of dollars pouring into Central America, Congress insisted on assurances that the administration had a "handle" on where the money was going and how it was being used. For example, as the *contra* war wound down in 1988 governmental auditors from the Congressional Accounting Office and a number of other agencies involved with aid programs were sent to the *contra* base camps in Honduras to investigate whether the supplies this country was providing the rebels were properly accounted for. The past allegations of misappropriations of aid money by the *contra* leaders and shoddy bookkeeping practices by CIA and Defense Department officials created a situation where a mini-army of accountants worked side by side with the *contra* army and the U.S. advisers.[22]

The issue of bureaucratic accountability continued on into the Bush administration, particularly with respect to the embarrassing revelations concerning the role of the CIA in retaining Manuel Noriega on the payroll as an intelligence link during the *contra* war despite his known participation in the drug trade and his close ties with the Medellin cartel of Colombia. The fact that Noriega was employed at cross purposes against one of President Bush's primary foreign policy objectives in the region pointed up the difficulty of developing coherent policies in a complex and competitive bureaucratic climate. While the CIA was using Noriega to provide the United States with what it felt was valuable intelligence and connections in Nicaragua, the Drug Enforcement Agency was working to stop the transshipment of cocaine through Panama.

THE LATIN AMERICAN SETTING

So far we have discussed those factors in the U.S. political system that shape public policy toward Latin America. But if this chapter is to give a complete picture of how government decisions are affected by human elements inherent in the policy-making and implementing processes, it is essential that we shift attention to the Latin American setting. Even though policy is initiated, formulated, and implemented within and through the U.S. government, the prospects for success depend in large part on whether the host country has the resources, the leadership, the management capability, and the will to transform the U.S. policy into national programs that meet the stated objectives.

One of the most critical problems in implementing U.S. policy in Latin America is that many of these countries lack the bureaucratic personnel to effectively administer U.S. programs, in particular those dealing with the use of aid monies for development projects. Although the United States channels millions of dollars in aid to Latin American countries yearly and sends thousands of specialists to this region to assist in the proper implementation of the assistance programs, the burden of success still rests largely on the shoulders of Latin American administrative staffs that are small and inexperienced in the management of large-scale and increasingly sophisticated policies. There is no question about the dire need for development capital and the positive response that such aid brings in Latin American governments, but with limited administrative resources the aid projects can be delayed, partially implemented, or, in the worst case, totally mismanaged.

Most of the difficulty with the administration of U.S. programs in Latin America is ensuring that the aid is properly delivered and that it performs the stated task. It is one thing to give country X $10 million for highway development, but quite another to channel that money into surveying crews, earth-moving equipment, and bridge construction. The actual construction of a stretch of road often depends on the expertise and managerial talents of government officials, who must assemble a team of workers and engineers in a country where all the components of highway development are not always readily available. Often in Latin America the government is literally starting from scratch when it takes on a modernization project. Even though the money may be there, success can never be guaranteed.

A much more serious delivery problem is the abuse of administrative power and the mishandling of foreign assistance. Some Latin American countries have reputations for administrative corruption and misuse of aid funds. Although such corruption exists in almost every nation, the funneling off of developmental aid by government officials in less developed countries can have a devastating effect on the overall modernization effort. One of the most serious instances of official corruption occurred in Nicaragua during the regime of Anastasio Somoza. An earthquake that destroyed much of the capital city of Managua in 1972 left thousands homeless. The plight of the Nicaraguans prompted public and private agencies in the United States and Europe to send millions of dollars worth of food, clothing, drugs, and medical equipment. Nicaraguan government officials were later found to have taken large portions of the aid and placed it in military warehouses to be sold on the black market. This blatant abuse of power further stirred up an angry population who saw their leaders make a profit on their misfortune.[23]

Besides these administrative bottlenecks in the implementation of U.S. aid policy are the challenges from Latin American political leaders. Modern U.S. presidents from Kennedy to Clinton have found that U.S. efforts to address an internal problem in a Latin America that has become more independently minded and attempts to force policy prescriptions on the region have met with increasing resistance. Even the prospect of losing U.S. aid and armaments has not served to move governments, because there are now other avenues for such assistance. The failures of the Clinton administration to quickly dislodge General Cedras and his repressive military cohorts in Haiti despite an economic embargo, international condemnation, and constant diplomatic pressure attests to the resistance of political leaders to U.S. pressure and the resiliency of governing regimes when faced with the enormous power that can be marshaled by a president.

It is important, in particular, not to overplay or generalize the resistance of Latin American leaders to U.S. policy. Even in countries like El Salvador and Honduras, where the United States was able to employ diplomatic and economic pressure in order to achieve its objectives, there are limits to mandating internal political behavior or government policy. The fact that they need us is complemented by the fact that we also need them. In countless incidents, U.S. and Latin American officials have expressed anger and dismay over either lack of cooperation or interference. Many times the impasse has been resolved by the U.S. officials recognizing that even though the money and policy prescription are ours, the country is theirs.

Finally, it is helpful to remember that these programs or initiatives are being implemented in a unique cultural environment that is not a mirror image of the United States. Decision makers who develop public policy for Latin America often assume that what we do for these people is in their best interest and destined to be successful, only to find out later that our presumptions about how things will work have been totally erroneous. The intentions may have been completely honest and sincere, but the policy prescriptions ignored the cultural setting where the policy was being implemented.

Some classic examples of culture shock in the implementation of U.S. aid policy in Latin America occurred in the area of population policy. The United States has for years encouraged the use of artificial birth control as a means of controlling Latin America's mushrooming population problem. In the 1960s and 1970s population control was seen as the answer to the food, housing, employment, and social service demands that were intensifying in many Latin American countries. But although birth control devices were popular means of family planning in the United States, when the Agency for International Development officials sought to develop similar programs in Latin America they encountered unexpected problems and in some cases stern government rebukes. Most of the problems occurred because the largely uneducated peasant population failed to understand the principles of artificial birth control. If peasants cannot read and if clinics are too distant, then an effective birth control program is difficult to manage.

But an even more serious problem in the population control policies fostered by the United States was the opposition of the Roman Catholic hierarchy and of nationalistic leaders. With local pastors castigating the use of birth control and praising the benefits of large families, U.S. officials faced their greatest roadblock to successful policy implementation. Population-control policy became entangled with church doctrine and with generations of belief that God looks favorably on the large family. Later on the population-control programs became further enmeshed in politics as nationalistic leaders questioned the motives of the United States in seeking to limit the rising birth rate in the region. Charges of "genocide" and antinatalism were heard with increasing frequency from critics who saw these programs as a new form of U.S. imperialism designed to weaken their nations by limiting growth.[24] Although there is growing support for contraceptive use in Latin America and the Clinton administration has reversed the Reagan policies of avoiding involvement in the issue of family planning, there is still vocal criticism of rich industrial countries like the United States pressing poorer, neighboring countries to limit their growth in the name of environmental and resource protection. The Catholic Church in a number of Latin American countries, at the United Nations Conference on Population in 1994, condemned the Clinton administration for advocating aggressive family planning programs, while environmentalists in Latin America reminded the United States that resource depletion and population growth are not necessarily associated because the industrial world and particularly the United States uses more of the world's resources than any other country.

CONCLUSION

As we have seen through these brief examples of U.S. policy formulation, the process of arriving at and implementing solutions to the problems, challenges, and threats emanating from Latin America involves more than the formal interaction between the executive and legislative branches. Even though we often see our relationship to Latin America in the form of a presidential address or a legislative debate, in reality there are more parts to the policy puzzle than we may have thought. Leadership, personality, data management, electoral politics, organizational snafus, and the Latin American political environment all make important contributions to the shape of the public policy. As a result, Graham Allison's Rational Actor model of decision making that we started with may have to be replaced by a more complex tool for describing the Latin American policy process. In the words of Howard Wiarda,

Today we would have to add some other "models" to Allison's list. These would doubtless include a "domestic politics model," a "media model," a "rival-interest group model," a "candidate reelection model," a "competitive think tanks model," and a "self-interest/self-aggrandizement model." These new perceptions of policy making are related to the more fragmented, more self-centered, less consensual society and polity that we have become in the past two decades.[25]

Although Wiarda's analysis calls into question the appropriateness of the Rational Actor model, his suggestions for replacements continue to suggest the importance of the human element in the formulation and implementation of Latin American policy. There may be more "actors" participating in the policy process and they may be pursuing more selfish, less rational objectives, but they nevertheless remind us that the decisions concerning the hemisphere are made by people and not faceless institutions. More important, the solutions to the myriad problems facing Latin America will in the end depend on the ability of leaders, from both the public and private sectors, rising above narrow interests and personal prejudices to develop policies that meet the needs of our neighbors while also achieving our own goals.

NOTES

1. Graham Allison, *Essence of Decision* (Boston: Little, Brown, 1971), pp. 10–38. See also John R. O'Neal, "The Rationality of Decision-Making During International Crises," *Polity* 20, no. 4 (Summer 1988): 598–622.

2. James David Barber, *The Presidential Character*, rev. ed. (Englewood Cliffs, N.J.: Prentice Hall, 1977).

3. Ibid., p. 337.

4. See Gary Wills, *Nixon Agonistes* (Boston: Houghton Mifflin, 1970) and Bruce Mazlish, *In Search of Nixon* (New York: Basic Books, 1972).

5. James Fallows, "The Passionless Presidency," *The Atlantic*, May/June 1979, pp. 33–46.

6. For a defense of Clinton foreign policy in Haiti and elsewhere, see Owen Harries, "My So-Called Foreign Policy," *New Republic*, October 10, 1994, pp. 24–31.

7. *News Briefing on Intelligence Information on External Support of the Guerrillas in El Salvador*, released by the Department of State and the Department of Defense, August 1984.

8. For a discussion of the Aristide-Helms affairs, see Pamela Constable, "Haiti: A Nation in Despair, a Policy Adrift," *Current History* 93 (March 94): 113–14.

9.   Irving Janis, *Victims of Groups Think* (Boston: Houghton Mifflin, 1972).

10.   See Robert Kennedy, *Thirteen Days* (New York: Norton, 1969), p. 8.

11.   Theodore Sorensen, *Kennedy* (New York: Harper & Row, 1965), p. 676.

12.   Bob Woodward, *The Commanders* (New York: Simon and Schuster, 1991), pp. 94–104.

13.   Barbara Kellerman, "Allison Redux: Three More Decision-Making Models," *Polity* 15, no. 3 (Spring 1983): 351–67.

14.   For a discussion of the new dilemmas of intervention, see Tony Smith, "In Defense of Intervention," *Foreign Affairs*, November/December 1994, pp. 34–46.

15.   See *Congressional Quarterly*, August 18, 1984, pp. 2037–39.

16.   Ibid.

17.   Karl Deutsch, *Politics and Government: How People Decide Their Fate* (Boston: Houghton Mifflin, 1980), p. 199.

18.   Ibid.

19.   Jerome Levinson and Juan de Onis, *The Alliance That Lost Its Way* (Chicago: Quadrangle, 1972), pp. 108–31.

20.   Abraham Lowenthal, *The Dominican Intervention* (Cambridge, Mass.: Harvard University Press, 1972), p. 148.

21.   See Seymour Hersh, "The Price of Power," *The Atlantic*, December 1982, pp. 31–58.

22.   See John Felton, "Special Report: Contra Outlook," *Congressional Quarterly*, April 2, 1988, pp. 835–41.

23.   See Penny Lernoux, "The Somozas of Nicaragua," *The Nation*, July 23, 1978, p. 1.

24.   José Consuegra, "Birth Control as a Weapon of Imperialism," in Terry McCoy, ed., *The Dynamics of Population Policy in Latin America* (Cambridge, Mass.: Ballinger, 1974), pp. 163–82.

25.   Howard Wiarda, *Finding Our Way? Toward Maturity in U.S. Latin American Relations* (Washington, D.C.: American Enterprise Institute for Public Policy Research, 1987), p. 210.

Part III

KEY ISSUES OF U.S.–LATIN AMERICAN RELATIONS

8

The Fragile Hold of Democracy

One of the major disappointments in our long relationship with Latin America is that we have been unable to successfully "graft" liberal democratic principles and practices onto the body politic of these nations. U.S. presidents and policy makers have often felt that the solution to the political instability in this region was the establishment of democratic institutions similar to those found in our country. Many Latin American countries took our advice and wrote constitutions, formed political parties, organized elections, and erected legislative chambers. And yet despite this flurry of institution building, Latin America has been unable to sustain a democratic tradition.[1]

The weakness of democracy in Latin America is the result of a strong authoritarian heritage that has made the process of establishing an alternative political system difficult. Efforts to introduce democratic reforms in Latin America were often undermined by conservative elites. Democracy, Latin American style, thus came to suggest elections that were not always final and were frequently threatened by intervention, constitutional guarantees that were subject to personal interpretation, and various separation-of-powers formulas for decision making that became structure without much substance.[2] The unique character of Latin American democracy has caused frustration among U.S. officials anxious to apply our political system in a Third World setting. What these officials have quickly found out is that transferring democracy from the United States to Latin America leads to the creation of a hybrid form of governance that combines new ideas with age-old customs and practices.

Although the Latin Americans have been unable or unwilling to develop a democratic tradition that mirrors our own, this has not stopped the United States from fostering a political climate conducive to reform, constitutionalism, human rights, and social justice. In fact, as revolutions erupted in Latin America, the United States increasingly came to view democracy as the primary means of containing Marxism.

If the communist revolutionaries promised the people a more equitable distribution of land and resources, we would counteract these promises by pointing to the freedoms and legal guarantees that were secured with the establishment of democracy.

But as the United States began competing for the hearts and minds of the Latin American people it faced a troublesome dilemma that raised questions about the strength of our commitment to democracy in this part of the world. The dilemma arose when the United States began to recognize the great difficulty of establishing democratic governance in a revolutionary setting. While admitting the need for major reform in many Latin American countries, the United States at the same time could not separate the importance of change from the prospect of communist influence in the revolutionary process. It is at this point that the United States began looking to the benefits of authoritarianism as a hedge against Marxism in the hemisphere. Alongside their commitment to democracy, U.S. presidents embraced military dictators from Trujillo in the Dominican Republic and Batista in Cuba to Somoza in Nicaragua. Our leaders were fully aware that these dictators headed repressive regimes, but chose to ignore the manner in which they governed because of their anti-communism and their willingness to welcome U.S. business executives. In a now-famous quote, allegedly attributed to President Franklin D. Roosevelt, Anatasio Somoza, Sr., was once described as "an S.O.B. but at least he's our S.O.B."

Official U.S. ties to Latin American dictators may have helped to stave off leftist revolutions, at least for a while, but they damaged our credibility as champion of democratic governance. The United States came to be recognized as a country that preferred stability to social change, even if that meant supporting repressive dictators. An even more serious consequence of our relationship with authoritarian leaders was that once they fell from power the United States could not easily influence the transition to a new form of government. We found ourselves facing either an inexperienced and weak democracy, because the dictators laid no foundation for popular rule, or Marxist guerrillas anxious to strip their country of U.S. influence.

As revolution spread to Central America, the dilemma over steadfast support of democratic principles versus toleration of authoritarianism as a means of containing Marxist revolution became an issue that divided presidential administrations, congressional leaders, professional foreign policy bureaucrats, and the U.S. populace. On one side were those who advocated a firm commitment to democracy in recognizing governments, providing aid, forming alliances, and influencing internal political conditions. This group, which might be described as the "reformists," felt that the United States gained only short-term security by supporting authoritarian regimes and damaged its image among the Latin Americans who sought to build strong democratic traditions.

In opposition to the reformists were those who saw themselves as taking a more pragmatic or realistic view of foreign policy formulation. These "realists" were not anti-democratic but were convinced that this country must make decisions based primarily on our interests and our national security. Foreign policy from the realist perspective placed concern for the state of democratic practice in Latin America behind the importance of ensuring that our position in the hemisphere was not threatened or compromised.

Once the Sandinistas were defeated at the ballot box in Nicaragua and the revolutionary struggle in El Salvador came to a grinding conclusion, democratization was viewed in policy-making circles less as an antidote to Marxism than as a system of governance that should be present in every nation of the hemisphere. Although quite different in their handling of foreign policy, the Bush and Clinton administrations stressed that elections, institution building, civilian rule, and human rights were essential requisites for development. With communism in retreat and leftists more interested in reentering mainstream society in the region, democracy became the sole standard of governance. U.S. officials and Latin Americans recognized that much needed to be done in order to strengthen the climate for democracy and to fashion workable systems of popular rule, especially in those countries where authoritarian dictators clung to power. But the days of ideological contests between communism and democracy were over. The issue of the 1990s in Latin America was how to ensure that democracy would survive and prosper.

To better understand the progression of democratization in Latin America let us return to the early days of the Reagan administration and examine this contest between communism and democracy and the gradual changes that occurred in U.S. policy as the region evolved and popular rule became the dominant governing model.[3]

THE DEBATE OVER AUTHORITARIANISM AND TOTALITARIANISM

In the November 1979 issue of the conservative magazine *Commentary*, Jeane Kirkpatrick, who would eventually be named President Reagan's UN representative, wrote an article entitled "Dictatorships and Double Standards." The article was destined to set off a major debate within foreign policy circles as to the proper approach this country should take in dealing with military governments in the Third World.[4] In the article Kirkpatrick stated that it was important for the United States to make distinctions between such authoritarian-military regimes as are found in some Latin American countries and the totalitarian regimes that are controlled by communists in the Soviet Union, North Korea, and Cuba. The article was written as a response to the Carter human rights policy, which disapproved of military governments in Latin America and went so far as to deny them military assistance.

To Kirkpatrick and to Reagan, who read the article and was impressed by the authoritarian-totalitarian distinction, the United States had lost valuable influence with some military governments because the Carter administration placed its commitment to human rights above its concern for maintaining good relations with traditional allies and staunch opponents of communist expansionism. From Kirkpatrick's point of view, the real violators of human rights were the communists with their totalitarian governing systems; the authoritarians, despite their penchant for employing harsh rule, had to be seen in a different light, especially if they shared common interests and concerns with the United States.

Once in office the Reagan administration began to follow a course of action that seemed to apply the authoritarian-totalitarian distinction made by Kirkpatrick and others. Among the first signs of this change in direction were the statements of Secretary of State Haig with respect to human rights violations attributed to Latin American military regimes. Rather than publicly criticize the authoritarian governments, the administration stated that it would follow a course of action described as "quiet diplomacy." The Reagan foreign policy team was clearly not willing to alienate right-wing governments as the Carter people had by calling attention to repressive rule. The new approach was that progress on human rights could be better achieved by firmly stating our opposition to such behavior in diplomatic exchanges rather than making our views known in the press or in international forums. Furthermore, Reagan sought to avoid what he felt was an uneven application of the Carter human rights policy in which only certain countries were singled out for public rebuke. Such unevenness (for example, criticizing Brazil's military government but saying little about the authoritarian rule in strategically important South Korea) in the Reagan view only further alienated military leaders and made our human rights policy appear hypocritical.

But if the Reagan administration was willing to overlook some of the repressive policies of authoritarian regimes and follow quiet diplomacy, it also showed a determination to alert the U.S. public and so-called apologists for Castro to severe human rights violations in communist Cuba. On a number of occasions President Reagan, Secretary of State Haig, and then–State Department official for human rights and humanitarian affairs Elliott Abrams castigated the Castro government for its treatment of political prisoners and its failure to defend basic human freedoms. In a speech in Washington in October 1983, Assistant Secretary Abrams demonstrated the administration's campaign to lay the onus of human rights violations on totalitarian governments when he said: "For too many years Fidel Castro had posed as a champion of liberty and has succeeded in concealing the totalitarian nature of his regime. Surely the time has come to identify Castro for what he is—one of the most vicious tyrants of our time, whose rule has brought ruin to his people."[5]

With this dual attitude toward human rights abuses and authoritarian rule the Reagan administration opened new diplomatic and economic channels to Latin American military governments that President Carter had shut off. A key initiative was undertaken with the Chilean government of General Augusto Pinochet. In spring 1981 the Chilean foreign minister visited with Vice President George Bush and Secretary Haig, the first such high-level contacts with Chile since 1977. The revival of these contacts coincided with the Reagan administration decision to reverse the Carter White House policy of voting against multilateral development loans to Chile because of its poor human rights record. By July 1981 the United States had voted yes on two international development loans to Chile totaling $161 million.

With the renewal of support for development loans it was not long before the Reagan administration resumed military sales to Chile. In October 1981 Congress cleared the way for military aid to Chile contingent upon the administration's certifying that "progress" had been made in the area of human rights. Soon afterward Chile was declared to have made "significant progress" and military assistance resumed— this despite reports from the United Nations Commission on Human Rights, which expressed its "indignation at the persistence and further deterioration of the human rights situation in Chile."

The shift in the Reagan administration policy toward Chile affected other authoritarian governments as well. By the end of the year the Reagan policy of rebuilding ties to authoritarian regimes had spread to Brazil, Uruguay, Argentina, Paraguay, Haiti, and Guatemala. Although none of these countries received substantial aid packages, it was clear that reports of human rights abuses were no longer a deterrent to providing economic or military assistance.

The Reagan rapprochement with Latin American military regimes was not achieved without considerable criticism from liberals in Congress, who sought to block the renewal of aid to right-wing dictatorships. In particular, the administration's efforts at strengthening its ties with Guatemala provided an example of this contest between the reformists and the realists. On June 10, 1981, the Department of Commerce approved a $3.1 million sale of military jeeps, cargo trucks, and spare parts to Guatemala. The sale of these vehicles had not previously been permitted by the State Department. The Reagan administration, however, transferred the items from a prohibited purchasing list to one that would allow the Guatemalan government to begin buying U.S. military equipment.

The military-equipment sale to Guatemala elicited a protest from fifty-four members of Congress, who felt that the Reagan administration's agreement undermined the clear intent of the Human Rights and

Military Assistance Amendment to the Foreign Assistance Act, which sought to stop the transfer of military materials to countries that violated human rights. The congresspersons pointed out to Secretary Haig that Guatemala had the worst record of human rights abuse in Latin America and that such aid would only provide a signal to the Guatemalan generals that the United States condoned their harsh rule.

The military sale to Guatemala in 1981 was but the first step in rebuilding our ties to the nation. In 1982, after meeting with Guatemalan leader General Rios Montt, President Reagan declared that Montt had received a "bum rap" on his human rights record, even though the human rights organization, Amnesty International, claimed that 2,600 civilians had been killed in the first four months of Montt's presidency. This report and others that documented the plight of over 50,000 Guatemalans who fled their country to seek haven in Mexico did not sway the administration from extending $10 million in economic support funds to Guatemala under the Caribbean Basin Initiative and supporting Guatemalan applications for international loans.

Although the Reagan administration followed a realist policy that renewed contact and aid with the more repressive states in Latin America, it is important to point out that the United States was not insensitive to human rights abuses or shy about registering its displeasure over the excesses of authoritarian regimes. In the final years of the Reagan presidency, the president and other high officials in the foreign policy bureaucracy criticized the repressive nature of the Pinochet regime and the reluctance of the ruling military to schedule democratic elections. The national referendum in 1988, in which Chileans voted no to the extension of Pinochet's rule, was supported by the United States and backed by abstentions on critical loan votes in international lending organizations.

The Reagan administration also had harsh criticism for the Haitian military and its bloody intervention in the presidential elections of November 1987. The subsequent cutback in U.S. aid, along with regular criticism of military rule and human rights abuse, prompted more moderate officers led by General Prosper Avril to take over power and begin building a governing system that could be supported by the United States and the world community of nations. The Reagan administration eventually did resume some aid disbursements to Haiti, but warned the military leaders about the necessity of bringing the nation toward democracy and the rule of law.

The fact that the Reagan administration did balance its realist-pragmatic vision of Latin America with a respectable human rights record points out that policy making never really exhibits extreme swings from one position to another. There may indeed be new emphasis placed on policies or approaches that a previous administration ignored, but by and large the U.S. position toward democracy and human rights in Latin America has been consistent over the years. While the Reagan administration had little interest in the near–moral crusade atmosphere that surrounded President Carter's human rights policies, it nevertheless showed an unwillingness to tolerate excessive government abuses or blatant attempts to prolong authoritarian rule. If there can be a criticism made of the Reagan approach to democracy and human rights in Latin America it is that the clear sense of movement on human rights and democratization achieved by President Carter was delayed as the new president sought to balance reformism with realism and preferred quiet diplomacy to forceful denunciations of repression and military rule.

DEATH SQUADS AND THE FIGHT FOR HUMAN RIGHTS IN EL SALVADOR AND HAITI

The fact that the debates concerning democracy and authoritarianism, realism and idealism occupied so much of the Reagan policy toward Latin America offered the Bush administration more opportunity to advance its objectives without becoming enmeshed in ideological and operational controversies. The issue of whether to support authoritarianism in the name of stability and good sense had been replaced by the tidal wave of democratization. President Bush was permitted the luxury of pronouncing democracy alive and well in Panama, Nicaragua, and Haiti and presiding over the end of the revolution in El Salvador where guerrillas became politicians. There would still be lingering questions during the Bush administration over the willingness of the United States to move beyond elections and commit the necessary resources to strengthen democracy and over its support for human rights and the rule of law. But those issues often generated less intensity and animosity than in the past as Washington and the countries of the region turned their collective attention away from authoritarianism.

With the onset of the Clinton administration, however, the democracy-authoritarianism, realism-idealism axis was turned on its head as the attempt to return exiled president Aristide to Haiti raised the question of how far the United States would go in order to protect and preserve democracy in the region. Critics of President Clinton's decision to send troops to Haiti in preparation for Aristide's return pointed out that restoring democracy was not in our national interest and not worthy of using U.S. troops. Many viewed Clinton as so rigid in his determination to restore Aristide to power and so committed to the principle of democratic governance in the hemisphere that he ignored the authoritarian style of leadership exhibited by the former priest turned politician and the fact that returning him to power would in no way create an immediate democracy. The lines between authoritarianism and democracy became increasingly blurry during the debate over Haitian policy and President Clinton's decision to use force to restart democracy raised questions as to whether good intentioned idealism had been taken too far.

The conflict between the advocates of a vigorous commitment to democratization and human rights and the supporters of stability and societal order within Latin American militaries can best be seen by examining the political violence in El Salvador in the 1980s and in Haiti during the early 1990s. Both countries tested the ability of the United States to establish a democratic system of government in a solidly authoritarian environment. Both countries have provided the realists and the reformists with a forum for their ongoing debate over the proper conduct of U.S. democratization policies in the Third World.

Of special concern to the reformists in El Salvador was the presence of right-wing death squads that roamed the countryside in search of civilians who supported the rebels or who were known as opponents of the government. These death squads were responsible for thousands of political murders (some human rights groups place the number at 40,000) and appeared to have the tacit consent of, if not direct leadership links to, key military officials.

This reign of terror from the right in El Salvador posed a dilemma for the Reagan administration. On the one hand it needed the support of the military in order to continue the war against the guerrillas, but at the same time it recognized that political violence undermined its overall strategy to develop a democratic framework. The administration thus had to walk a narrow line in El Salvador as it mixed public criticism of the death squads with increased military aid for the government. This balancing act is best seen in the response of the former U.S. ambassador to El Salvador, Deane Hinton, to a question from reporters concerning the death squads:

You have a government that is trying after 50 years of dictatorship to play by democratic rules. It is carrying out social reforms. . . . This is a government that is trying, under terrific pressure from an armed terrorist movement supported by Cuba and Nicaragua. They have had an effort to correct the [human rights] abuses. Of course they are terrible, and they are unacceptable, but these people are going in the right direction.[6]

But if U.S. officials saw progress in human rights, the Congress was less impressed and decided to pressure the Salvadoran leaders to move more quickly to secure personal liberties. The International Security and Development Cooperation Act, passed in 1981, tied military aid to El Salvador for fiscal 1982 and 1983 to the president's certification, at 180-day intervals, that El Salvador was making progress toward securing human rights protection. The act required the president to certify that El Salvador:

1. is making a concerted and significant effort to comply with internationally recognized human rights;

2. is achieving substantial control over all elements of its own armed forces, so as to bring to an end the indiscriminate torture and murder of Salvadoran citizens by these forces;

3. is making continued progress in implementing essential economic and political reforms, including the land reform program; and

4. is committed to the holding of free elections at an early date and to that end has demonstrated its good faith to begin discussions with all major political factions in El Salvador that have declined their willingness to find and implement an equitable political solution to the conflict, with such solution to involve a commitment to: (a) a renouncement of further military or paramilitary activity and (b) the electoral process with internationally recognized observers.

The certification process became a bone of contention between Congress and the Reagan administration. White House officials felt that certification tended to cloud the issue of stopping communist expansionism in El Salvador and placed unrealistic goals of government reform on a nation that had only recently begun to develop democratic institutions. Nevertheless the Reagan administration submitted the certification as a precondition of the aid process.

In most instances the certification reports filed by the administration showed progress in three major areas targeted for change: agrarian reform, human rights violations, and election preparations. In the third certification report of February 1983 Assistant Secretary of State for Inter-American Affairs Thomas O. Enders stated that El Salvador "continues to advance" toward the attainment of the three goals that "democracy is little by little emerging." To support its claim of progress the administration provided data on the so-called Land-to-the-Tiller agrarian reform program and on the reduction of human rights violations. According to the third certification report, more than 20 percent of the arable land had been redistributed since U.S. aid to El Salvador had begun, with some 550,000 *campesinos*, or 25 percent of the rural population, benefiting from the reform effort. But despite the claims of success, the administration also admitted that progress had slowed because of guerrilla activity, the intransigence of private owners, and footdragging by the Salvadoran government. Nevertheless, the Reagan administration took pains to tout the successes achieved and published numerous charts to defend its agrarian reform program in El Salvador.

In the area of human rights the third certification report was cautiously optimistic. The report showed a diminishing of human rights abuses but at a slower rate than that indicated in the second certification report. Overall the Reagan administration sought to present a picture of movement toward a climate of respect for human rights in El Salvador, but it is important to point out that despite the decline in the number of civilian deaths attributed to political violence during this 180-day period, the number still was near 400.

The optimism expressed by the Reagan administration in the third certification report was absent in the fourth report of July 1983. Secretary of State George Shultz, who delivered the report, bemoaned the lack of progress in El Salvador: "It is evident that the record falls short of the broad and sustained progress which both the Congress and the administration believe is necessary for the evolution of a just and democratic society in El Salvador."[7]

A major disappointment of the administration was the failure of the Salvadoran judicial system to prosecute those responsible for the killings of four U.S. churchwomen and the murder of four other U.S. citizens. As a result, Congress in 1983 added an amendment to the 1981 legislation that required certification be also contingent on the Salvadoran government's bringing to justice those responsible for the murders. The footdragging and corruption of the Salvadoran judicial system had long been a concern of the United States, but as the Congress put increased restrictions on the aid package, the Reagan administration seemed more open in its criticism. In fact in the fall of 1983 the U.S. ambassador to El Salvador went so far as to name those military officials who were known death-squad leaders. Furthermore, a speech by Vice President Bush during a state visit to El Salvador reflected U.S. concern about the violence and its impact on the leftist revolution. As the vice president stated in his speech:

These right-wing fanatics are the best friends the Soviets, the Cubans, the Sandinista commandantes, and the Salvadoran guerrillas have. Every murderous act they commit poisons the well of friendship between our countries and advances the cause of those who would impose an alien dictatorship on the people of El Salvador.[8]

The lack of progress toward alleviating the human rights problem in El Salvador increasingly led the Reagan administration to criticism, not only of right-wing death squads, but also of the certification process. The White House viewed the certification as a "snapshot" of the current situation in El Salvador that did not reveal "the long term, evolutionary processes." Furthermore the administration felt that the certification had a negative impact on the war effort. The Salvadoran government, it was claimed, could not adequately mount military campaigns against the rebels if its line of supply was "in constant danger of being shut off."

President Reagan's opposition to the certification process became quite clear in November 1983, when he killed a bill, through the use of his pocket veto, that would have extended certification for another year. Although the extension was approved by both the House and the Senate, and had bipartisan support of the Senate Foreign Relations Committee, Reagan felt that the certification hindered his ability to strengthen our ties with the current Salvadoran government. In the president's mind the prospect of a communist victory in El Salvador was much more serious than the slow pace of the government toward reform and democratization. Secretary of State Shultz had a more candid appraisal of the president's veto when he stated that in the next scheduled certification the administration would have found it "very difficult" to show progress in the area of human rights; rather than jeopardize the aid package for El Salvador, the administration decided to veto the certification extension.

The battle over the merits of certification did not diminish with the president's veto. The Kissinger Commission, for example, recommended that the United States continue to link military aid to El Salvador to "periodic reports" on demonstrated progress in democratization and human rights. The commission further suggested that sanctions be employed (denial of visas, deportations, and investigations of financial dealings in the United States) against foreign nations who were connected with the Salvadoran death squads. President Reagan expressed displeasure over this recommendation, but it was not seen as a major limitation of his ability to channel aid to El Salvador, especially since the Kissinger Commission also called for a massive injection of economic and military assistance to Central America and in particular to El Salvador.

The battle between human rights advocates determined to end the brutality in El Salvador and U.S. government officials concerned about alienating anti-communist military leaders continued during the Bush administration. The murder of the six Jesuit priests during the 1989 assault on San Salvador so angered members of Congress and the Catholic religious community worldwide that public attention began focusing on issues such as the rule of law and civilian control of the military rather than on the value of containing the spread of communist revolution. Congress, led by the influential House Rules Chairman Joseph Moakley of Massachusetts (a graduate of Jesuit Boston College), became a champion of the cause of bringing the officers responsible for the murder to justice. Moakley and Jesuit leaders from the United States and Europe maintained pressure on the Bush administration by demanding that the government of President Cristiani and the Salvadoran judicial system bring the killers to trial.

When the Bush administration continued to stress the dangers of the guerrilla threat in El Salvador and appeared incapable of convincing the military to address the matter of the Jesuit murders, Congress moved decisively to cut military assistance in half and threatened more aid reductions until justice was served. The action of Congress and the public positions taken by members of Congress, such as Joseph Moakley, forced the Salvadoran government to bring the officers to trial and eventually to prison. In retrospect, the pressure placed on the Salvadoran government by Congress over the Jesuit murders was instrumental in moving the peace process forward. With little assurance that military assistance would continue and the Bush administration growing weary of the Central American crisis, the sad trail of death that had marked life in El Salvador since 1980 came to an end.

Although the killing came to an end with the UN–brokered agreement in 1992, U.S. policy in El Salvador continued to come under intense scrutiny, especially as investigations began over numerous incidents of atrocities and mass murder during the civil war. In particular, the United Nations Truth Commission, which was formed as part of the peace agreement, began examining rural areas, such as the village of El Mozote, where hundreds of villagers were killed by the U.S.–trained Atlactl Brigade, an elite group of counterrevolutionary fighters. The mass graves in villages like El Mozote cast new light on the military training programs of the United States. Although American personnel were not present when the mass killings occurred, the association of the United States with human rights abuse and the failure of training programs to influence the behavior of Salvadoran units like the Atlactl Brigade was another damaging blow to our image in the region.[9]

When the Clinton administration took power and the scene shifted from El Salvador to Haiti, the issue of human rights abuse and the position of the United States toward that abuse resurfaced. The military government of General Raoul Cedras waged an unrelenting war of repression against supporters of President Aristide despite threats from the United States, the Organization of American States, and the United Nations. Estimates of Haitians killed or disappeared from the signing of the Governor's Island Accord in 1992 to the decision to invade the country in 1994 were over 3,000. The execution of Catholic priests, the use of orphans as target practice, and the brutal rapes of women became commonplace occurrences as the military regime sought to intimidate the civilian population. President Clinton used the repression by the Cedras government as the centerpiece of his decision to send troops to Haiti. The need to stop the killing in Haiti was defined by the president as a compelling national interest despite the criticism of many in Congress who felt that the United States had no valid reason to use force to return Aristide to power. President Clinton, however, stood firm in his belief that upholding democracy and responding to the humanitarian needs of the Haitian people were important objectives to pursue. As the president states in his address to the American people:

The United States must act here to protect our interests to stop the brutal atrocities that threaten tens of thousands of Haitians, to secure our borders and preserve stability and promote democracy in our hemisphere, to uphold the reliability of commitments others make to us.[10]

EL SALVADOR: ELECTIONS
AND THE MOVE TO DEMOCRACY

What did seem to take some heat off of the death-squad issue and certification was the election of José Napoleon Duarte as president of El Salvador. Despite the refusal of Robert D'Aubuisson to concede defeat, raising the specter of future right-wing opposition, Duarte received the ceremonial sash in June 1984, with Secretary George Shultz and a large contingent of congressional and administrative notables in attendance. In his acceptance speech Duarte set the tone for his administration by pledging to end the political violence and to maintain a rule of law. Although there were many both in and out of El Salvador who doubted Duarte's ability to attain human rights progress, especially in the light of his poor standing among conservative military officers, both the administration and Congress gave their support to the new president. One news report even stated that President Reagan sent his personal representative, General Vernon Walters, to El Salvador to inform military officials that a coup attempt against Duarte would spark a prompt reversal of U.S. support for El Salvador.

The Reagan administration's attempt to solidify Duarte's power base was but one example of the U.S. effort to bring democracy to El Salvador. During the preliminary election in March and the runoff in May the United States channeled millions of dollars in both technical aid and controversial covert political assistance to the country. In the early stages of the electoral process the United States was concerned primarily with ensuring that the Salvadorans would be able to conduct a major vote count. To achieve this, $10.5 million in economic support funds were used to provide the Central Election Council with new computer equipment to facilitate the tabulation of votes and for technical assistance and international observers to witness the elections. U.S. monies were allowed to purchase paper ballots and ink and hire an accounting firm to verify the vote count.

But as the prospect of a victory by the rightist Robert D'Aubuisson became the real possibility, the Reagan administration used the CIA to funnel assistance to the Duarte camp. U.S. Senator Jesse Helms of North Carolina, a long-time foe of Duarte, charged that the CIA had given $360,000 to Duarte's Christian Democratic party and $100,000 to a third-party candidate, Francisco Guerrero, in order to help defray the costs of their campaigns. The monies went to pay for precinct organizers, radio and television advertisements, computer voter registration, and political consulting fees. No monies were given to the D'Aubuisson camp.[11]

Helms's charges brought up questions of a rigged election (Helms even suggested that the U.S.–supplied election computers were preprogrammed to ensure a Duarte victory) and forced many to wonder how independent the new president would be. The Reagan administration, for its part, publicly denied favoring Duarte but privately admitted that Duarte was its choice for president. Working with D'Aubuisson, who was not committed to the reform agenda of the United States, would simply have been impossible and his election certainly would have caused Congress to curtail its foreign aid support.

In the end the Reagan administration got what it wanted in El Salvador's first attempt in fifty years at democracy: a reform president who presided over a country with a new constitution (not surprisingly quite similar to our own), an electorate that appeared supportive of the new democracy, and a spirit of change that held promise for a more peaceful future. But the United States also faced a war that was spreading, a guerrilla army that seemed intent on weakening the democratic institutions, and rightists who remained fearful that reform meant compromise with and not defeat of the communists.

The Salvadoran experiment in democracy from June 1984 through the conclusion of the Reagan presidency faced increasing threats to its stability and integrity. After a brief decline in deaths by right-wing death squads and a relative calm in the guerrilla war, the government of President Duarte came under attack as new rounds of political violence and rebel activity thrust El Salvador and its shaky democracy into its most serious challenge. By the fall of 1988 the Salvadoran Catholic Church reported 91 death squad and army killings; while the Farabundo Martí National Liberation Front (FMLN), the main guerrilla group, was becoming bolder in its attacks against government installations and talking boastfully about a final offensive to bring the Duarte government down just like the Sandinistas had done to Somoza.[12]

If the return of death squads and guerrilla warfare was not enough to weaken the Salvadoran democracy, the rightist element in El Salvador still led by Roberto D'Aubuisson was making significant gains among the electorate. D'Aubuisson's ARENA party won a number of seats in the Salvadoran legislature and was viewed by many observers as a future power broker in the country. Officials in the United States were clearly worried about the shift to the right in El Salvador, especially since President Duarte was diagnosed as having cancer and would not be a candidate for reelection. Duarte's illness, coupled with extensive factional disputes in the ruling Christian Democratic party, created an open field for the 1989 presidential elections.

The elections became even more open when in early 1989 the guerrilla forces in a surprise announcement pledged to participate in the political process. In return the rebels demanded a six-month delay in the election from March to September and a pledge by the military to remain in their barracks when elections are held. The proposal by the rebel army was seen by some as an attempt to bolster the chances of left-wing parties who were participating in the electoral process, while others felt that the rebels were acknowledging that the possibility of a successful final offensive was remote and that it was time to compromise with the national government.

Under heavy pressure from the military, outgoing president Duarte refused to agree to the rebel proposal. The 1989 presidential election was thus held in an atmosphere of heightened tension as the leftist rebels pledged to shut the country down and stop the elections. On election day Salvadorans went to the polls amid heavy security, power outages, and frequent gunfire. Despite the efforts of the guerrillas, El Salvador staged its second presidential election and chose ARENA party candidate Alfredo Cristiani. The Bush administration expressed cautious support for Cristiani hoping that he would be able to separate himself from rightists in his party and begin addressing the long list of social problems facing the country. The concerns of the United States were heightened soon after Cristiani took office, when a new wave of assassinations against public officials and civilians began and the leftist rebels expanded their guerrilla war to include the capital city of San Salvador.

The Bush administration thus quickly realized that El Salvador had become less a shining example of democratic reform and more a troubled country where the trappings of democracy masked a nation beset by internal discord and a powerful revolutionary threat. The inability of the Salvadorans to build on the election of 1984 and establish a stable democracy points up the fragile nature of popular government in countries where there are weak institutions, little experience in democratic practice, and an economic base that is largely dependent on foreign trade, aid, and investment. Although many public officials were reluctant to make comparisons with Vietnam, the fact that the United States was propping up a government ($4.5 billion through 1989) that was unpopular and unable to control the right or the left signaled that the Bush administration would have to make some hard decisions in the future concerning economic support, political preference, and the most practical way to fight a revolutionary movement that could not be ignored.

Despite the questionable state of democratic governance in El Salvador in 1989 and the continued wave of violence, there were signs that a momentum was building for creating a political system where partisan disputes were heard peacefully within democratic institutions. In particular the Cristiani administration was becoming convinced that the civil war had reached an untenable stalemate. There was, of course, opposition from hardline elements within the military who refused to consider any negotiations that might lead to a diminution of the armed forces position in Salvadoran politics or to a purge of officers tied to human rights abuse. But by 1990 elites in El Salvador were becoming increasingly aware that the United States was not going to pump hundreds of millions of dollars into a military solution to the civil war and that they were out of step with the forces of democratization in

Central America. With rebel leaders also showing interest in a peaceful settlement and international pressure mounting, the decision to come to an agreement was obvious, despite military opposition. The long and complex negotiations that led to the New Year's Eve 1991 UN–brokered peace accord hinged on fundamental democratization issues, such as civilian control of the armed forces, an independent judiciary, and guarantees of basic human rights. After a number of false starts and military inspired roadblocks the negotiators were able to agree on a number of key changes to the 1983 Constitution including a redefinition of the responsibilities of the armed forces, a narrowing of the jurisdiction of military courts, a new system for electing Supreme Court justices, and changes in electoral laws involving party participation and voter registration. With the groundwork laid for a return to democracy, the United Nations, in concert with a number of Latin American countries and eventually the Bush administration, was able to iron out a final agreement in New York City that satisfied the military.[13]

The arrival of peace and democracy to El Salvador turned the world's attention away from Central America and allowed the politicians and the people to rebuild the economy and the governing system. When media attention did return to El Salvador it was in connection with the 1994 presidential elections, which were considered a guidepost to the depth of democratic governance. The victory of Conservative candidate Jose Calderón Sol in the election was a major disappointment to the leftist movement and its candidate, former rebel Reuben Zamora. There were charges of fraud and intimidation but little in the way of sustained demonstrations or calls to arms. El Salvador had settled into a new stage in its development, one in which democratic practice was accepted and opposition politics remained within the system. It is much too early to conclude that democratization has been solidified in El Salvador because the institutional framework remains weak and the political elite are insecure, but in a relatively short period of time El Salvador has moved from a revolutionary battleground to a quiet democracy going about its business without the conflict that divided the country for twelve years.

With El Salvador behind it, the Clinton administration entered office with new democratic challenges. Such countries as Mexico, Colombia, Venezuela, the Dominican Republic, and Panama all held elections in 1994. These elections were viewed as important guideposts for determining how resilient popular rule was in the region. In each case the United States was anxious to see a smooth electoral process and transfer of power because in many of these countries there were potentially explosive issues that could tarnish the legitimacy of democratic government. In Mexico the issue was the longstanding control of power in the hands of the Institutional Revolutionary Party; in Colombia the influence of the drug cartels in the electoral process was a concern; in Venezuela the fragile oil democracy was reeling after years of corruption and military unrest; in the Dominican Republic the aging president, Joaquín Balaguer, was likely to control the electoral outcome; and in Panama the first election since the invasion of 1989 would reveal the extent to which that country had developed a workable democracy.

Fortunately for the Clinton administration these electoral contests were conducted with a minimum of controversy or unrest. In Mexico the Institutional Revolutionary Party continued its reign in power in what many felt was the most open election since 1929; in Colombia Ernesto Samper gained a victory despite charges that he received campaign funds from the Cali drug cartel; in Venezuela the elder statesman Rafael Caldera took office and brought a sense of calm to the country in the Dominican Republic Joaquín Balaguer won the presidency for the seventh time, but not until he pledged to call early elections in 1996; and in Panama Ernesto Balladares, representing the party of imprisoned dictator Manuel Noriega, won an easy victory and promised a continuation of democratic government and good relations with the United States.

For the Clinton administration the smoothness of the electoral contests in Latin America were reassuring, particularly when compared to the dilemma of restarting Haitian democracy after nearly three years of military rule. Factoring out the crisis in Haiti, Latin America in the 1990s appeared to be building a democratic tradition that was able to weather the storms associated with economic crisis, corruption, and social unrest. There was still doubt as to the staying power of democracy, especially since the benefits from the market system and the new trading arrangements had not trickled down to the vast majority of the people. But for the Clinton administration the outward signs of democracy—voting, registration, elections, inaugurations, and the peaceful transfer of power—signaled that the twin forces of capitalism and democracy were working hand in hand to stabilize the region.

DEMOCRATIC STRATEGIES

Developing a democratic system of governance in Latin America is, as U.S. officials have found out over the years, a long, evolutionary process that is filled with obstacles and major disappointments. Abraham Lowenthal, author of *Exporting Democracy: The United States and Latin America*, echoes this view when he states,

Democracy is not an export commodity; it cannot simply be shipped from one setting to another. By its very nature, democracy must be achieved by each nation, largely on its own.[14]

Because there have been and continue to be alternative models of government present in Latin America, specifically the authoritarian model and revolutionary Marxism, U.S. policy makers have had to formulate strategies that will strengthen the prospects of democratization. Although the United States may approach the democratization process differently from country to country, it is possible to describe four strategies that have served as the basis upon which our democratization policy in this region is formed.

Negotiated Settlement or Victory?

As the guerrilla war in El Salvador dragged on, there were increased calls for a negotiated settlement. The Contadora countries—Colombia, Mexico, Panama, and Venezuela—feared that without a diplomatic solution to the hostilities the revolution could trigger an expansion of fighting that might engulf the entire region. But negotiating a settlement to a civil war in which the moderate Duarte government was locked in battle with revolutionary guerrillas posed a problem of massive proportions. Beside the fact that both sides represented differing socioeconomic classes, supported opposite development ideologies, and were receiving assistance from competing world powers, there was also the presence of the United States, which had special national security interests in this region and was determined to influence the outcome of the war.

Although many Latin American leaders believed that the United States was the key to a negotiated settlement in El Salvador, the Reagan administration often appeared intransigent and uninterested when dealing with representatives of the rebels. Officially the Reagan administration supported a negotiated settlement in El Salvador and even named former Florida senator Richard Stone as a special envoy to Central America in 1983 to begin talks with the leftists, but there was evidence that despite the diplomatic overtures, government officials like Ambassador Stone were expected to follow a hard line toward the rebels and were often criticized for their efforts on behalf of a diplomatic settlement. State Department officials such as the former assistant secretary for inter-American affairs Thomas O. Enders, former ambassador to El Salvador Deane Hinton, and special envoy Stone all encountered opposition in the White House when they appeared flexible on key negotiating points. All three subsequently left their posts and were transferred to other duties or left government service.

The personnel shifts within the State Department coupled with the certification veto, the military buildup in Honduras, and the requests for more weapons aid for El Salvador signaled to many administration critics that this country was moving closer to embracing a military solution to the war. However, administration spokespeople disputed the charges of militarization, claiming that the United States fully supported the efforts of the Contadora group and its twenty-one objectives for establishing peace and democratic governance in Central

America.[15] After initially downplaying the efforts of the Contadora group, the Reagan administration began to find value in Contadora's goals of reducing foreign military personnel in Central America, ending subversion, stopping the flow of weapons, and achieving a peace treaty for the region. Langhorne Motley, the then-assistant secretary of inter-American affairs, revealed the Reagan administration's apprehension regarding the prospects for peace in Central America. Motley stated, "it is certainly too soon to conclude that an effective regional agreement can be achieved. Moreover, there should be no illusions that a treaty alone will resolve the crisis."[16]

Once Elliott Abrams became assistant secretary of state the focus of attention shifted from being defensive on its commitment to negotiations to a bold offensive in support of Central American military capability and containment of communist expansionism. The Contadora process was largely ignored by Abrams as the administration concentrated on advancing the *contra* war, building up its presence in Honduras, and training Salvadoran troops in anti-guerrilla warfare. There was of course lip service paid to negotiations, but the underlying theme of U.S. policy in the region was a military defeat of Marxist revolution.

The conflict between the Reagan administration and most Latin American leaders over a military solution to the war in El Salvador points up the vastly different approaches to stability in the region. At the crux of the debate was the president's concern that the government formed out of a negotiated agreement would be democratic in nature and have a political and governmental climate responsive to the interests of the United States. The Reagan administration, with its inherent mistrust of the rebels, was wary of entering into negotiations that might lead to the dismantling of democratic institutions or the emergence of a leadership group that pulled the country away from its ties to the United States. Because of its fears of the possible outcome of negotiation, the Reagan administration hedged its bets by supporting peace negotiations while at the same time showing its willingness to use military means as an alternative approach to establishing a pro–U.S. democracy.

As evidence of the problems that negotiating a settlement in El Salvador has posed for the United States, one need only look at the administration's response to the so-called power-sharing proposals that were popular early in the Duarte presidency. Power sharing is a formula for negotiations in which the military-backed government in El Salvador allows the guerrillas a role in running the country. The success of power sharing would, however, most likely require the United States to pressure hard-line military officials to accept the new formula or face a curtailment of military assistance. In order to ensure the success of power sharing, and to guard against the rebels using this arrangement to gain an advantage, the supporters of this plan suggested that a peace-keeping force be sent to El Salvador for an extended period while a provisional government formulated a permanent system that included the left in national decision making.[17]

The power-sharing formula was rejected outright by President Reagan. He argued that this avenue to negotiations allows the rebels "to shoot their way into power." Moreover, the president felt certain that the rebels would use any truce to advance their positions in the countryside. Finally, Reagan seemed unwilling to place any serious pressure on the current military establishment despite its failure to prosecute the war successfully and its weak commitment to democratic principles. From the administration's perspective, the only proper form of power sharing was for the rebels to participate in national elections.

Although George Bush sent clear signals that he did not intend to rely on a military solution to revolution in Central America, he was guided by the belief that negotiations must not compromise the democratization process in El Salvador. The rebel offensive of November 1989 created a serious dilemma for the Bush administration as it saw the process of a negotiated settlement of the civil war destroyed in a few short days. On the one hand critics of the Cristiani government complained that its refusal to negotiate with the FMLN forced the rebels to renew the fighting, while supporters of the Salvadoran government said the rebels were merely using the peace process as a time of regrouping for the so-called final offensive. Although President Bush continued his support for the Cristiani government, it was clear that the administration understood that there were limitations on what it could do in El Salvador. Congressional support for aid was in jeopardy and the claim of a regional security threat diminished markedly after the Panama invasion to remove Manuel Noriega and the election of Violeta Chamorro in Nicaragua. By February 1990 Secretary of State James Baker was telling Congress, "We believe this is the year to end the war through a negotiated settlement which guarantees safe political space for all Salvadorans."[18]

The support by the United States of a negotiated settlement in El Salvador enhanced the momentum for meaningful talks between the FMLN and the Cristiani government. During most of 1990 the two sides worked out their differences under the watchful eye of the Bush administration and Congress. The incentive to negotiate was further enhanced by Congress reducing military assistance by 50 percent in October 1990. Although the Salvadoran military balked at proposals to limit their power and reduce their ranks, the threat of a complete aid cutoff convinced the Cristiani government to force the military to compromise.

As for the Bush administration, it continued to hold the position that a steady aid stream for El Salvador could be attained, even restoring some aid to the military in early 1991. But when Congress, in August 1991, moved even further to restrict aid to El Salvador, the Bush administration began openly supporting the peace process and called upon the United Nations to become involved. With the Salvadorans now engaged in productive talks and the United States on board with the UN effort to achieve an accord, the agreement to end the fighting was signed on December 31, 1991. The Bush administration praised the agreement and committed $250 million for reconstruction projects in El Salvador.[19]

Dollars and Democracy

One of the primary requisites of a stable and thriving democracy has always been a prosperous economic climate. The onset of a recession or the presence of hyperinflation has often led to internal dislocations as various social groups scramble to adjust to the economic crisis. At this stage, democratic regimes are severely tested. Many times, in the face of these socioeconomic disruptions, democratic governments are unable to cope, especially when they institute corrective measures that create even more unrest. It is not long before the military enters to restore order.

The internal economic situation in El Salvador (and for that matter all of Central America) was dismal. The war with the guerrillas severely disrupted the traditional export sector. In the course of the war, guerrillas destroyed 55 of El Salvador's 260 bridges, less than half of the country's railway rolling stock was operative because of military engagements, and electrical power was frequently shut off to many parts of the country. The war also displaced thousands of peasants who could no longer work their land for fear of being killed in a skirmish. Added to this is the fact that prices for staple crops like coffee, cotton, and bananas plummeted while oil costs doubled. The result was that El Salvador's gross domestic product dropped by one-third during the height of the war, its population endured 40 percent unemployment, and the cost of staple food commodities skyrocketed.

Under these circumstances the prospects for democratic development in El Salvador were slim. Because of the economic disorder created by the guerrilla war, the United States sought to provide a kind of "economic shield" behind which the government and the people could rebuild their economy and, in the process, strengthen the chances for democratic rule.

In two major provinces where guerrilla activity was prominent, the United States in concert with the Salvadoran military was active in providing assistance and expertise in order to restore public services and to ensure that the guerrillas would not be able to disrupt the agricultural economy. The expectation was that this program would allow twenty-eight of El Salvador's forty-two largest farm cooperatives to resume normal operations.[20]

The shield program was part of a larger aid effort designed to replace the losses El Salvador has experienced from export-import imbalances. For example, for fiscal 1989 the Reagan administration requested $902 million in bilateral assistance to Central America of which $389 million was targeted for El Salvador. Much of the aid for El Salvador was in the form of Economic Support Funds and was designed to help the country repair bridges and roads damaged by the guerrillas, to purchase raw materials and consumer products, and to assist in addressing the severe balance-of-payments crisis faced by the government.

The U.S. aid commitment to El Salvador was founded on more than just a concern for the economic rejuvenation of the country. The Reagan administration was conscious of the connection between economic development and democratization. In his now-famous April 27, 1983, speech to Congress the president stated clearly our democratic strategy in El Salvador:

"We will support democracy, reform, and human freedom. This means using our assistance, our powers of persuasion and our legitimate leverage to bolster humane democratic systems where they already exist and to help countries on their way to that goal."[21]

In the view of the White House, democracy does not come about merely through the holding of elections, the reform of the land system, and the protection of human rights, but also by massive injections of aid, which creates a climate of stability so that democratic institutions can gain a foothold. Democratization takes time and the only way to gain time is by providing aid to conduct the war and to strengthen the internal economy that is ravaged by war. In this sense our dollars are "buying time" for democracy. As the Kissinger Commission stated in its support of increased aid to El Salvador: "There might be an argument for doing nothing to help the government of El Salvador, there might be an argument for doing a great deal more. There is, however, no logical argument for giving some aid, but not enough."[22] See Table 8.1 for a listing of U.S. aid to Central America from 1980 to 1986.

Not everyone in Washington decision-making circles accepted the argument for connecting aid and democratization. Critics of the administration believed that no amount of money was going to bring a democratic system to El Salvador. The aid, in their view, was merely going to prop up a government that was only faintly democratic, uncommitted to real socioeconomic reforms, and in reality controlled by conservative authoritarians who were not likely to relinquish power. The aid might indeed buy time, although not to assist in establishing a democratic environment, but rather to right the leftists and to solidify further the hold of the right.

Table 8.1
U.S. Aid to Central America, 1980–86

Country	Economic Aid	Military Aid
Guatemala	$646.0 million	$ 19 million
Honduras	1.0 billion	431 million
El Salvador	2.3 billion	726 million
Nicaragua		
to Sandinistas (1979–82)	119.0 million	
to *contras*	132.0 million	77 million
	(humanitarian aid)	
Costa Rica	926.0 million	34 million

Source: U.S. State Department.

The dispute over the role of military and economic aid and democratic development was a basic one and certainly went to the heart of what this country was hoping to achieve in El Salvador. The principle of using our dollars to buy time so that the Salvadoran military could fight the rebels while the civilian leaders formed a stable and functioning democracy became a key strategy of the Carter, Reagan, and Bush administrations. The problem with this strategy was that presidents often saw this commitment as open ended, with little in the way of dollar or time limitations. Moreover, the buying time strategy often created the impression that just a little more money and time could succeed in stopping the rebels or achieving democratization. In Vietnam optimists referred to "the light at the end of the tunnel." El Salvador was not Vietnam in large part because policy makers eventually came to realize that there had to be limits to the financial commitment of the United States.

Of course once the peace agreement in El Salvador was signed, the connection between dollars and democracy did not come to an end. Estimates for the postwar rebuilding of El Salvador ran as high as $1 billion with key targeted areas, such as assistance to the combatants to reenter civilian life, land reform programs, health and educational projects, and major injections of infrastructure monies. The Bush administration, for its part, pledged $250 million to aid El Salvador and worked with the European Community and the Inter-American Development Bank to provide a total of $175 million in assistance. This was clearly a good start, but as the crisis in El Salvador faded from view, the level of U.S., European, and Inter-American assistance declined.

When the Clinton administration came into office the Haiti crisis became the locus for the debate over the connection of dollars and democracy. The decision by President Clinton to ratchet up the economic embargo against the military regime had a devastating impact on the Haitian people and rekindled the Vietnam war era discussion of whether the United States was destroying the country in order to save it. Once the decision was made to enter Haiti with U.S. military personnel, President Clinton told Congress and the American people that the United States would commit hundreds of millions of dollars to the rebuilding of the shattered Haitian economy. In fact when U.S. soldiers entered the city, officers carried satchels with hundreds of thousands of dollars to begin construction work as an immediate "spark" to the economy. Estimates of the initial cost of the rebuilding program ranged from $500 million to $1 billion with long-term cost projections in the billions.[23]

The Clinton administration recognized that the success of Haitian democracy rested more on the performance of President Aristide than on the regular injection of huge amounts of U.S. assistance. Nevertheless, Haiti had fallen so far so fast that the flow of aid dollars into the country became the critical ingredient for establishing some semblance of stability and permitting the newly restored government the opportunity to construct a democratic system that had a chance of surviving. Dollars do not bring democracy, but in Haiti dollars became the lifeblood of a weak government that needed more than the presence of U.S. soldiers to remain in power.

Building Institutions—Training Democrats

As a result of the Kissinger Commission's recommendations on Central America, the Reagan administration went beyond the pouring of dollars into countries like El Salvador and began developing a series of programs designed to build democratic institutions and train people to run those institutions. The Kissinger Commission stated that the democratic strategy of the United States in Central America should be to "support democratic processes and institutions by backing free and competitive elections, the administration of justice, technical training and the development of leadership skills."

To achieve these objectives the Reagan administration targeted the institutionalization and training components of democratization. The most visible of these programs was the National Endowment for Democracy (NED). Established by Congress in 1983 the charter of the NED stresses "that private institutions in free societies can contribute to the development of democracy through assistance to counterparts abroad." Four institutes make up the NED: The AFL-CIO's Free Trade Union Institute, the Center for International Private Enterprise of the U.S. Chamber of Commerce, and the National Democratic and National Republican Institutes for International Affairs. These institutions administer a wide range of programs from leadership training and civic education to regional political parties, development of electoral machinery, and support for workers' federations. Since its inception a number of specific programs have been implemented in

Central America, such as grants to the Caribbean/Latin American Action organization to establish a so-called nonpartisan studies center in Guatemala, to the New National party in Grenada and the Conservative party in Nicaragua, to an organization called PRODEMCA (Friends of the Democratic Center in Central America) that allegedly funneled newsprint to the anti-Sandinista newspaper *La Prensa*, and to an anti-Castro group called the Cuban National Foundation.

Besides working through such institutions as the NED, the Reagan policy makers also developed important programs in the area of judicial administration. Because of the poor human rights records of countries like El Salvador and Guatemala, the United States felt the need to assist those governments in judicial reform. The United States provided Central American countries with assistance to train judges, prosecutors, and legal personnel; to improve court administration; to modernize law codes; to train criminal investigators; and to strengthen case reporting systems. Moreover, the United States also lent its support to the UN–affiliated Latin American Institute for the prevention of Crime and Treatment of Offenders (ILANUD), which also assists in training court personnel and improves the collection of criminal data and systems. U.S. officials are firm in their belief that the human rights climate in countries like El Salvador and Guatemala will improve only when the court system has capable administration and an efficient system of prosecution.

The U.S. initiative that gained the most attention in the area of democratization was the effort by the Reagan administration to assist in the electoral process of Central American nations. In El Salvador in 1982, 1984, 1985, and 1989 and in Guatemala and Honduras in 1985, the United States provided key assistance to assure the success of the voting process. The United States provided ballot paper and ink and technical assistance to computer operators at election headquarters. The Agency for International Development (AID) also provided monies to train poll monitors in Guatemala and provide for election observers in Honduras and El Salvador. The AID also showed a willingness to cooperate and provide financial assistance to the Inter-American Center for Electoral Assistance and Promotion (CAPEL). CAPEL provides a wide range of election services to governments in Latin America, including proper vote-counting procedures, educational programs for voters, seminars on election law formation, and development of computerized voting lists. From the State Department perspective CAPEL is "building a valuable network of individuals and institutions committed to promoting well-administered, free and competitive elections."

The United States also directed its energies to strengthening Central American and Caribbean legislatures. AID funds were appropriated to promote exchanges among parliamentarians from the region and to develop programs that enhance the skills necessary for effective policy making in a legislative setting. Legislative programs were developed in El Salvador, Guatemala, and Honduras to strengthen information management and analysis and administrative support services. Although legislative programs were less visible than the judicial and electoral ones, they nevertheless were viewed as critical if democratic institutions were to survive and prosper.

The final part of this effort by the United States to strengthen institutions in emerging democracies like El Salvador, Guatemala, and Honduras was to so-called people-to-people programs. Although many Americans think of the Peace Corps as our main people-to-people enterprise, the Reagan administration expanded the number of contacts with Central America as a way of introducing our democratic way of life. The United States Information Agency developed a pilot program called the Central American Program for Undergraduate Scholarship to bring thousands of Central American students to the United States every year. At the same time AID expanded the Partners of the Americas program, which develops links with U.S. civic and community groups like the Rotary Club. These educational and community contacts, plus the already substantial ties between U.S. labor unions and Central American unions, have created a broad-based initiative to educate the people of this vital region about the United States and democracy.

These programs instituted and supported by the Reagan administration reveal the extent to which the United States attempted to go beyond "buying time with dollars" by building a stronger institutional and human foundation for democracy in Central America. Realistically, however, the success of democracy in countries like El Salvador depended less on these programs and more on what the United States did to strengthen the economic climate in the region. Education, technical training, institution building, and goodwill can only go so far if war and a sagging economy create a fragmented and unstable political climate.

The importance of joining institution building with economic progress was also seen during the Bush administration. The U.S. intervention in Panama removed Manuel Noriega and restored democracy, but the stability of the country rested on restructuring the Panamanian Defense Forces (PDF), which had been used by Noriega to maintain a tight control of political opposition. Within days of the removal of Noriega, the United States began purging anti-democratic officers from the PDF and completely redefining its mission. U.S. military trainers and military police officers were brought in to create a new public force that was designed as a national police department with traditional responsibilities for upholding the law rather than maintaining an authoritarian regime in power.

Such rebuilding of key governing institutions like the PDF spread to other countries, especially those that were involved in responding to the drug trade. The Bush administration worked closely with countries like

Bolivia, Colombia, and Peru to modernize and train their anti-narcotic forces so that they could challenge drug smugglers who often had more sophisticated equipment than the government. The United States also continued its efforts to professionalize the security and judicial systems of drug producing countries where rampant corruption had limited the ability of those nations to advance the war on drugs. From the perspective of the Bush administration, one of the major challenges to democratic stability in Latin America was the power of the drug cartels, which in countries like Colombia acted as nearly sovereign states and openly flaunted the central government.

Rebuilding public institutions like the PDF and anti-narcotic units, however, was not the only objective of the Bush administration. Because of its support for liberalized market economies and free trade the Bush administration stressed a kind of "de-institutionalization" as it tried to pressure Latin American governments to dismantle state enterprises, cut government budgets, and streamline payrolls. The push for privatization of the state's role in Latin American economies was joined with a vigorous effort to promote U.S. investment in the region and the formation of trade agreements that opened the doors to expanded exchange of goods, capital, and services. In many respects the Bush administration was institution building from the private side of the ledger as it touted the role of the corporate sector in strengthening the Latin American economy.

As for the Clinton administration its commitment to institution building centered on Haiti and the enormous task of restarting democracy after three years of military rule. The United States saw its mission as a two-pronged effort of restarting democratic practice while simultaneously dismantling the old authoritarian system. One of the first tasks of the U.S. occupation forces was to secure the parliament building in Port au Prince and invite legislators who had been in hiding to return to their elected responsibilities. This action was followed by restoring the mayor of the capital city, Evans Paul, to his rightful position and handing over the radio and television facilities to the government. Before the United States could begin the process of strengthening the basic democratic institutions in Haiti it had to regain them and declare them legitimate.

While this legitimizing action was occurring U.S. troops were dismantling the private militias and political organizations that the military had used to intimidate the opposition. Early in the occupation U.S. troops killed ten police officers in the northern city of Cap Hatien. This action was immediately followed by the destruction of the police station by angry citizens. Later in Port au Prince, U.S. soldiers, to the cheers of hundreds of Haitians, took away the militia leaders associated with the Front for Progress and Advancement in Haiti (a political and paramilitary organization used by the military to intimidate the people) in a clear sign that the old institutions of repression would not be tolerated.

Despite the early successes of the United States in restarting democracy, Clinton administration officials were not naive in their realization that institution building would be a long and difficult process. Haiti has had little in the way of a democratic tradition, and its democratic institutions are but a framework with little substance. In the coming years the United States can be expected to administer a number of training programs designed to give Haiti's struggling democracy the tools to manage its own affairs.[24]

Holding the Center Together

The long-term success of democratization in Latin America is not contingent only upon a stable economy and strong institutions. An even more pressing concern is the development of a leadership elite that represents the values of modernization, compromise, and reform and that occupies the center of the political spectrum. In countries like El Salvador and Haiti, where there is a severe disagreement over the governmental rules of the game and where the revolutionary situation has tended to polarize the citizenry, it is extremely difficult for leaders with centrist political views to establish a base of support. What makes the situation even more problematic is that El Salvador and Haiti have a corps of military leaders who have little training in or use for the techniques of moderation and compromise. Responsible for maintaining order and often holding the reins of govermental power, the military high command has consistently been reluctant to accept civilian leaders whom they view as too weak to stand up to the rebels or too willing to succumb to the pressures for major socioeconomic reform.

Given the vast economic and social gulfs present in El Salvador and Haiti and the suspicion that accompanies leaders willing to accept a moderate course of action, the United States has had to work hard to ensure that the governments in that country are not captured by extremists, whether from the right or from the left. Our position has been that democracy will work best when leaders are in power who seek to create a broadly based government willing to establish policies that address the needs of the people. Relying on our own experience with democratic politics, administration policy makers are convinced that finding the middle way in El Salvador and Haiti will enhance the establishment of a stable democracy.

Those who have sought to establish a viable democracy in El Salvador insisted that if the United States were truly interested in strengthening the center it must press for a major shake-up of the military. Supporters of a shake-up point to moderates within the officer ranks who would be more amenable to democratic reforms, respect for human rights, and a negotiated settlement of the war. Although

Presidents Duarte and Cristiani promised to replace some of the worst human-rights abusers in the military ranks, conservative staff officers who make up individual graduating classes, or *tandas*, continued to dominate the process of appointment, promotion, and retirement. As a result the United States found it difficult to criticize or intimidate its allies with the Salvadoran military, for fear of alienating them at a time when they were not needed. Our reluctance to criticize military behavior lessened the influence of moderate politicians who had been trying to control the military, if for no other reason than to establish their own base of power.

Thus, the United States was working at cross purposes in its democratization of El Salvador. On the one hand it praised the benefits of elections, civilian leaders, and socioeconomic reform, while at the same time continuing to provide a largely anti-democratic, anti-reform military with the assistance necessary to fight the rebels. Fortunately, the UN agreement that ended the war addressed the issues of military reform, human rights guarantees, and restructuring the security and police forces with the result that key officers were reassigned or left their positions. What the United States had been reluctant to press the governing elites for during the civil war was achieved, albeit belatedly, and after years of unrelenting repression.

The task of holding the center in Haiti must be approached from a different perspective, particularly since the civilian leader, exiled President Aristide, was the focus of an intense debate over whether he indeed represented moderate politics or was a violent extremist (and perhaps a Marxist) bent on retribution against the military and the elite. The Clinton administration was taken to task by Congress for promoting Aristide's return when it was not clear whether the Haitian president had democratic credentials and could be counted on to bring the nation together. Opponents of Aristide's return stressed the speech in which he openly advocated the "necklacing" of his opponents (lighting a rubber tire and placing it around the neck of those viewed as agents of the military or the elite) as an example that Haiti would be thrust into renewed unrest once Aristide returned.

Proponents of Aristide's return stressed that the exiled president was not only the legitimate leader of Haiti but that his years out of the country had made him a more sophisticated democrat who recognized his need to move toward the center and convince wary members of the business class and the military that he would work toward reconciliation rather than retribution. Much of the concern about Aristide hinged on how he would deal with those in the military and para-military units accused of repression and whether he would crack down on retaliatory attacks on members of the upper class. In the case of Haiti, the future of democratization rested squarely on whether the national leader was willing to moderate his views on amnesty and class warfare in the name of stability and his own legitimacy. In the time that he has been back in power Aristide has appeared more willing to co-operate with the business elites and not use his opposition to rouse the masses to retribution.

Holding the center in El Salvador and Haiti will be a true test of whether democratization has a chance of succeeding. Unfortunately, the power of the military and the intransigence of economic elites makes the task of moderate leaders that much more difficult. Supporting reform and training a professional military, as the United States is currently doing, may not be enough to stem the temptation of elites to return to authoritarianism when faced with uncertainty and the pro-spect of a redistribution of national decision-making power. The estab-lishment of democratic governments in El Salvador and Haiti is a complex and extremely sensitive process that requires major sacrifices from all segments of society. If the United States hopes to see democracy firmly entrenched in El Salvador and Haiti, it may have to remind the key power contenders that the politics of the center thrive on com-promise and a willingness to accept change.

DEMOCRACY AND LATIN AMERICAN POLITICS

The U.S. attempts to support democracy in Latin America have, as we have seen, been marked by disappointment and frustration. The absence of an electoral tradition, the intransigence of conservative elites, the brutality of some military factions, and the weakness of the internal economy have all contributed to the slow pace of democratic development. The problems encountered by the United States as it seeks to bring democracy to the region make it necessary that a more basic question be asked before decision makers in Washington devise strategies for enhancing the democratization process or criticize elites for failing to live up to our model of governance. It is essential that the United States understand what it can realistically achieve in the way of democratization.

Democracy, as we know it, is a form of government in which the people play a major role in the process of leadership selection and policy making. But as we also know, there are various forms of democratic practice in the world today. In the United States we are of course familiar with our own federal republican system founded on the prin-ciples of separation of powers and checks and balances, while our allies in Europe have largely parliamentary systems based on party majori-ties and coalitional rule.

Both the United States and Western Europe are, however, quite different from El Salvador and Haiti. Democracy in El Salvador and Haiti is being constructed with a unique set of internal conditions and historical legacies. Just as in any country that is starting anew, El Salvador and Haiti cannot be expected to develop a form of government that ignores the social relations, the cultural mores, the political jealousies, and the economic separations present there.

In sum, what can be expected in those Latin American countries where the United States seeks to introduce and secure democratic governance is something best described as "conditional democracy," a form of democracy that borrows from the Western model found in the United States and Europe, but which shapes that model in a manner that fits the special conditions found in its own country. To many in the United States this may seem to be a disappointing prospect especially in light of the efforts that have been made to establish a liberal democracy that follows our system closely. Yet it is important to remember that our influence will always be limited, and no matter how hard we seek to place our mark on these emerging democracies, the host country will inevitably make adjustments either to assert its independence or to respond to the realities of internal politics.[25]

NOTES

1. See Howard J. Wiarda, "Is Latin America Democratic and Does It Want To Be? The Crisis and Quest of Democracy on the Hemisphere," in Howard J. Wiarda, ed., *The Continuing Struggle for Democracy in Latin America* (Boulder: Westview Press, 1980), pp. 3–24.

2. Fernando Henrique Cordoso, "On the Characterization of Authoritarian Regimes in Latin America," in David Collier, ed., *The New Authoritarianism in Latin America* (Princeton: Princeton University Press, 1979), pp. 33–60.

3. As background for this discussion see Thomas Carothers, *In the Name of Democracy: U.S. Policy Toward Latin America in the Reagan Years* (Berkeley: University of California Press, 1991).

4. Jeane Kirkpatrick, "Dictatorships and Double Standards," *Commentary* 70 (November 1979): 34–45.

5. Address by Elliott Abrams, Assistant Secretary for Human Rights and Humanitarian Affairs, United States Department of State, Bureau of Public Affairs, Current Policy No. 518.

6. From an interview with Deane R. Hinton, U.S. Ambassador to El Salvador, on ABC-TV's "This Week with David Brinkley," March 6, 1983.

7. George Shultz, Department of State *Bulletin*, September 1983, p. 84.

8. From a dinner speech given by Vice President George Bush, "San Salvador, El Salvador," December 11, 1983, as reported in the U.S. Department of State, Bureau of Public Affairs, Current Policy No. 533.

9. See Guy Gugliotta and Douglas Farah, "When the Truth Hurts," *Washington Post Weekly Edition*, March 29–April 4, 1993, pp. 6–7.

10. "Clinton Speaks on Haiti," Boston *Globe*, September 19, 1994, p. 1.

11. See *Congressional Quarterly*, May 12, 1984.

12. See Sam Dillon, "Dateline El Salvador: Crisis Renewed," *Foreign Policy* 3 (Winter 1988–89): 153–70.

13. Pamela Constable, "At War's End in El Salvador," *Current History*, March 1993, pp. 106–11.

14. Abraham Lowenthal, *Exporting Democracy: The United States and Latin America* (Baltimore, Md.: The Johns Hopkins University Press, 1991), p. 402.

15.   "Administration Defends Its Peace Policy in Central America," Boston *Globe*, February 5, 1984.

16.   Ibid.

17.   Piero Gleijeses, "The Case for Power Sharing in El Salvador," *Foreign Affairs* 61, pp. 1048–63.

18.   Terry Karl, "El Salvador's Negotiated Settlement," *Foreign Affairs*, Spring 1992, p. 153.

19.   Ibid., p. 162.

20.   "Economic Growth and the U.S. Policy in Central America," U.S. Department of State, Bureau of Public Affairs, Current Policy No. 509.

21.   President Ronald Reagan, Address to Joint Session of Congress, April 27, 1983.

22.   Henry Kissinger, New York *Times*, January 12, 1984, p. 1.

23.   Mark L. Schneider, "Haiti Recovery Program," in U.S. State Department *Dispatches*, November 7, 1994, pp. 753–54.

24.   Institution building from the Haitian perspective can be found in David Jacobson, "Haitians on Haiti: An Embarrassing Presence," *New York Review of Books*, November 3, 1994, pp. 37–38.

25.   See Howard J. Wiarda, "Can Democracy Be Exported? The Quest for Democracy in United States/Latin American Policy," paper prepared for the Inter-American Dialogue on United States–Latin American Relations in the 1980s, sponsored by the Latin American Program of the Woodrow Wilson Center for Scholars (Washington, D.C., 1983). See also Howard Wiarda and Ieda Siqueira Wiarda, "The U.S. and South America: The Challenge of Fragile Democracy," *Current History*, March 1989, pp. 113–16.

9

Responding to an Ever-changing Region

As U.S. power grew in Latin America, the term "sphere of influence" was used more often to describe our relationship to the nations in this region.[1] As a result of our superior military strength (and our willingness to use it), aggressive business organizations anxious to open new markets, and a series of U.S. presidents committed to promoting the United States as a major force in international politics, the interests of this country reigned supreme in Latin America. But the most important function of the Latin American sphere of influence was to serve as our security screen and first line of defense against foreign intervention. By ensuring that other major world powers did not gain a foothold in the region, the United States strengthened its defenses and lessened the prospect that the Western Hemisphere would become a center of international conflict.

Today the United States remains the premier military force in the hemisphere, we continue to control the largest blocs of trade and investment, and more recent presidents seem just as committed as their predecessors to ensure that this country maintains its hold on Latin America.

And yet amid these constants, there is change and a realization that the old ways of doing business are gone. In almost every facet of Latin American life there are signs of independence, foreign competition, and new modes of operation. Whereas in the past the United States thought nothing of directing the internal economic and political development of Latin American countries, today these nations fiercely resist attempts at outside intervention and on occasion have been bold enough to lecture presidents on the failure of inter-American relations.

A changing domestic political climate has contributed to the erosion of U.S. power in its traditional sphere of influence. It is extremely difficult for presidents to "carry big sticks" or "civilize" the Latin Americans without facing a barrage of criticism and a complex of laws and procedures designed to limit executive decision making. Although there may still be support in this country for a continuation of U.S. dominance in the Western Hemisphere, the opportunity to use our power has diminished. The U.S. public policy agenda today has become enormously crowded and the American public has become more demanding. A slow but steady realignment of our relationship with the nations of Latin America attracts less attention than crime statistics and health care reform. Yet while issues from the domestic scene dominate the attention of the American public, an equally significant set of changes is occurring in the hemisphere that will have a profound impact on our economic well-being, our power, and, ultimately, our security.

SOURCES OF CHANGE IN OUR SPHERE OF INFLUENCE

The challenges faced by the United States in its sphere of influence did not develop overnight. In the twenty-five years since John F. Kennedy took office, a series of events have contributed to the erosion of our influence in the Western Hemisphere.

U.S.–Latin American relations have undergone a number of significant changes in the contemporary era. These changes cover a wide range of issues and conditions from increases in foreign competition to dwindling foreign policy resources to new developments in trade liberalization to renewed emphasis on regional cooperation. So as to better understand the current state and future direction of U.S.–Latin American relations let us examine these sources of change at close range.

The Global Economy and the Rise of Competition

One of the most significant developments affecting Latin America in the contemporary period is the change required by the global economy. For a part of the world that looked to the United States for trade opportunities and placed more emphasis on import substitution strategies than export promotion, Latin America was quickly forced to restructure its economies and expand its trade horizons in order to survive in a world that had clearly changed. As Latin American leaders pushed for more open investment climates and sought to liberalize restrictive tariff systems, the countries of the region became attractive centers for multinational corporations, foreign banks, and a new wave of smaller traders anxious to gain access to the Latin American market. While this meant new opportunities for U.S. business, it also meant that Latin America was much more willing to look elsewhere for trade and investment. The United States began to face stiff competition from a number of countries that previously had been inactive in Latin America. Countries like Japan, Germany, Taiwan, South Korea, Spain, and Canada along with some of the emerging Latin American industrial powers, such as Brazil and Mexico, challenged the long-standing position of the United States as the primary source of trade and investment in the region.[2]

Even though the United States remained the largest trader and investor in Latin America, the influx of foreign competition reduced this country's share of the market and allowed the nations of this region to seek alternative sources of capital for development projects. Moreover, the huge bills incurred by Latin Americans when the Organization of Petroleum Exporting Countries increased its oil prices forced many countries to expand sources of their financing and diversify their economies, both of which diminished their traditional dependence on the United States. The Organization of Petroleum Exporting Countries oil price escalation of the 1970s also strained relations between the United States and Latin America, when hemispheric nations looked to this country to provide them with greater access to our markets for their exported goods. The response from the United States, which at the time was experiencing a severe balance-of-payments crisis of its own, was either to deny entry or to pass protective legislation that increased trade barriers.

To many Latin Americans our reluctance to assist them was not surprising, but it drove a wedge further into a relationship that was deteriorating. The Latin American reaction to our trade policies was unusually hostile and was expressed in terms that signaled a new-found independence and a determination never to permit its future to depend on U.S. goodwill or self-interest. As a result, the leaders of many Latin American nations became more aggressive in their trade talks with the United States and intensified their efforts to open up their economies to new sources of trade, aid, and investment. The days of one-sided commerce and financial relations with the United States were over.[3]

Many Latin American economies have undergone vast changes in the past years. The monoeconomies in which staple crops provided the bulk of the foreign exchange largely disappeared (except perhaps in Central America), as have the U.S.–dominated trade relations. By widening their trade horizons, Latin Americans have come to recognize that sources other than the United States can contribute to their economic development. Latin American economies are now more regionally focused with major trading blocks formed, such as MERCOSUR for the Southern Cone countries, CARICOM for the Caribbean nations, the Andean block and the Central American Common Market. Inter-American trade is also on the rise and is expected to be a key source of economic vitality in the region in coming years. Moreover, Latin American countries have been eager to gain greater access to the European Community and are beginning to make modest inroads into Slavic Europe and the former Soviet Union. Government and business leaders are actively pursuing trade and capital formation arrangements on a worldwide scale and, in the process, have left the United States without the assurance that its commercial and financial interests will be offered primary consideration.

Dwindling Foreign Policy Resources

After years in which Latin American countries saw the United States as their chief benefactor, trading partner, and source of development capital, the 1980s ushered in a new era in which the United States consciously contributed to its own declining influence in the region.

A few examples will serve to highlight the domestic conditions that have diminished U.S. presence and influence in Latin America:

1. President Clinton's FY 1995 international affairs budget is not only restructured under six specific foreign aid objectives—promoting U.S. prosperity through trade, building democracy, promoting sustainable development, promoting peace, providing humanitarian assistance, and advancing diplomacy (rather than in terms of geographic regions as was the case in the past), but the request of $20.7 billion in outlays is a decrease of over $1 billion from FY 1994. Although the State Department continues to target significant funds for Haiti, antinarcotic operations in the Andes, and investment promotion throughout the hemisphere, traditional aid programs that have been targeted to Latin America in areas such as development assistance in the past have been scaled back. This restructuring and reduction has not gone unnoticed in Latin America where countries have seen their aid allocations from the United States severely cut back. Increasingly the Latin American countries have had to rely on private non-governmental organizations to replace U.S. foreign aid. With Republicans, such as Senator Jesse Helms (N.C.), heading the Senate Foreign Relations Committee and regularly railing against foreign aid, the Latin Americans are not hopeful that the downward trend will abate any time soon.

2. To accompany the decline in aid assistance for the region there has also been a severe reduction in U.S. personnel representing official U.S. interests. Again because of budgetary reductions, the corps of U.S. diplomatic, military, and aid personnel has dwindled since the late 1960s. The term "American presence" in a country has been altered as a result of the budget cuts and has seriously affected our ability to report accurately about events, represent vital U.S. interests, inform host countries of U.S. policy, and provide neighboring countries with a helping hand.

These examples of a declining interest and involvement in the Western Hemisphere suggest that the United States may be in the process of rethinking its traditional commitments to the region and reordering its foreign policy priorities. It is important, however, not to interpret these examples of change as a break with the past and a deemphasizing of our "special relationship." What appears to be happening in hemispheric relations is that in the post-communist world, where U.S. domestic budget deficits are considered more of a threat than unrest in countries near our borders and U.S. corporate executives are more visible as representatives than diplomats, our policy toward Latin America is undergoing a kind of structural downsizing. Solutions to regional problems are not seen solely in terms of public programs and problem solvers are not necessarily public officials. Moreover, the days of grand scale Latin American policy with huge injections of aid and personnel are likely gone. The new Latin American environment or market economies and global perspectives have diminished the role of government as the definer of inter-American relations and transformed it into a kind of caretaker as other players and other institutions move to the forefront.

Also the view of Latin America from policy-making centers in Washington and corporate boardrooms in New York are beginning to compartmentalize the region and develop initiatives on a country-by-country and subregional basis. This, of course, is not necessarily a new approach, but the view that Latin America is no longer a singular entity that must be dealt with in its totality is being accepted with greater regularity. There will still be a "Latin American policy" of the United States in the future, but it will often be overshadowed by a "Central America," "Caribbean," "Andean," and "Southern Cone" policy. The special relationship between the United States and Latin America may have reached a level of maturity whereby this country begins to recognize differences and treats its hemispheric neighbors as individual entities.

THE GLOBAL ECONOMY AND LATIN AMERICAN LIBERALIZATION

One of the profound changes to affect Latin America and also U.S. relations with Latin America did not come as a result of revolution, military overthrow, or democratic elections. Rather Latin American civilian leaders who entered office in the 1980s and 1990s recognized the importance of opening their economies to the realities of a new global economy. Led by visionary presidents such as Carlos Salinas of Mexico and Carlos Menem of Argentina, many Latin American nations introduced economic policies that have been defined under the umbrella term of liberalization. As a result, the lifting of restrictive tariffs, the privatization of state enterprises, the removal of barriers to foreign investment, the reduction in government spending and hiring, and the reform of national currencies and credit policies became accepted methods of restructuring national economies.

Even though Latin American leaders embraced liberal economic reforms as a response to the onrush of the global economy, there was also a critical linkage to the United States. Government officials in the region, many of whom received advanced degrees from prestigious U.S. universities and were influenced by market principles such as the monetarist Chicago School economics of Milton Friedman, were instrumental in implementing changes to their economies. These so-called "techni-yuppies," such as Mexican Finance Minister Guillermo Ortiz and Chile's financial architect of liberalization, Hernan Buchi, saw first hand how capitalism works while they studied in the United States and were determined to introduce that system once they were put into positions of governing responsibility.

With civilian presidents and key advisors convinced that liberal reforms needed to be in place, the infatuation with the backbone of Latin American economies since the 1950s was dismissed and dismantled. Although the replacement of the old economic system with one more attuned to the new global economy brought short-term hardship in the way of unemployment, pay freezes, social welfare cutbacks, and general uncertainty, Latin American leaders were convinced that they could no longer rely on the engine of the state to drive their countries forward.[4]

As Latin America moved through this transition the Bush administration kept the pressure on Latin American leaders to adopt market principles. During the late 1980s, when debt renegotiations took place, Secretary of State James Baker, working with U.S. banks, achieved breakthrough agreements with countries like Mexico, Costa Rica, and Venezuela that were based on the understanding that a restructuring of debt and even the forgiveness of debt had to be linked with major changes in the manner in which Latin America ran its economy and did business. The Enterprise for the Americas Initiative also built on the debt renegotiations to enforce the need to create a climate responsive to investment, free trade, and market principles.

The changes in the Latin American economy were greeted with great anticipation in the United States and other industrial nations anxious to enter economies where the private sector was welcomed and where new opportunities abound. In the initial stages U.S. and European corporations became involved in buying state enterprises and transforming them into private entities. Once it became apparent that Latin American nations were serious about economic reform, investment levels skyrocketed, corporate executives swarmed into the region, and new businesses were born with lightning speed. Latin America became a center of foreign economic activity. Stock markets flourished, North American consumer products (and their logos) flooded the region, and Latin Americans increasingly became employees of foreign car manufacturers, fast food outlets, and mall chains.

In a few years Latin American economies had changed from being controlled by the state to being in the hands of private investors and foreign corporations. In the process economic relations between Latin America and the United States have never been more cordial and cooperative as both sides are in agreement over the accepted governing system (democracy) and the most effective economic system (capitalism). But as David Rockefeller, the honorary chairman of the Council of the Americas, warns,

As the societies of this hemisphere move away from an over-dependence on government, new and more flexible institutions will have to take responsibility for addressing and hopefully, for solving the immense problems of poverty, violence, disease and environmental degradation that we all face. That may be the greatest challenge for the private sector.[5]

The End of Communism

No change in the international scene has had a more profound impact on Latin America and inter-American relations than the collapse of communism. As the Marxist dominoes fell in Eastern Europe and the Soviet Union, shock waves were felt in Cuba, Nicaragua, El Salvador, and throughout a region where leftists depended on communist financial, ideological, and logistical support. Marxist revolution, which once was touted as the answer to the evils and injustices of capitalism in the hemisphere, became outmoded and irrelevant as the twin forces of democracy and market economy surged to the forefront of Latin American consciousness.

The end of communism had a particularly devastating effect on the Latin American left. Castro, already reeling from a faltering socialist economy, could not count on the Soviet aid that at one time was as much as $11 million per day. Castro berated Soviet leader Gorbachev in 1989 for straying from the orthodox line, but his criticism had little influence as the bearded communist no longer was regarded as the legitimate alternative voice in the region. By 1990 the Sandinistas were in disarray as the U.S. economic embargo and their own failings turned their movement into an unpopular regime. In neighboring El Salvador the years of fighting had taken their toll as the combatants, especially the Marxist Farabundo Martí National Liberation Front, sought a peaceful resolution of the war and promised to reenter Salvadoran society as democratic politicians. And in Peru, the radical Marxist guerrilla leader Abimael Guzman was captured by the government of Alberto Fujimori and his violent organization, the Shining Path, quickly faded from view.[6]

In a matter of a few years Marxism, which had so dominated the landscape of Latin America since Castro's triumphant entrance into Havana, had been relegated to rear guard actions in hopes of rallying peasants and urban dwellers to action. But with little money, no international leadership, and no convincing message leftist leaders were incapable of mounting any effective challenge to the status quo. The peasant uprising in the Chiapas province of Mexico in 1993 was viewed by some as a new beginning of leftist revolutionary activity, but the leaders of the revolt seemed more interested in gaining concessions from the government than pursuing a wider movement for radical change. There was still isolated guerrilla activity in Colombia, Peru, and Guatemala but the challenge posed by these groups did not threaten the system.[7]

From the standpoint of U.S. security interests, the collapse of communism worldwide and the failure of the Marxist left to sustain movements of radical change allowed Washington to turn its attention elsewhere and scale down its aid commitment to the region. Castro continued to be a problem but not as a center of revolutionary promotion. In fact the United States now faced a weakened adversary who appeared anxious to mend fences and reenter the hemispheric mainstream. Both the Bush and the Clinton administrations toyed with the idea of reevaluating the isolation of Cuba but faced firm opposition from the Cuban-American community and conservatives who argued that recognizing the Castro regime would solidify his hold on power. What stands for U.S. policy toward the last bastion of communism is a kind of tense waiting game as the United States waits for the Castro regime to collapse, all the while knowing that the United States is facing a foe who has survived for over thirty years and will not give up power easily.[8]

THE EFFECT OF THE NORTH AMERICAN FREE TRADE AGREEMENT

The passage of the North American Free Trade Agreement (NAFTA) not only solidified a trading relationship with Canada and Mexico but also convinced Latin America that the United States was committed to the global economy and willing to negotiate new terms of trade with its neighbors. Within days of NAFTA's passage Latin American leaders were talking about being included in the expansion of the agreement. Caribbean and Central American officials reminded U.S. Trade Representative Mickey Kantor about the natural extension of the agreement to the region closest to U.S. borders. Also Argentine and Chilean leaders made the claim that their booming economies were correctly positioned to participate in a free trade relationship with the United States. With a number of so-called framework agreements already in place that outline the parameters of free trade with the United States, many Latin American countries see the prospects for achieving a free trade zone from Anchorage to Antarctica as good. The announcement by the Clinton administration at the Summit of the Americas that it would press Congress to include Chile as the next member of NAFTA further brightened the prospects for achieving the hemispheric free trade zone.

The Latin Americans, however, are not waiting patiently for the United States to include the nations of the hemisphere in NAFTA. They are taking steps now to implement new agreements that expand an already vibrant free trade climate. For example, Mexico, Colombia, and Venezuela signed a trade pact that would reduce tariffs among the three countries by 35 percent in its first year. Colombia also announced that an agreement had been reached with Venezuela and the Central American countries to initiate a free trade agreement.

Another plus for moving the NAFTA bandwagon forward was the six-month report card on how the agreement affects U.S.–Mexican trade. In the first half of 1994 bilateral trade rose 17.5 percent from $42.9 billion to $50.3 billion. Furthermore, Mexico's trade with Canada also increased dramatically with a 33 percent surge to $1.7 billion. The bulk of the trade increase was in Mexican exports of computers, autos, and auto engines while Mexican imports from the United States were concentrated in capital goods, such as machinery. The trade picture in the post-NAFTA period also had a positive impact on investment as capital flows increased by some 31 percent.

The sense of optimism over the first months of NAFTA were shattered by the financial crisis in Mexico in late 1994 and early 1995. After years of ignoring the overvaluation of its currency and its enormous trade deficit, the government of Ernesto Zedillo changed economic policy and quickly devalued the peso. The devaluation touched off a flood of selling in the Mexican stock market and nervous foreign investors lost millions. With confidence in the Mexican economy plunging daily the Clinton administration spearheaded an $18 billion financial rescue package, of which the United States assumed a $9 billion line of credit. Although the devaluation decreased the cost of Mexican exports to the United States, many U.S. businesses were concerned that the higher cost of selling their goods in Mexico would severely compromise the objectives of NAFTA. These fears were supported by 1995 trade figures, which showed a $1.6 billion deficit with Mexico after a $350 million surplus in 1994.

Besides the downturn in trade, political leaders in the United States, especially from border states and industrial states that would be affected by higher costs in Mexico, began questioning the value of NAFTA. Their argument was that the devaluation would not only weaken U.S. exports to Mexico but also spur a new exodus of migrants from south of the border in search of cheaper goods and jobs as the economy entered a new, unstable phase.

Although leery about Mexico's future, many business leaders remained cautiously optimistic that hemispheric integration was on the fast track and could not be derailed by the Mexican crisis. The actions of the Clinton administration helped bolster the peso, and many Mexican leaders were urging calm and a longer view. The government of Ernesto Zedillo promised renewed privatization and government belt-tightening in its effort to put at ease the concerns of North American investors. The devaluation crisis, however, was clearly a major blow to

the Mexican economy and to NAFTA. With billions in trade and investment at stake, the government of Mexico, in concert with the United
States, set to work immediately to rebuild the image of its country as a
solid and stable business partner.

The Mexican devaluation crisis may have raised serious questions
about the wisdom of economic integration in the hemisphere, but there
remains a clear sense of movement in Latin America to achieve the
trade zone as quickly as possible. In many respects the Latin Americans
are ahead of the United States in seeing the potential for a region-wide
trade zone. Unfortunately, the United States, despite its support of
NAFTA, continues to view the European Community, the Pacific Rim,
and Slavic Europe as having greater potential for expanding markets
and capital investment. The peso devaluation reinforced the view in the
United States that economic stability is still years away in Mexico and
perhaps in all of Latin America.

THE MOVE TO MULTILATERALISM

U.S. policy in Latin America has come a long way from the days
when the Johnson administration browbeat the Organization of
American States (OAS) into supporting its intervention of the
Dominican Republic. Recent presidents have been careful to advance
policy initiatives, whether economic, political, or military, with the cooperation if not the involvement of hemispheric nations. Ronald Reagan
invaded Grenada under the auspices of the Organization of Eastern
Caribbean States, George Bush advanced his Enterprise for the
Americas Initiative by praising the importance of cooperation and
calling for a regional trade zone, and Bill Clinton's Haiti policy was
fashioned around UN and OAS participation.[9]

U.S. policy makers have embraced the concept of multilateralism as
a foundation of the U.S. relationship with Latin America. Besides peace
keeping and regional security, which are often at the core of multilateral
cooperation, key areas of Latin American development, such as aid
programs, debt relief, infrastructure formation, environmental protection, refugee assistance, narcotics control, and nuclear non-prolifer-
ation, are increasingly organized along international and regional lines
so that the United States does not appear to be dictating policy or
controlling the decision making. In a major overhaul of the United
States Agency for International Development (USAID) in 1993, for
example, top officials made it clear that the agency would

Give much greater priority to leveraging multilateral cooperation [because]
expanding the involvement of other donor groups not only serves the objective
of more effective assistance but has the additional benefit of strengthening
cooperation among the community of democratic nations that contribute the
bulk of the world's development assistance.[10]

After developing a reputation in the hemisphere as the preeminent power willing to go it alone in order to influence if not control events, the United States has come to the realization that it does not have the economic resources to respond to the problems in the hemisphere or the political will to sustain a police action. The United States remains the largest aid donor in the hemisphere and, as evidenced by the interventions in Grenada, Panama, and Haiti, is not shy about using force when pursuing its interests. But modern presidents are much more conscious about having their administrations portrayed as directing the destiny of the countries in the region. Working with the United Nations or the OAS now lends a legitimizing factor that presidents and State Department policy makers are anxious to use as they build support for their policies in Congress and among the American people.

Also the United States has emphasized the importance of multilateralism in its efforts to strengthen democratic government in Latin America. The Clinton administration has shown strong support for the OAS's Democracy Unit, which is designed to ensure open and free elections in the hemisphere. The Clinton administration has also supported the formation of more informal multilateral organizations such as the Four Friends Plus One formula to advance Central American peace. And, of course, the Clinton administration relied heavily on UN resolutions in implementing the economic sanctions against Haiti and in forming the twenty-five–nation coalition that participated in the peace keeping operation. As Clinton's Assistant Secretary for Inter-American Affairs, Alexander Watson, states,

The OAS and the UN are now very effectively fulfilling specific roles in resolving conflicts in the region. The OAS role in the defense of democracy is deeply supported by Latin American countries as well as by the United States.[11]

PEOPLE AS A NATIONAL SECURITY THREAT

National security has been the bedrock of U.S. foreign policy during the Cold War period, but the collapse of communism forced a reevaluation of national security and the threats to which the United States must pay particular attention. In this new era of foreign policy making, arguments are being made that national security threats must be redefined in different terms and that the United States must adjust its actions in ways that respond to different types of national security threats. As to Latin America, national security is increasingly being defined as events or circumstances that have an impact on the domestic scene.

Under the new interpretation of national security the migration of thousands of Latin Americans to the United States has risen to the top of the list of events and circumstances that are viewed by many

Americans as posing a threat to the United States. With the American public regularly focused on Haitian and Cuban boat people, Mexicans crossing the Rio Grande into Texas, and states like California and Florida transformed into dual societies of Spanish and English cultures, opinion polls point to a condition of fear and unease as U.S. citizens begin to see the arrival of Latin Americans as threatening their way of life, their jobs, and their pocketbooks.[12]

Government officials are beginning to recognize that the American public views Latin American migration to the United States in terms of a national security threat. The Clinton administration, after promising in the 1992 campaign to reverse the Bush policy of turning back Haitians on the high seas, refused entry of the boat people and instead placed them in makeshift holding camps in Guantanamo, Cuba. Later, as the tensions with the Cedras government in Haiti created a new wave of migrants, Clinton closed off the exodus to Guantanamo and Florida as public pressure intensified. Although the resolution of the crisis in Haiti was couched in terms of democratization and the return of an elected president, there was a clear undercurrent of concern in Washington and in states like Florida that a failure to return Aristide would unleash a larger flow of migrants to U.S. shores.

But while the Haitian outflow of people may have been curtailed with the return of Aristide (indeed hundreds of Haitians returned from Guantanamo and from exile in the United States), the deteriorating situation in Cuba may pose the next migration and national security dilemma for the United States. In August 1994 disgruntled Cubans began a new exodus to the United States. With the Castro government's tacit consent, over 20,000 Cubans left the Havana area on crudely made rafts and headed for Miami. After at first permitting the entry of the Cubans, the Clinton administration heeded the concerns of Floridians and abruptly ordered that the Cubans be turned around at sea or taken to Guantanamo with no guarantee of entry into the United States. The Clinton administration took the policy one step further by negotiating an agreement with the Castro government to ensure that the Cubans would patrol their own shores and deter the migrants from launching their rafts.[13]

These very visible migrations to the United States are small in comparison to the regular movement of people from Mexico to the United States. Despite increased border patrol activity, concrete walls that separate the two countries at key entry points, and more vigorous checks of employers who use illegal immigrants in the workplace, the Mexicans continue to come. Washington policy makers state that as NAFTA strengthens the Mexican economy, the migration will diminish, but this is little consolation to Californians and Texans who have become hostile to the flood of immigrants into their states. Political movements to deny welfare and educational benefits to illegals have been successful as evidenced by the passage of Proposition 187 in

California, and the continued effort to make English the official language in those states with high Hispanic populations points up the high level of resistance to immigration. These movements are growing throughout the country.

Experts who look at migration see the movement of people as a public policy problem that will face industrial countries like the United States for years to come. There is hope that more vibrant economies in the region will halt the exodus, but with populations growing ever larger in Latin America and immigrant communities in places like Miami, Los Angeles, San Antonio, and New York providing an attractive destination, the debate over how to handle this new wave of arrivals to our shores will continue. The difference, however, between this debate and those in the past is that the migration is being played out against the backdrop of national security concerns as white Americans fear that they may be losing their grip on their country to Hispanics.

THE END OF THE DRUG WARS

There is perhaps no foreign policy issue relating to Latin America that differentiates the 1980s from the 1990s more than the war on drugs. The Reagan and Bush administrations placed enormous emphasis and resources on curbing the flow of drugs from Latin America. During the Bush presidency, when the United States invaded Panama to end the Noriega dictatorship, drug policy overshadowed other areas of hemispheric relations. Placing drug interdiction high on its foreign policy agenda in Latin America was in many respects a response to the urban violence and the widespread fear that illegal narcotics were undermining the social order in the United States. As President Bush said at the San Antonio Drug Summit in 1992,

Drug traffickers corrupt our young people. They bring violence to our democracies and destroy our hemisphere's natural environment. This is a new kind of transnational enemy, well-financed, ruthless, well-organized, and well-armed, a foe who respects no nation's sovereignty or borders. The struggle to defeat the narco-traffickers requires cooperation, commitment, and it will not be won overnight. But make no mistake, defeat the traffickers we will.[14]

George Bush backed up his rhetoric with dollars during his years in office. With the announcement of the Andean Strategy in 1989, the United States pledged $2.2 billion from 1991–95 to advance the drug war in Colombia, Peru, and Bolivia. A major portion of the assistance was for military and police aid, although leaders in the three countries emphasized the need to concentrate on funding for development and crop replacement as keys to successfully ending the cultivation of coca and marijuana. The Bush administration, however, was committed to the militarization of the war on drugs and formulated its aid requests in the area of surveillance equipment, narcotics control training, and the construction of fire bases deep in the jungles where cocaine laboratories were located.

As the war on drugs progressed during the Bush years, signs of tension and internal disagreement appeared both in this country and throughout Latin America. Despite the money and the bold talk of destroying the drug traffickers, the United States continued to make only a peripheral impact on the flow of narcotics across its borders. By the beginning of the Clinton presidency many in and out of government were taking a dim view of the war on drugs. As one analyst stated,

The decade of the 1980s witnessed intense pressure on the part of the U.S. government to install an anti-drug national security regime in the hemisphere. These efforts failed because Washington did not establish a legitimate, credible and symmetrical framework capable of coping with the multiple problems presented by international drug production, smuggling and use.[15]

With the onset of the Clinton administration it soon became clear that the United States would not make the drug war a high priority. Early on the White House downsized its internal drug policy unit and delayed the announcement of the drug czar, former New York police commissioner Lee Brown. In fact, where the Bush drug czar, William Bennett, was constantly thrust into the forefront of the drug policy debate, Lee Brown became a little-noticed advocate for tough drug measures and spoke infrequently on the Latin American aspect of the drug problem. The Clinton administration was clearly interested in concentrating its efforts on education and prevention in the United States rather than militarization and interdiction in Latin America.

The Clinton administration's lack of interest in the Latin American aspect of the drug problem by may be associated with a number of successes by regional governments in combating the drug kingpins. The murder of Pablo Escobar, the Medellin cartel chief, by Colombian police; the crackdown on narcotics induced terrorism by Peru's President Fujimori; and the change of government in Haiti, a known transshipment site for drugs entering the United States, has encouraged those in government who have been fighting the war against the drug smugglers.

But these small victories in Latin America are overshadowed by the Clinton administration's seeming lack of interest in using war and the theme of war for responding to the drug crisis in this country. There has been no sense of urgency in the Clinton White House to pursue drug smugglers or spend millions on spy satellites and radar equipment. In fact, the Clinton administration entered into a major dispute with the Colombian government over whether the United States would permit the use of its radar equipment to shoot down planes suspected of transporting drugs. The argument made by U.S. officials was that the United

States did not want to be party to any errors in judgment that would bring down a plane with innocent people on board. There was, however, one significant victory during the Clinton administration—a money laundering operation (code name Operation Dinero) in which the Justice Department set up a phony bank in the Caribbean and convinced members of the Cali drug cartel to use the bank for its drug transactions. The sting operation led to scores of arrests and put a temporary crimp in the drug operation.[16]

The reluctance of the Clinton administration to follow in the tradition of Reagan and Bush and wage war against drug cartels in Latin America does not mean that the flow of drugs into the United States has diminished or that the power of the drug kingpins has waned. In fact an argument can be made that the drug cartels are becoming bolder and more pernicious in the pursuit of profits and power. Charges that Colombia's President Ernesto Samper actively solicited campaign contributions from the Cali cartel signaled that the drug kingpins may have normalized relations with the government and become a legitimized interest group in the Colombian political system. In Mexico the violence waged by the drug gangs claimed the life of Guadalajara's Catholic archbishop and may have been responsible for the execution of prominent political leaders. And in Central America the sharp drop in U.S. aid for the governments of El Salvador and Nicaragua and the departure of Colonel Noriega in Panama has stimulated the drug trade as a new generation of drug entrepreneurs ply their trade in a more open economic climate and without the watchful eye of the United States.

The Clinton administration points with pride to the decline in cocaine use in the United States and the wide range of educational and prevention programs that are making a dent in crime related to drugs in many urban centers. But while there have been signs of improvement, new narcotics enter the United States from Latin America. Countries that previously were on the fringes of drug cultivation and processing like Brazil, Chile, and Argentina are now deeply enmeshed in the drug trade. And perhaps most importantly the violence related to the drug enterprise and drug use in the United States and Latin America continues. The political war announced by the Bush administration may be over but the real war in the United States and in Latin America continues unabated.

THE MORE THINGS CHANGE . . .

In this climate of newness and change that is the Latin America of the 1990s it is important to emphasize that relations with the United States are surprisingly revolutionary. Although revolution connotes radical change and upheaval, the word itself derives from the Latin, *revolver*: to return to. In many respects what is happening in U.S.–Latin

American relations is a return to an earlier period of political, economic, and military interaction. Despite the fact that Latin America today is a region that has formed a mature relationship with the United States by opening its economy to trade and investment and downplaying its nationalistic proclivities, the consequences of these developments in terms of how the United States operates in the hemisphere are strangely reminiscent of how it conducted its business during the heyday of Roosevelt's Big Stick, Taft's Dollar Diplomacy, and Wilson's civilizing interventionism.

If we review the previous sections on how change has reshaped the relationship between Latin America and the United States what is obvious is that U.S. ties to the region are driven by corporate interests and shaped by private rather than public contacts. U.S.–Latin American policy is now akin to the days at the turn of the century when American capitalists roamed the region in search of new opportunities. The U.S. government saw itself during this era as charged with assisting and protecting these business interests by arranging contacts, smoothing paperwork, and ensuring that governments would provide a stable economic environment. There was little talk of huge public sector programs or major injections of government capital to address the needs of the Latin American nations. Rather, the United States stressed that private development was the key to bringing these nations into the twentieth century. U.S. foreign policy in Latin America was in a real sense U.S. business policy. There might have been some grumbling in the region over the use of the corporate sector to represent U.S. interests, but key elites in Latin America welcomed the attention and the dollars that the businesses brought into the region.

Also during this early period of Roosevelt, Taft, and Wilson the United States defined its political mission in terms of good government and stability. The Roosevelt Corollary articulated the obligation of the United States to stop chronic wrongdoing and fashion a policeman's role in the hemisphere. The Bush administration invaded Panama to remove Noriega and restore democracy. A few years later, Bill Clinton sent troops to Haiti to restore President Aristide, whom Clinton praises in terms that are close to Wilson's boast of promoting the election of good men in South America. This may not be a new era of the Big Stick in Latin America, but it certainly is a time when the United States military is being called upon to be a policeman for the region and a force for modernization and reform.

What may be the most critical tie between the turn-of-the-century U.S. policy approach toward Latin America and the contemporary relationship is the desire of Washington officials to foster stability in the region so that other, more pressing international concerns can be addressed without the distractions from our neighbors. Just like it did in the Big Stick era, the United States views Latin America as an area of opportunity but not as a high priority zone of diplomatic and economic attention. Latin America is indeed our neighbor and we must focus on events and trends in our neighborhood, but for U.S. policy makers there are far more important political and economic horizons in the Pacific Basin, Europe, and the former Soviet bloc. We therefore often look over our shoulder at Latin America and when instability erupts in the hemisphere, whether it is in 1905 or 1995, feel an obligation to act, but it is more out of annoyance than real concern.

As the title of this section suggests, relations between the United States and Latin America may have gone full circle. This revolutionary aspect of our ties to the region may be bothersome to those who want the United States to follow a more activist model of foreign relations where diplomats, advisors, consultants, aid officials, information officers, and other public employees distribute money, run programs, and guide the political fortunes of the Latin American governments. But in the Latin America of the 1990s, U.S. policy is returning to a time when governments stepped aside and let the marketplace advance. U.S. interests and public presence was directed mainly toward ensuring that friends of the United States were in office to help advance U.S. economic interests.

NOTES

1. See Jan F. Triska's discussion of spheres of influence in his *Dominant Powers and Subordinate States: The United States in Latin America and the Soviet Union in Eastern Europe* (Durham, N.C.: Duke University Press, 1986).

2. See Barbara Stallings and Gabriel Szekely, *Japan, the United States and Latin America: Toward a Trilateral Relationship in the Western Hemisphere* (Baltimore, Md.: The Johns Hopkins University Press, 1993).

3. For background see H. Jon Rosenbaum, "U.S. trade and Investment Policy toward Latin America," in *Trade, Aid and U.S. Economic Policy in Latin America*, edited by Howard Wiarda and Janine Perfit (Washington, D.C.: American Enterprise Institute, 1983).

4. See Moises Naim, "The Four I's of Reform," *Hemisfile*, July/August 1994, pp. 8–12.

5. David Rockefeller, "Latin America, Next Steps," *Washington Report*, Winter/Spring 1994, pp. 12–14.

6. See David Scott Palmer, ed., *Shining Path of Peru* (New York: St. Martin's Press, 1992).

7. See Timothy Wickham-Crowley, *Guerrillas and Revolution in Latin America: A Comparative Study of Insurgents and Regimes Since 1956* (Princeton, N.J.: Princeton University Press, 1992).

8. Eleana Cardoza and Ann Helwege, *Cuba After Communism* (Cambridge, Mass.: MIT Press, 1992).

9. For a view of the Clinton position on multilateralism, see Warren Christopher, "Supporting Democracy and Prosperity Through the OAS," Remarks at an OAS luncheon, Washington, D.C., March 26, 1994, in U.S. Department of State, *Dispatch*, April 4, 1994, p. 186.

10. USAID Officials, "USAID and Foreign Aid Reform." Testimony before the Subcommittee on International Economic Policy, Trade, Oceans and Environment of

the Senate Foreign Relations Committee, Washington, D.C., July 14, 1993, in U.S. Department of State, *Dispatches*, July 26, 1993, pp. 527–28.

11.   Alexander Watson, "U.S.–Latin American Relations in the 1990s: Toward a Mature Relationship." Address before the Institute of the Americas, La Jolla, California, March 2, 1994 in U.S. Department of State, *Dispatch*, March 4, 1994, p. 154 . For a critique of U.S. multilateralism with respect to Haiti see Ian Martin, "Haiti: Mangled Multilateralism," *Foreign Policy*, Summer 1994, pp. 72–89.

12.   For background, see Margery Tietelbaum, *Latin American Migration North* (New York: Council on Foreign Relations, 1986).

13.   Pamela Constable, "US, Cuba Set to Talk to Halt Flood of Refugees," Boston *Globe*, August 28, 1994, p. 1.

14.   President Bush, "San Antonio Drug Summit: The Challenges of Supply and Demand." Remarks at Opening Session, February 27, 1992, in U.S. Department of State, *Foreign Policy Bulletin*, May/June 1992, p. 57.

15.   Bruce M. Bagley and Juan G. Tokatlian, "Dope and Dogma: Explaining the Failure of U.S.–Latin American Drug Policies," in Jonathan Hartlyn, Lars Schoultz, and Augusto Varas, eds., *The United States and Latin America in the 1990s: Beyond the Cold War*, op. cit., p. 232.

16.   David Andelman, "Money Laundering: The Drug Money Maze," *Foreign Affairs*, July/August 1994, pp. 94–108.

Conclusion: The United States and the New Latin America

The formulation of U.S. foreign policy is tied to what is perhaps the most elusive concept in politics: national interest. Although on the surface it may appear that arriving at policy decisions that are compatible with what is good for this country is a relatively simple procedure, in reality it is very complex and highly controversial. The difficulty comes not in disagreement over the broad interests of this country, such as maintaining the defense of our economic interests abroad. Rather, debates about foreign policy and the national interest have arisen over the proper application of our power in the world and the domestic impact of that application. As President Clinton's National Security Advisor Anthony Lake states,

When the pursuit of American ideals is not perceived both at home and abroad as rooted in American interest, the result is confusion and suspicion. When American policy is seen to be defined solely in terms of realpolitik, it loses much of its natural character, strength and appeal.[1]

Anthony Lake's comments on the tension between ideals and realpolitik in U.S. foreign policy highlights the contemporary dilemma facing the United States as it operates in a vastly changed world and hemisphere. In Latin America the debate over our involvement in reestablishing democracy in Haiti struck at the core of this internal tension over ideals and realpolitik. In a real sense the issues surrounding our involvement in Haiti highlighted the fact that the United States is at a critical juncture in foreign policy making and foreign policy implementation.

What appears to be happening is that the more traditional objectives of U.S. foreign policy that flow from a Cold War understanding of national interest are running up against a more contemporary set of objectives that flow from a new set of international and regional conditions. Whether this new set of conditions goes by President Bush's

New World Order or President Clinton's concept of enlargement of market democracies, clearly national interest is being defined as a result of these changes. The Latin American policy positions of the United States are especially affected by this tension between the old and the new. The concerns over communist expansionism, revolution, and instability that guided U.S. policy for much of the post–World War II era are now being replaced by concerns over migration and trade uncertainty as the hemisphere changes and the policy agenda shifts in order to respond to those changes.[2]

In concluding this book we examine more closely this dynamic tension of traditional and modern definitions of national interest within the Latin American policy of the United States. In the following pages we will explore this tension by showing how the changing character of international and regional relations has forced a reappraisal of what national interest means and how it should be advanced. The blending of the traditional and the modern — the Cold War and the New Order — will provide a more complete picture of the challenges faced by the United States as it seeks to influence events and conditions in the region closest to its borders.

THE NEW HEMISPHERIC SECURITY

Defining national interest in terms of national security has undergone a major transformation since the 1980s. The Reagan administration made the revolutions in El Salvador and Nicaragua into direct threats to the security of the United States. But the days of huge aid packages, military advisors, forward bases, and *contras* are past. With Cuba focused internally, Russia incapable and unwilling to exert influence outside its borders, and revolutionary Marxism no longer attractive, the security of the United States is not threatened by communist expansionism and the prospect of falling dominoes ending, as President Reagan warned, in Harlingen, Texas.

In a few years the conditions for defining national security have shifted from revolutionary and strategic threats to human threats as illegal immigration, drug smuggling, and environmental catastrophes have now captured the attention of the American public and political leaders. Where President Reagan warned about the prospect of communist expansionism threatening our borders sometime in the future, illegal immigrants, drugs, and the effects of environmental neglect are, today, posing real challenges to the United States.

In the Latin American policy climate of the 1990s the relationship between national interest and national security is tied to what happens in California or Florida or Texas and not what happens in Havana or, for that matter, Moscow. National security is now truly national as public opinion focuses on how Latin America affects the domestic scene rather than how Latin America can compromise our security or our preeminence in the hemisphere. The foreign policy agenda of the United States in the western hemisphere is now driven by concerns over whether Hispanic immigration will compromise our American way of life, drugs will further escalate urban violence, or ecological decline in the Amazon rainforest will destroy the delicate environmental balance that we have taken for granted.

With national interest as national security undergoing such a historic transformation, policy makers in Washington and, indeed, the average citizen in the United States must think anew about what it is that threatens the United States. The fact that we as a country have only begun to see national security in a new light means that policy makers have yet to develop new strategies for responding to these problems and challenges. Unlike communist expansionism and revolution, which posed a direct threat to our dominance in the region, problems like illegal immigration, drugs, and environmental neglect are more complex and difficult challenges that cannot be solved by the traditional modes of military containment. These new national security challenges are not only global in scope but also domestic in impact. Pursuing the national interest in our Latin American policy will thus become increasingly problematic with few easy answers. The 1990s have new slogans such as "Stop Immigration," "Just Say No," and "Save the Rainforest" to replace the rhetoric of the Cold War, but the new security agenda of the United States in Latin America will not be attained with the kind of political consensus that often accompanied the call to arms against communism.[3]

THE NEW HEMISPHERIC STABILITY

The United States has consistently presented itself as an eager supporter of stable governments throughout Latin America. Championing stability, even if it meant aligning with dictators, became recognized U.S. policy not only because of the regularity and calm that accompany such a political situation but also because our economic interests could be more easily protected and could prosper in countries that maintained public order. Although this support of stability often cost us in terms of image and moral leadership, the returns to our trading and corporate sectors overshadowed the negative results.

Today the United States continues to be concerned with stability in the region, to ensure that democratic governments deepen their hold on the body politic, and to support the new market approach. What is different about our obsession with stability in Latin America is that Washington policy makers have become more committed to developing an institutional framework to protect the U.S. investment in democracy and capitalism. For example, the United States is a signatory of the Santiago Agreement, which pledges the nations of the hemisphere to protect governments threatened by authoritarian rule. The United

States has also been more active in bolstering the Inter-American Commission on Human Rights, which has worked long to establish the rule of law in Latin American governments. There is a clear commitment on the part of recent administrations to put into place the mechanisms to guarantee that political stability in Latin America will be attained with a democratic context.[4]

So, too, with the advance of market economies in the region. The United States is unwavering in its support for tariff liberalization, regional trading blocs, debt restructuring, and multilateral investment funds. There is no turning back from the global economy now that the North American Free Trade Agreement has been passed and the General Agreement on Tariffs and Trade accords have been ratified. But if the new system of economic development does not create prosperity at the low end of the social ladder then political stability under a democratic regime may be threatened. As the influential Inter-American Dialogue stated in a position paper on the future of the Americas

The United States government should have a key role in fighting against poverty and inequality in Latin America—through its influence on the policies and priorities of the international financial institutions, with its own bilateral aid programs, and in its extensive communications with all Latin America and Caribbean governments.[5]

There is without question a new confidence in Latin America that is fueled by the belief that the countries of the region have reached a stage in their development where democracy is more secure and the market approach is gaining acceptance. Political leaders understand that there is much to lose from a return to political instability and economic uncertainty. But there is also a lingering fear in the region that democracy and capitalism have to deliver to offset the frustration and anger of the masses that can be found close to the surface of politics. The United States, as the champion of democracy and capitalism in Latin America, has an enormous responsibility to provide the leadership and resources to sustain stability. It will not be enough to tout the mantra of elections and trade as the keys to Latin American stability and prosperity. The United States must take the initiative to fashion the institutions, develop the multilateral arrangements, and press for assistance to ensure that democratic capitalism remains in place and takes Latin America forward.

A NEW COMMITMENT TO CHANGE

One of the most difficult problems that has faced the United States in less developed countries is its inability and perhaps unwillingness to accommodate the forces of change. As a superpower with vital interests in all parts of the world, the United States has often been cautious and conservative when faced with changes in the political, social, and economic order of the Third World. In many instances, the caution and conservatism were natural responses because defense installations, corporate investment, access to precious minerals and resources, and valuable trade markets were affected by upheaval.

This concern with the potential or real impact of change on our interests has often clashed with the views of Third World leaders and intellectuals who interpreted our interest in maintaining the status quo as the result of power politics, greed, and the desire to control. The perception of the United States as selfish and insensitive to the needs and aspirations of the less developed world became a commonly accepted viewpoint, particularly in Latin America where many in the region could not understand the arrogance and neglect associated with our foreign policy.

It is difficult these days to characterize U.S. policy toward Latin America as anti-change or reflecting arrogance and neglect. The United States has become the agent of change in the hemisphere as it pushes for economic restructuring, free trade, open elections, and stronger democratic institutions. The Latin Americans look to the United States for leadership in their drive for greater democratization. In some instances the Latin Americans have accused the United States of not moving quickly enough to bring change, such as the creation of the hemispheric free trade zone.

But what the United States will have to guard against is concentrating its efforts for change in the business, trade, and professional sectors while ignoring the need to reform the living conditions and employment opportunities for those still mired in poverty. Despite the fanfare of change, 45 percent of the people in Latin America remain in poverty; the per capita income for Latin America in 1992 was 7 percent lower than in 1981. This huge army of the unemployed and underemployed in Latin America will be looking to the United States for answers if the global economy that we are promoting does not respond to the needs of the desperately poor.

The United States is currently benefiting from elite support in Latin America for its brand of economic change. If there is little trickle down effect from the market reforms, then the United States will be pressed by the Latin Americans for more development assistance and financial support. It is at this point that the Latin Americans will see if the United States is a new agent of social change or merely the old practitioner of market access and corporate profiteering. The popular uprising of disgruntled peasants in the Chiapas region of Mexico may be a warning bell for the United States and to its elite partners in Latin America.

The excitement generated by change in Latin America is real and infectious. Furthermore, the positive image of the United States as the agent of change is a welcome development, especially after generations of nationalistic antagonism toward the gringos. The challenge for the future of U.S.–Latin American relations is that Washington policy makers become as excited about change at the grassroots level as they are about reductions in tariffs and cutbacks in government spending.[6]

THE NEW HUMANITARIANISM

The United States, probably more than most countries of the world, views itself as a nation that has attempted to form a governing system committed to the principles of liberty, equality of opportunity, and the rule of law. Our nation takes pride in its reputation as a protector of human dignity, a leader in the field of equal rights, and an advocate of honesty and integrity in government. Yet despite the widespread support for the place of idealism in the U.S. political process, a principled approach to policy making has had, on occasion, a negative impact on our relations with other countries. Presidents and members of Congress have made decisions in the name of some lofty goals only to realize later that a more pragmatic course of action would have served the national interest better.

The difficulty in determining the proper role of idealism in the conduct of foreign policy making not only has created problems in our relations with other governments and in addressing critical issues in international politics but also has been a fundamental source of divisiveness in U.S. society. Since most people in the United States believe that this country should be a model for the rest of the world, actions by public officials that ignore our basic principles or tarnish our image as a democratic model complicate the process of achieving a consensus on the national interest.

As a result of the social divisions that erupted over our involvement in the Vietnam conflict and the Carter administration's staunch support for governmental policies that reflected moral standards, foreign policy making can no longer be evaluated only in terms of strategic considerations, trade opportunities, and potential threats to our power and influence. The national interest also includes such concerns as whether our foreign policy is committed to enhancing democratic practice, pressing for strong human rights, and achieving meaningful social and political reform. In the view of the proponents of a more principled foreign policy, U.S. interests also are served when this country shows that it can rise above security and economic considerations and make decisions that empower people, strengthen the quality of life, and reinforce social justice.

The relationship between moral principles, good governance, societal reform, and the national interest of the United States has become even more pronounced in recent years. Beginning with our involvement in Somalia to aid a starving country and continuing in Haiti to bring back democracy, the United States has moved beyond a commitment to human rights to what can best be described as a new humanitarianism. Although there remain many in governing circles in Washington who believe that this country is meddling in the affairs of other countries and spreading itself too thin by responding to human tragedies in distant places, the linking of humanitarianism and national interest has entered the foreign policy arena.

No matter how ambivalent Americans are about using their troops as doctors, road builders, and instructors rather than fighters, the reality of the post–Cold War world is that the demands of the United States as the premier world military power fall under the general heading of humanitarian. The United States no longer faces 10,000 tanks in Europe or thousands of ICBMs targeted at its heartland, but it does face a world of hungry people, abusive government, grossly mal-distributed resources, and angry masses willing to use force in order to settle old scores. The dilemma that is presented to the United States by the new humanitarianism is when to use power and wealth in another country. Although Haiti is close to the United States, the decision by the Clinton administration to intervene touched off a firestorm of criticism that conditions in Haiti, no matter how sad, did not warrant military invasion in the name of humanitarianism. The fact that President Clinton, like Bush before him in Somalia, ignored the opposition and pressed ahead points up the legitimacy of the new humanitarianism in U.S. foreign policy.

The people of the United States have always wanted to believe that their government's course of action was not only sound and practical but also designed to further their vision of a good society. The recent emphasis on using U.S. power and resources to champion humanitarian causes may not be firmly established with the body politic, but it is clearly becoming a new mission for the United States in a vastly changed world.[7]

THE NEW PARTNERSHIP

This discussion of the key ingredients of national interest would not be complete without commenting on the importance of maintaining friendly relations with our neighbors. This book began by describing how the United States has often taken Latin America for granted. Relying on stereotypes, exuding arrogance, and generally ignoring opportunities to deepen understanding, the U.S. government has in most instances only gone through the motions of friendship. Despite the slogans, the periodic state visits, the cooperative ventures, and the multilateral conferences, the United States has never really treated the nations of Latin America as a friend would: appreciating differences, accepting criticism, making few demands, and minding one's own business.

Our friendship problem with Latin America derives in large part from the inequality that separates the power and abundance of the United States from the uncertainty and poverty present in Latin America. This gap, which has led to decades of U.S. dominance and exploitation, may have served our interests, but it also created ill will and nationalistic fervor that translated into obstacles to trade and investment along with growing interest in diversifying relations outside the hemisphere. Over the years the United States lost touch with the people of Latin America, in particular the young people. We have forgotten how to make friends; we have failed to recognize that money does not necessarily buy friendships or control events; we have neglected to realize the connection between keeping friendships alive and our own best interests. As former U.S. ambassador to the Organization of American States Sol Linowitz stated:

We must understand that solutions to hemispheric problems cannot be manufactured in Washington and imposed on Latin America. They must be forged as cooperative undertakings between the United States and Latin America. Unilateral initiatives are rarely effective, and understandably antagonize our Latin American neighbors. We need the cooperation of Latin American countries just as much as they need ours—and we must work hard to obtain it. Common problems must be addressed jointly. Our fundamental goal must be to restore a sense of trust and partnership in U.S.–Latin American relations.[8]

To bolster inter-American friendship the United States may have to take some risks with new governments, pressure old allies to make concessions, and be more aggressive in its own efforts to win the hearts and minds of the masses. In short, it will take a total reevaluation of our relationship with Latin America and its people and a reexamination of what kind of friend we want to be—one who seeks to control from a position of superiority or one who seeks to build a partnership and cooperate from a position of neighborliness.

In order to achieve this new partnership the United States may be wise to remember a few simple guidelines as it works with the Latin Americans in this vastly changed world.

1. Proclaiming the market system as the key to development is not enough. The United States must work to ensure that the new economic system being put in place in the region works for everyone and not just for those who happen to be talented or in the right place at the right time.

2. Democratization needs to be seen as a process and not as an event, such as an election or the return of a popular leader. Institution building is the key to a stable and progressive Latin American political system. The United States has the capability to strengthen Latin

American democracies if it concentrates on making legislatures work, professionalizing the military, training judges and prosecutors, and inculcating key values, such as the rule of law and bureaucratic integrity.

3. Latin America is a definable region; the United States should treat it as such and move toward developing policies that link this region together. There are wonderful opportunities to pursue in the western hemisphere if the United States rids itself of the piecemeal approach to economic relations. The old adage that there is strength in numbers applies to the western hemisphere just as it does to military confrontations.

4. To achieve a mature relationship and seek a partnership with the Latin Americans the United States must fashion its policies to meet its neighbors as equals. There is no better way to sustain the market economy and democracy than to work side by side with the Latin Americans, learn from them, and help them create economic and political systems that reflect their own unique values and conditions. Resorting to arrogance and paternalism will not suffice in the 1990s— nor should it.

NOTES

1. Anthony Lake, "Defining the National Interest," *Proceedings of the Academy of Political Science* 34, no. 2 (1981), in Chau T. Phan, ed., *World Politics 82/83* (Guilford, Conn.: Annual Editions, 1983), p. 8.

2. Anthony Lake, "From Containment to Enlargement." Address at Johns Hopkins University, School of Advanced International Studies, Washington, D.C., September 21, 1993.

3. Madeline K. Albright, "Use of Force in a Post–Cold War World." Remarks to the National War College, National Defense University, Fort McNair, Wasington, D.C., September 23, 1993.

4. See the discussion of the strategies to protect democracy in Inter-American Dialogue, *Convergence and Community, the Americas in 1993* (Aspen, Colo.: Aspen Institute, 1993), pp. 21–40.

5. Ibid., pp. 55–56.

6. Michael Kryzanek, *Latin America: Change and Challenge* (New York: HarperCollins, 1995), pp. 283–91.

7. See President Clinton, "Confronting the Challenges of a Broader World," Address to the UN General Assembly, New York City, September 27, 1993.

8. Sol Linowitz, "Latin America: The President's Agenda," *Foreign Affairs*, Winter 1988–89, pp. 45–62.

Selected Bibliography

Ad Hoc Working Group on Latin America. *The Southern Connection: Recommendations for a New Approach to Inter-American Relations*. Washington, D.C.: Transnational Institute, 1977.

Agee, Philip. *Inside the Company: CIA Diary*. Middlesex, England: Penguin Books, 1975.

Allison, Graham T. *Essence of Decision: Explaining the Cuban Missile Crisis*. Boston: Little, Brown, 1971.

Ameringer, Charles D. *The Democratic Left in Exile: The Anti-Dictatorial Struggle in the Caribbean, 1945–1959*. Coral Gables, Fla.: University of Miami Press, 1974.

Arnson, Cynthia J. *Crossroads Congress, The Reagan Administration and Central America*. New York: Pantheon, 1989.

Atkins, G. Pope, ed. *South America in the 1990's*. Boulder, Colo.: Westview Press, 1990.

____. *Latin America in the International Political System*. New York: Free Press, 1977.

Bailey, John M. "U.S. Military Assistance to Latin America." *Journal of Inter-American Studies and World Affairs* 14 (1972): 469–87.

Bailey, Samuel L. *The United States and the Development of South America, 1945–1975*. New York: New Viewpoints, 1976.

Barber, William F., and C. Neale Ronning. *Internal Security and Military Power: Counterinsurgency and Civic Action in Latin America*. Columbus: Ohio State University Press, 1966.

Barnett, Richard S., and Ronald E. Muller. *Global Reach: The Power of the Multinational Corporations*. New York: Simon & Schuster, 1975.

Bender, Lynn D. *The Politics of Hostility: Castro's Revolution and U.S. Policy*. San Juan: Inter-American University, 1974.

Blachman, Morris, William LeoGrande, and Kenneth Sharpe. *Confronting Revolution: Security Through Diplomacy in Central America*. New York: Pantheon, 1986.

Black, George. *The Good Neighbor: How the United States Wrote the History of Central America and the Caribbean*. New York: Pantheon, 1989.

Black, Jan Knippers. *Sentinels of Empire. The United States and Latin America Militarism*. New York: Greenwood Press, 1986.

Blasier, Cole. *The Hovering Giant: U.S. Responses to Revolutionary Change in Latin America*. Pittsburgh: University of Pittsburgh Press, 1976.

Bodenheimer, Suzanne. *The Ideology of Developmentalism: The American Paradigm-Surrogate for Latin American Studies*. Beverly Hills, Calif.: Sage, 1971.

Bonner, Raymond. *Weakness and Deceit: U.S. Policy and El Salvador*. New York: Times Books, 1984.

Bonsal, Philip W. *Cuba, Castro and the United States*. Pittsburgh: University of Pittsburgh Press, 1971.

Bosch, Juan. *Pentagonism: A Substitute for Imperialism*. Translated by Helen R. Lane. New York: Grove, 1968.

Bradford, Colin I., and others. *New Directions in Development: Latin America, Export Credit, Population Growth and U.S. Attitudes*. New York: Praeger, 1974.

Buckley, Tom. *Violent Neighbors: El Salvador, Central America and the United States*. New York: Times Books, 1984.

Bunau-Varilla, Phillipe. *The Great Adventure of Panama*. New York: Doubleday, 1920.

Bundy, William P. "Who Lost Patagonia? Foreign Policy and the 1980 Campaign." *Foreign Affairs* (Fall 1979): 1–27.

Calcott, Wilfred Hardy. *The Caribbean Policy of the United States, 1890–1920*. Baltimore: Johns Hopkins University Press, 1942.

____. *The Western Hemisphere: Its Influence on United States Policies to the End of World War II*. Austin: University of Texas Press, 1968.

Chace, James. *Endless War*. New York: Vintage, 1984.

Chilcote, Ronald, and Joel Edelstein, eds. *Latin America: The Struggle with Dependency and Beyond*. New York: Halsted, 1974.

Cockroft, James D. *Neighbors in Turmoil: Latin America*. New York: Harper & Row, 1989.

Commission on United States–Latin American Relations (Linowitz Commission). *The Americas in a Changing World*. New York: Halsted, 1974.

Cornelius, Wayne, ed. *Immigration and U.S.–Mexican Relations*. San Diego: University of California Press, 1981.

____. *America in the Era of Limits: Nativist Relations to the "New" Immigration*. San Diego: University of California Press, 1982.

Cotler, Julio, and Richard R. Fagen, eds. *Latin America and the United States*. Stanford, Calif.: Stanford University Press, 1974.

Council for Latin America. *The Effects of United States and Other Foreign Investments in Latin America*. New York: Council for Latin America, 1970.

Crassweller, Robert D. *Trujillo: The Life and Times of a Caribbean Dictator*. New York: Macmillan, 1966.

____. *The Caribbean Community: Changing Societies and U.S. Foreign Policy*. New York: Praeger, 1972.

Cruz, Arturo. *Memoirs of a Counter-Revolutionary Life with the Contras, the Sandinistas and the CIA*. New York: Doubleday, 1989.

Davis, Harold E., Larman C. Wilson, and others. *Latin American Foreign Policies*. Baltimore: Johns Hopkins University Press, 1975.

Davis, Nathaniel. "U.S. Covert Action in Chile, 1971–1973." *Foreign Service Journal* 55 (November 1978): 10–14, 38–39, 56; (December 1978): 11–13, 43.

Dominguez, Jorge I. "Consensus and Divergence: The State of the Literature on Inter-American Relations in the 1970's." *Latin American Research Review* 13 (1978): 87–126.

____. *U.S. Interests and Policies in the Caribbean and Central America*. Washington, D.C.: American Enterprise Institute for Public Policy Research, 1982.

Dominguez, Jorge, and Rafael Hernandez, eds. *U.S. Cuban Relations in the 1990's*. Boulder, Colo.: Westview Press, 1989.

Donzer, Donald M. *Are We Good Neighbors? Three Decades of Inter-American Relations, 1930–1960*. Gainesville: University of Florida Press, 1959.

Draper, Theodore. *Castroism: Theory and Practice*. New York: Praeger, 1965.

____. "The Dominican Intervention Reconsidered," *Political Science Quarterly* 86 (1971): 1–36.

Dreier, John C., ed. *The Alliance for Progress*. Baltimore: Johns Hopkins University Press, 1962.

____. "New Wine and Old Bottles: The Changing Inter-American System." *International Organization* 22 (1968): 477–93.

Duncan, W. Raymond. "Castro's New Approach Toward Latin America." *World Affairs* 133 (March 1971): 275–82.

____. "Soviet Policy in Latin America Since Khrushchev." *Orbis* 15: 643–69.

Einaudi, Luigi, ed. *Beyond Cuba: Latin America Takes Charge of Its Future*. New York: Crane, Russak, 1974.

Eisenhower, Milton. *The Wine is Bitter: The United States and Latin America*. Garden City, N.Y.: Doubleday, 1963.

Erisman, Michael, and John Martz, eds. *Colossus Challenged: The Struggle for Caribbean Influence*. Boulder, Colo.: Westview Press, 1982.

Fagen, Richard, and Olga Pellicer. *The Future of Central America*. Stanford, Calif.: Stanford University Press, 1983.

Farer, Tom. *The United States and the Inter-American System*. St. Paul, Minn.: West Publishing Co., 1978.

Feinberg, Richard. "Central America: No Easy Answer." *Foreign Affairs* (Summer 1981): 1121–46.

Ferguson, Yale. *Contemporary Inter-American Relations: A Reader in Theory and Issues*. Englewood Cliffs, N.J.: Prentice Hall, 1972.

Fontaine, Roger W. *Brazil and the United States*. Washington, D.C.: American Enterprise Institute for Public Policy Research, 1974.

Francis, Michael. "Military Aid to Latin America in the U.S. Congress." *Journal of Inter-American Studies* 6 (July 1964): 389–404.

Frank, Andre Gunder. *Capitalism and Underdevelopment in Latin America: Historical Studies of Chile and Brazil*. New York: Monthly Review, 1967.

____. *Latin America: Underdevelopment or Revolution?* New York: Monthly Review, 1969.

Fuentes, Carlos. "Farewell Monroe Doctrine." *Harpers* (August 1981): 29–35.

Gaspar, Edmund. *United States–Latin America: A Special Relationship?* Washington, D.C.: American Enterprise Institute for Public Policy Research, 1978.

Gil, Federico G. *Latin American–United States Relations*. New York: Harcourt Brace Jovanovich, 1971.

Goldhamer, Herbert. *The Foreign Powers in Latin America*. Princeton, N.J.: Princeton University Press, 1982.

Gordon, Lincoln. *A New Deal for Latin America: The Alliance for Progress*. Cambridge, Mass.: Harvard University Press, 1963.

Gutman, Roy. *Banana Diplomacy: The Making of American Policy in Nicaragua, 1981–87*. New York: Simon & Schuster, 1988.

Hahn, Walter F., ed. *Central America and the Reagan Doctrine*. Boston: Center for International Relations (Boston University), 1987.

Hamilton, Nora, and others. *Crisis in Central America: Regional Dynamics and U.S. Policy in the 1980s*. Boulder, Colo.: Westview Press, 1988.

Hansen, Roger D. *Central America: Regional Integration and Economic Development*. Washington, D.C.: National Planning Association, 1967.

____. *U.S.–Latin American Economic Policy*. Washington, D.C.: Overseas Development Council, 1975.

Hanson, Simon G. *Five Years of the Alliance for Progress*. Washington, D.C.: Inter-American Affairs, 1967.

____. *Dollar Diplomacy Modern Style: Chapters in the Failure of the Alliance for Progress.* Washington, D.C.: Inter-American Affairs, 1971.

Hayes, Margaret Daly. "Security to the South: U.S. Interests in Latin America." *International Security* 5 (Summer 1980): 130–51.

Hilsman, Roger. *The Politics of Policy Making in Defense and Foreign Affairs.* New York: Harper & Row, 1971.

Horowitz, Irving Louis, ed. *Rise and Fall of Project Camelot.* Cambridge, Mass.: MIT Press, 1967.

Horowitz, Irving Louis, Josue de Castro, and John Gerassi, eds. *Latin American Radicalism.* New York: Random House, 1969.

Immerman, Richard. *The CIA in Guatemala.* Austin: University of Texas Press, 1983.

Karnes, Thomas L. *The Failure of Union: Central America, 1824–1960.* Chapel Hill: University of North Carolina Press, 1961.

____, ed. *Readings in the Latin American Policy of the United States.* Tucson: University of Arizona Press, 1972.

Kessley, Francis. "Kissinger's Legacy: A Latin American Policy." *Current History* 12 (February 1977): 76–78.

Kirkpatrick, Jeane. "The Hobbes Problem: Order, Authority and Legitimacy in Central America." *AEI Public Policy Papers.* Washington, D.C.: American Enterprise Institute for Public Policy Research, 1981.

Kryzanek, Michael. "President Reagan's Caribbean Basin Formula." *AEI Foreign Policy and Defense Review* (June 1982): 29–36.

Lake, Anthony. *Somoza Falling, The Nicaraguan Dilemma: A Portrait of Washington at Work.* Boston: Houghton Mifflin, 1989.

Langley, Lester. *The United States and the Caribbean in the Twentieth Century.* Athens: University of Georgia Press, 1976.

LeoGrande, William. "The Revolution in Nicaragua: Another Cuba?" *Foreign Affairs* (Fall 1979): 28–50.

LeoGrande, William, and Carla Anne Roberts. "Oligarchs and Officers: The Crisis in El Salvador." *Foreign Affairs* (Summer 1980): 1084–1103.

LeFeber, Walter. "Inevitable Revolutions." *Atlantic Monthly* 249 (June 1982): 74–83.

Leiken, Robert S., ed. *Central America: Anatomy of Conflict.* New York: Pergamon Press, 1984.

Lernoux, Penny. *Cry of the People.* New York: Penguin Books, 1982.

____. "The Kirkpatrick Doctrine for Latin America." *Nation* 239 (March 28, 1981): 361–64.

Levinson, Jerome, and Juan de Onis. *The Alliance That Lost Its Way: A Critical Report on the Alliance for Progress.* Chicago: Quadrangle Press, 1972.

Lewis, Gordon K. *Notes on the Puerto Rican Revolution.* New York: Monthly Review, 1975.

Lieuwen, Edwin. *Arms and Politics in Latin America.* New York: Praeger, 1961.

____. *Generals vs. Presidents.* New York: Praeger, 1964.

____. *U.S. Policy in Latin America.* New York: Praeger, 1965.

Lowenthal, Abraham F. "Foreign Aid as a Political Instrument: The Case of the Dominican Republic." *Public Policy* 14 (1965): 141–60.

____. "'Liberal', 'Radical', and 'Bureaucratic' Perspectives on U.S.–Latin American Policy: The Alliance for Progress in Retrospect." In *Latin America and the United States: The Changing Political Realities*, edited by Julio Cotler and Richard R. Fagan. Stanford, Calif.: Stanford University Press, 1974.

____. *Partners in Conflict: The United States and Latin America.* Baltimore: Johns Hopkins University Press, 1987.

____. "Ronald Reagan and Latin America: Coping with Hegemony in Decline." In *Eagle Defiant: United States Foreign Policy in the 1980s*, edited by Kenneth Oye, and others. Boston: Little, Brown, 1983.

Lowenthal, Abraham F., and Albert Fishlow. *Latin America's Emergence: Toward a U.S. Response*. New York: Foreign Policy Association, 1979.

Martin, John Bartlow. *Overtaken by Events: The Dominican Crisis From the Fall of Trujillo to the Civil War*. Garden City, N.Y.: Doubleday, 1966.

Martz, John, ed. *Latin America, The United States and the Inter-American System*. Boulder, Colo.: Westview Press, 1980.

____. *United States Policy in Latin America: A Quarter Century of Crisis and Challenge 1961–1986*. Lincoln: University of Nebraska Press, 1988.

Matthews, Herbert. *The Cuban Story*. New York: Braziller, 1961.

____. *Fidel Castro*. New York: Simon & Schuster, 1969.

May, Ernest R. *The Making of the Monroe Doctrine*. Cambridge, Mass.: Harvard University Press, 1975.

Mecham, Lloyd. *The United States and Inter-American Security, 1889–1960*. Austin: University of Texas Press, 1961.

Menges, Constantine. *Inside the National Security Council*. New York: Simon & Schuster, 1989.

Middlebrook, Kevin, and Carlos Rico, eds. *The United States and Latin America in the 1980s*. Pittsburgh: University of Pittsburgh Press, 1986.

Molineau, Harold. *U.S. Policy Toward Latin America from Regionalism to Globalism*. Boulder, Colo.: Westview Press, 1986.

Morgenthau, Hans J. "A Political Theory of Foreign Aid." *American Political Science Review* 56 (June 1962): 301–9.

Munro, Dana G. *The United States and the Caribbean Republics, 1921–1933*. Princeton, N.J.: Princeton University Press, 1974.

Needler, Martin C. *The United States and the Latin American Revolution*. Boston: Allyn & Bacon, 1972.

Newfarmer, Richard, ed. *From Gunboats to Diplomacy: New U.S. Policies for Latin America*. Baltimore: Johns Hopkins University Press, 1984.

Pastor, Robert A. "Congress' Impact on Latin America: Is There a Madness in the Method?" In *Report of the Commission on the Organization of the Government for the Conduct of Foreign Policy* 3, app. 1. Washington, D.C.: Government Printing Office, 1975.

____. "Our Real Interests in Central America." *Atlantic Monthly* (July 1982): 27–39.

____. *Condemned to Repetition: The United States and Nicaragua*. Princeton, N.J.: Princeton University Press, 1987.

Pastor, Robert A., and Jorge Castenada. *Limits to Friendship: The United States and Mexico*. New York: Knopf, 1988.

Perkins, Dexter. *The United States and Latin America*, rev. ed. Baton Rouge: Louisiana State University Press, 1966.

____. *The United States and the Caribbean*, rev. ed. Cambridge, Mass.: Harvard University Press, 1966.

Perloff, Harvey S. *Alliance for Progress*. Baltimore: Johns Hopkins University Press, 1969.

Peterson, Harold F. *Argentina and the United States, 1810–1960*. Albany: State University of New York, 1964.

Petras, James, ed. *Latin America: From Dependence to Revolution*. New York: John Wiley, 1973.

Petras, James, and Morris Morley. *The United States and Chile: Imperialism and the Overthrow of the Allende Government*. New York: Monthly Review, 1975.

____. "Economic Expansion and U.S. Policy in Central America." *Contemporary Marxism* (Summer 1981): 69–88.

Petras, James, and others. *Latin American Bankers, Generals and the Struggle for Social Justice.* Totowa, N.J.: Rowman and Littlefield, 1986.

Pike, Frederick B. *Chile and the United States, 1880–1962.* South Bend, Ind.: University of Notre-Dame Press, 1963.

Poitras, Guy. *The Ordeal of Hegemony. The United States and Latin America.* Boulder, Colo.: Westview Press, 1990.

Rangel, Carlos. *The Latin Americans and Their Love-Hate Relationship with the United States.* New York: Harcourt Brace Jovanovich, 1977.

Reynold, Clark, and Carlos Tello, eds. *U.S.–Mexico Relations.* Stanford, Calif.: Stanford University Press, 1983.

Rockefeller, Nelson. *The Rockefeller Report on the Americas.* Chicago: Quadrangle Press, 1969.

Ronning, C. Neal. *Law and Politics in Inter-American Diplomacy.* New York: John Wiley, 1963.

____, ed. *Intervention in Latin America.* New York: Knopf, 1970.

Sack, Roger E., and Donald L. Wyman. "Latin American Diplomats and the United States Foreign Policymaking Process." In *Report of the Commission on the Organization of the Government for the Conduct of Foreign Policy* 3, app. 1. Washington, D.C.: Government Printing Office, 1975.

Schoultz, Lars. *National Security and United States Policy Toward Latin America.* Princeton, N.J.: Princeton University Press, 1987.

Sheehan, Edward R. F. *Agony in the Garden: A Stranger in Latin America.* New York: Houghton Mifflin, 1989.

Sigmund, Paul E. "Latin America: Change or Continuity?" *Foreign Affairs* 60, no. 3 (1982): 629–57.

Slater, Jerome. *The OAS and United States Foreign Policy.* Columbus: Ohio State University Press, 1967.

Stallings, Barbara, and Robert Kaufman, eds. *Debt and Democracy in Latin America.* Boulder, Colo.: Westview Press, 1988.

Stepan, Alfred. "The United States and Latin America: Vital Interests and the Instruments of Power." *Foreign Affairs* 58, no. 3 (1979): 659–52.

Szulc, Tad. *Dominican Diary.* New York: Delacorte, 1965

____, ed. *The United States and the Caribbean.* Englewood Cliffs, N.J.: Prentice-Hall, 1971.

Theberge, James D., ed. *The Soviet Presence in Latin America.* New York: Crane, Russak, 1974.

Vaky, Viron P. "Hemispheric Relations: Everything is Part of Everything Else." *Foreign Affairs* 59, no. 3 (1981): 617–47.

Valenta, Jiri. "The U.S.S.R., Cuba and the Crisis in Central America." *Orbis* (Fall 1981): 715–46.

Welles, Sumner. *Naboth's Vineyard: The Dominican Republic, 1844–1924.* New York: Payson and Clarke Ltd., 1928.

Wesson, Robert, ed. *U.S. Influence in Latin America in the 1980s.* New York: Praeger, 1982.

Wesson, Robert, and Heraldo Munoz, eds. *Latin American Views of the U.S.* New York: Praeger, 1986.

Whitaker, Arthur P. *The United States and South America: The Northern Republics.* Cambridge, Mass.: Harvard University Press, 1948.

____. *The United States and Argentina.* Cambridge, Mass.: Harvard University Press, 1954.

____. *Nationalism in Latin America.* Gainesville: University of Florida Press, 1962.

White, Richard Alan. *The Morass: United States Intervention in Central America.* New York: Harper & Row, 1984.

Wiarda, Howard. *In Search of Policy—The United States and Latin America.* Washington, D.C.: American Enterprise Institute for Public Policy Research, 1984.

___, ed. *Rift and Revolution: The Central American Imbroglio.* Washington, D.C.: American Enterprise Institute for Public Policy Research, 1984.

___. *The Democratic Revolution in Latin America: Implications for U.S. Policy.* New York: Holmes & Meier, 1990.

Williams, Edward J. *The Political Themes of Inter-American Relations.* Belmont, Calif.: Duxbury, 1971.

Wood, Bryce. *The Making of the Good Neighbor Policy.* New York: Columbia University Press, 1961.

___. *The United States and Latin American Wars, 1932–1942.* New York: Columbia University Press, 1966.

Index

ABOUT THE AUTHOR

MICHAEL J. KRYZANEK is a Professor of Political Science at Bridgewater State College in Massachusetts. In addition to the first two editions of this work, he is the author of *Leaders, Leadership, and U.S. Policy in Latin America* (1992), coauthor of *The Dominican Republic: A Caribbean Crucible*, second edition, (1992), and *Latin America: Change and Challenge* (1995).

ISBN 0-275-95083-2

9 780275 950835

90000>

HARDCOVER BAR CODE